for Ava

for Ava

VERA TWOMEY

MERCIER PRESS

MERCIER PRESS

Cork

www.mercierpress.ie

Back cover images (*Top to bottom*): © John Delea, Vera Twomey, John Delea, Fachtna Roe, James O'Driscoll

ISBN: 978 1 78117 683 2

A CIP record for this title is available from the British Library

Printed and bound in the EU.

The greatest achievement in life is to lose fear. When you are no longer afraid, you are free. Once this happens you will achieve any goal, in time, with focus and determination.

Vera Twomey

Dedication

For Ava, of course. Sophia, Michael and Elvera-Mae have infused my life with joy, happiness and love. They are a constant reminder of what childhood should be about. To my husband, Paul, who has been beside me every step of the way and is still there. You helped to lighten my load on so many occasions, I hope I helped to lighten yours. In memory of my late father, Michael, who was a mighty man. To my wonderful mother, Katty, for your unconditional support and love throughout the years. The family would be lost without you.

Contents

Foreword

I've had the privilege of meeting many remarkable people in my role as a public representative in the Irish parliament; however, occasionally someone truly inspiring crosses my path. Vera Twomey most certainly falls into that category. As much as this is a book about dealing with a child's terrible illness and fighting for medical justice, it is essentially a book about a mother's love and devotion to her daughter. It isn't until we're tested that a person learns what they are capable of and how strong they can be. This story teaches us profound lessons about friendship, solidarity and the human condition.

I first met Vera and her husband, Paul, in May 2016, in Leinster House. They had come to highlight the desperate situation they faced regarding their daughter Ava's health and how they were committed to doing anything they could to alleviate her immense suffering. Vera's impassioned plea struck a chord and after listening to her speak I knew that something had to be done in terms of legislation for medicinal cannabis. That meeting would start the process and the development of a deep friendship that helped bring the issue to the national stage.

Vera's campaign to gain access to medicinal cannabis for Ava has captured the public's imagination and they readily took this extraordinary family's plight to their hearts. Her dauntless will and determination in taking on an obdurate establishment was both inspirational and moving. The narrative that played out was one of institutional resistance and inherent conservatism, within both the political and medical spheres, in relation to access to medicinal cannabis. Her sheer devotion and commitment to Ava drove Vera to anything and everything in securing the necessary treatment.

Vera's fight for Ava is one no family should ever have to endure. Their enormous sacrifice will hopefully make it easier for others in the future to avoid the monumental obstacles that were placed in their way. I am more confident than ever that access to medicinal cannabis will happen in Ireland. It is inevitable. The winds of change have fundamentally altered people's awareness of its enormous benefits.

History will show that it was one woman, exhibiting incredible courage and conviction, who took on the system, won the right to obtain access to medicinal cannabis for her daughter, and paved the way for so many who will benefit from her heroic struggle. Vera always said to me, 'Gino, we need somebody inside and outside the parliamentary gates to win.' I'm glad to have played a role in the past few years, but ultimately it is people like Vera Twomey who have begun to open the gates for the many people who may benefit from the use of medicinal cannabis to help alleviate their pain and suffering.

On that afternoon in May 2016, when I first met Vera and Paul, I didn't realise what lay ahead, much less its significance. Since then I have developed a deeper awareness and appreciation of the courage exhibited by so many carers and ill people living in Ireland. Their courage is infectious and, together with dogged persistence and solidarity, we can move forward to success. Now that is something truly worth fighting for.

Gino Kenny, TD

A Normal Day

'I have sadness in me, I have anger in me,
I have heartbreak in me.'

– Ellen DeGeneres

It was early in 2016 and just a normal day, or as normal as it ever gets when one of your children suffers from a serious, chronic illness. Ava's epilepsy had long since taken over our lives. Every waking moment was consumed by it. I operated under constant fear and tension, waiting for the next seizure. It was coming, though you never knew when – but as sure as day it was coming. We had reached a stage where Ava was having several seizures almost every day, with over twenty on a bad day. They may have varied in extent and severity, but each one was an agonising experience, full of pain and terror.

I was in the kitchen that day, doing the washing and chatting away with my mother, Katty. The door between the kitchen and sitting room was open, so I'd occasionally snatch a glance at the children playing, to see that they were okay. You know yourself – when it's quiet, it's usually time to investigate what they're up to.

The constant illness had sapped the strength from my six-year-old daughter. Ava had been out of sorts over the last few days, with another ear infection that raised her temperature, along with other alarm bells for an impending seizure, like how her previous night's sleep had been very disturbed. The family needed to be vigilant. Being sleep-deprived had become part of daily life, as we monitored Ava through the night for seizure activity.

Bang.

A cry of distress came from the sitting room.

I rushed in, with my mother following right behind.

Ava was lying on the sofa, her torso stiff as a poker but her arms and legs jerking uncontrollably. She had a fixed, far-off look in her eyes. She wasn't in the room any more; the seizure had her.

I needed to control my worry and, to be honest, keep myself from panicking. You go into automatic pilot mode when a seizure strikes; you tell yourself, 'Keep calm, you know what needs to be done, just do it.'

While my mother stayed with Ava, I ran back into the kitchen. Reaching up, I got the rescue medicine, Buccolam, from its appointed place, high up in the press. It's powerful stuff and not to be used lightly. It may stop a seizure – though not always – but either way it would leave Ava zonked out for several hours afterwards. No, it wasn't to be used lightly at all. Still, it was all that was available.

My mother told me, 'Twenty seconds, Vera', as I hurried back into the sitting room. We still had time; it might stop of its own accord. You had to wait five minutes before administering the rescue medication, so it was an agonising waiting game, kneeling beside Ava, praying for it to stop. After five minutes she exclaimed, 'Vera, it's not stopping.' She was right; if anything the seizure was growing in intensity, with more powerful muscle spasms. It was time, so I gave Ava the medicine, hoping it would halt the attack.

Afterwards, I looked up at my mother. 'What do you think, is it easing off at all?'

She looked down at me with a pained expression. 'No, Vera, she's not coming out of it. I think it's nearly time to phone for the ambulance.'

You needed to wait to see if the rescue medication would work before the next step: the emergency ambulance call. But my mother was right; we were at that stage now.

I made the call.

Whoever answered the phone on the other end recognised the number. 'Hello, Vera, is that you? Is Ava having a seizure again? How long? Okay, we're on our way.' The call-outs were so regular that there was no need to provide an address.

I had a few short moments to phone my husband, Paul, who was at work, with the bad news and try to organise things for my mother, who'd mind the rest of the children. I also rushed to put some essentials in a bag for the looming hospital stay.

The ambulance arrived from Macroom in less than fifteen minutes. Ava was still seizing. Working quickly – we were well used to the procedure by now – she was gently lifted into the ambulance and off we sped. About twenty minutes later, we arrived at the hospital in Cork city.

So here we were, back in the Cork University Hospital (CUH) Accident and Emergency room again. How thoroughly sick of that room I was. Some of the most upsetting, distressing moments of my life have taken place there. The doctors and nurses surrounded Ava, trying to stop the attack. 'How about if we try phenytoin?' suggested a junior doctor.

'But doctor, that takes half an hour to have an effect,' I protested. I'd been through this process so many times.

'Yes, oh, yes, that's right, Mrs Twomey, it does. Have you experienced this before?'

'Yes I have, too many times, and that one isn't suitable; it's never worked quickly enough for Ava.'

While this discussion was going on the seizure stopped as suddenly as it had begun. It had lasted about forty minutes from beginning to end. It had been a bad seizure, powerful. Another shocking day, but far from the worst.

Ava looked wretched and completely exhausted lying in the hospital bed. As I gently held her hand and stroked her hair, trying to give her some comfort from the pain or at least let her know she wasn't alone, I wondered to myself: how did my family end up in such a terrible predicament?

Much more importantly and more urgently, I strove to think of a way to alleviate her suffering and give her a chance at a better, healthier life. As I held her hand, I silently assured her, 'Ava darling, I promise we're going to make it happen.'

I

Early Days

'To get the full value of joy, you must have
someone to divide it with.'

– Mark Twain

Growing up, the most dramatic event to happen to our family had to be the time our house was destroyed by lightning. This occurred when I was just one year old, so I'm relying on my parents' recollection for this. We were all gathered in the kitchen for the evening, when a bolt of lightning struck the house and set it ablaze. The force of the strike dislodged a beam from the roof, knocking both my parents unconscious.

My father, Mike, awoke to find himself surrounded by flames. At the time, he wasn't aware that his scalp had been split open by the falling beam. He just scooped up my mother, who was still slumped unconscious in her chair, and snatched me from my playpen, where I was apparently standing gazing at the surrounding fire. The tremendous power of the lightning strike had also somehow blown the kitchen door off its hinges, so he quickly carried us out of the developing inferno, saving our lives.

The phone line was down, however, so the fire brigade couldn't be called. Dad stood in the yard, holding us both, and watched as the flames consumed our home. A small mercy was that the wind blew the flames and sparks away from the hay and animal sheds, saving the farm business. For the next year and a half, we lived in Uncle Mick's mobile home at the side of the yard, until our new bungalow was built, which is our home to this day. I spent the rest of my childhood being referred to as the 'girleen' who had survived the fire.

My earliest memories are of accompanying my father as he worked on the farm. I'd feel very grown-up and responsible when he'd let me participate in some little odd job or other. I didn't realise it at the time, but I had an idyllic childhood growing up in Aghabullogue village. There was an entire farm to explore and play in, save for a small number of dangerous, out-of-bounds locations. And sure, if you strayed onto the neighbouring farm, that was no problem.

The school I attended was a throwback to an earlier era. The heating was provided by old-style stoves, the desks retained the place for an inkwell used by previous generations, and when it came time to go to the toilet – 'Teacher, *an bhfuil cead agam dul go dti an leithreas?*' – we had to venture outside to a separate building to reach the bathrooms. Our school was small, but a strong part of the bedrock of the village community. Everyone knew and looked out for everyone else, and to a great extent the community hasn't changed in that respect, which is in itself a lovely thing.

Playtime revolved around the local obsessions of hurling and Gaelic football. Occasionally, when the rain was pouring down and confined us to the playground's gravel surface, we would switch to soccer, but we were back to hurling as soon as conditions permitted. Playing hurling was the major pastime and my best friend, Irene, and I would look forward to the hay being cut, so we could play a match out in the freshly cleared field. It would be just the two of us and our imaginary teams winning glory for the village, or, if we were lucky, her cousins would call and there'd be enough children for two actual teams. Then we'd get stuck in and no quarter was asked for or given. It was all great fun and was normal enough for my generation growing up in Aghabullogue, but extraordinary at the same time when I look back and compare it to the more structured play of children today.

The older and more capable you got, the more responsibility you were given. You'd be expected to 'muck in' with jobs around the farm. When the hay was baled in the summer, my cousin and I would be drafted into stooking the bales (forking the hay into a heap). We'd spend hours in the fields, stooking, chatting and larking about. At the end of our shift, we'd get a spin back in the trailer as the bales were brought into the hay shed. Our financial reward was a shiny fifty pence piece, which at the time seemed like a fortune. Those fifty pence pieces burnt a fierce hole in our pockets, because as soon as we received them we'd be off to the shop. A delicious Cornetto would relieve us of our hard-earned wages for the day. It was also a common enough occurrence to be following the cows down the road to the fields for the night after they were milked, while in the autumn, I can remember myself and my friends heading out to the hedgerows and collecting baskets and baskets of blackberries that my mother made into jam. They were great, carefree times.

As I grew up, I'd often look at my parents' strong bond and wonder would I manage to be as decent and successful in my life as they were in theirs. Daddy diligently taught me to be honest and to 'Tell the truth and shame the devil'. Just being around my parents and seeing how they conducted themselves taught me so much about how to live my life. 'Do your best; once you give your best effort that is all that can be expected. Keep trying, no matter what the result' was a creed that they preached and lived by. They both had a strong sense of justice and of what is right. Dad would say, 'If a fella's wrong, you don't put up with it. Don't lie down and take it, rather stand up and fight back.' That would prove to be valuable advice in the years ahead, and maybe more of their spirit was passed on to me than I realised.

***

Meeting Paul was one of the most significant things to happen in my life. The joy at the time was unbounded; it was a whirlwind, a happy dream. Having the right person beside me, a real friend, someone who 'gets me', is the greatest gift I could possibly have received. Humour, a sharp wit and kindness are all traits he has in abundance and, along with my mother, he's been my best friend and closest ally in the years since. Any ideas I'd have were teased out and discussed together at length, and his ability to see things differently to me usually resulted in us, together, making better decisions.

Paul and I got married in February 2009, the honeymoon followed, and soon after the news came that a baby was on the way. Was I ready? No. I don't think anyone is ever really ready for such a life-changing event, even if they reckon they are. As the year progressed, I gradually got bigger, and bigger, and bigger. Eventually I reached the stage where I just hoped the pregnancy would be over soon as I could barely walk. But sure, the baby would arrive soon, I reminded myself, and from then on everything would be wonderful.

Looking back now, I can still remember all the plans I had: I was going to teach the child Irish from birth; Spanish would follow later and classical music would be on the agenda from an early age. It surprised me how other parents simply nodded and smiled knowingly when I told them my plans.

In Marie Morgan's bestselling book on hypnobirthing, she outlines the many benefits of a drug-free birth and that was the way I wanted it to be. The baby had other ideas, however, and it took a labour of thirty-eight hours for my little angel to arrive into the wide world. She didn't seem interested in being born at all, but an emergency Caesarean section later and there she was.

I'll never forget those first moments seeing her, despite the drugs. Because I had taken all of the drugs available: the gas and air and two epidurals. But, in the end, she was there and she was so beautiful. I thought she must belong to someone else, because someone so beautiful couldn't be my baby.

It was 3.14 p.m. on 29 November when I first met Ava Barry. She had all the appearances of a healthy baby: she was a good weight, had a healthy appetite and no issues were noticed by the maternity hospital staff. It had been a long labour, but everything seemed fine.

Ava was christened soon after she arrived home. In the following weeks, she adopted the usual routine of any baby: sleeping, feeding, nappy changes, naps, some crying and more feeding. I floated around in a fog of happiness and joy, gradually getting used to the constant changing of tiny nappies and gaining in confidence holding my beautiful little girl. Really, it all became so normal and the birthing books were placed back

for Ava

on the shelves as I began to listen, as you do, to my mother more and more.

As time trundled along I thought of Ava's future and wondered what she would enjoy as she grew up: would she play hurling? Would she be mad for Irish dancing?

The sky was the limit.

2

Falling into a Nightmare

'Without health, life is not life;
it is only a state of languor and suffering …'

– Buddha

Late 2009 and early 2010 was a brutally cold winter. It was a really severe one for us in Aghabullogue and we were actually snowed in for a few days, which was unusual. Ava had a doctor's appointment scheduled for the beginning of February, but on the day it was impossible for us to drive to Macroom town because of the bad weather, so it was slightly delayed.

We eventually made it to the doctor's and following the appointment nothing appeared out of the ordinary, nothing to indicate that we should have any concerns.

Bang.

Ava's first seizure began at eight o'clock that night. She suddenly let out a loud exhalation of breath, as her body contorted violently. A feeling of horror, such as I'd never experienced before, washed over me as I rushed over and held her in my arms. I did everything I could to keep her safe, as it was obvious that she was suffering some type of seizure.

Ava's body was taken over by the seizure. It was so violent, so long and without mercy. Her eyes had a fixed stare and her little body jerked and twisted in pain as I screamed, panicking, 'Jesus, she's gone, Mam, she's gone, she's gone. Get Paul, where's Paul? Call the ambulance. Oh my God, she's gone.'

The ambulance was called and I immediately rang Paul, who was out repairing agricultural machinery in Blarney. I screamed, 'Get back home, get back, it's bad, as soon as you can.' I held Ava as best I could, as her little body continued to violently jerk. Her legs, her arms and her little facial muscles all jerked uncontrollably as she made the most distressing noises. I was inconsolable. Mother tried to reassure me, 'He's coming, he's on his way.' In my shock I had to be reminded where Paul was coming back from, even though I had known just moments before.

I cried and shouted out, 'No, no, please God, not Ava, please don't take her, please God, don't take my baby now. Make it stop.'

We put a car at the top of the lane, as instructed by the ambulance crew, and had every light on in the house. Paul arrived home before the ambulance got there. His total shock at what greeted him as he entered the house only heightened my awareness that the situation was really bad.

The ambulance reached the house as the seizure was stopping. It had lasted forty-five minutes. They crew asked about Ava's medical history and did their checks of heart rate, blood sugar and blood oxygen. Their practiced professionalism helped to reassure me that Ava was in the best possible hands and, with that, we quickly drove to CUH.

One of the ambulance personnel that night was a woman named Jenny, and we were lucky to have her with us as we sped through the darkness. Jenny and I were in the back with Ava and I really believed that she was going to die. Her face had turned blue and only changed to a frightening grey colour after an oxygen mask was placed on her face. It was horrifying.

While in the ambulance, she started having another seizure. The crew were kept busy attending to Ava and reassuring me that we'd arrive at the hospital soon, but it was impossible to miss the concerned glances cast between them. I sat beside my daughter with tears streaming down my face and what felt like a vice-like grip closing around my throat.

We arrived at the hospital and were led straight through the A&E. Paul tried to keep up with the ambulance in his car, but couldn't, and arrived in the hospital about twenty minutes after us, by which time Ava was in the resuscitation room. The doctors and nurses surrounded her, while I stood by, blankly watching what was going on.

This second seizure was as bad as the first. When it eventually stopped, Ava had a line in her tiny arm, giving her various emergency anti-seizure medications. Later, we were moved up to the 'Ladybird' children's ward. Here we met Colm. He was one of the nurses who supervised Ava that night, and he couldn't have been kinder and more considerate in dealing with two very distraught and bewildered parents. We both stayed for the night in Ava's room, sitting in the chairs beside the bed and thinking over the terrible event. I had an ominous, sick feeling in the pit of my stomach as, for the first time, I truly learned the meaning of having a 'sleepless night'.

The next morning we were advised that Ava was going to be kept in and that we would meet the public paediatric neurologist the following day. When the neurologist arrived, Ava was much improved. The neurologist told us that Ava didn't have a febrile convulsion (a seizure associated with a fever or high body temperature, but without any serious underlying health problem) and because she had had a number of seizures she most likely had some form of epilepsy. They had ordered blood tests to determine what kind of epilepsy. We were blessed with the thorough nature of the neurologist's investigations. I believe that even at that early point our neurologist suspected that Ava's epilepsy wasn't generalised epilepsy.

The three possible types of epilepsy were explained to us as: generalised, hereditary and, the rarest and most unlikely form of epilepsy, a mutated gene. But because this is extremely rare, we were told not to worry about it. However, I grew more concerned when I learned that Ava's blood samples were being sent out of the country to be tested. I wasn't aware if this was the standard procedure, but my guess at the time was that it was not. Adding to my concern about the type of epilepsy Ava might have were the length and severity of the seizures.

We were released home from the hospital after a number of days and given Ava's first medication, the barbiturate (a class of drugs that act as central nervous system depressants), phenobarbital.

Back at home, I had a constant feeling of worry that something really bad, over which I had no control, was taking place. We weren't in a fog of happiness any longer; no, dark clouds had moved in and lingered over our lives. Although we kept telling each other that it was going to be okay, in reality we all knew that it was really bad. But hope is a curious thing, and until the results of the blood tests returned we held on tight to hope and prayed that there was nothing seriously wrong with Ava's health.

***

There is a nondescript, old-fashioned corridor to the left as you go into the A&E area of CUH. It has holding areas named after rivers: the Bandon suite, the Blackwater suite, and so on. Long rows of chairs line both sides of the corridor. The sense of apprehension was unreal as we walked down to our appointed suite, inside which were more chairs and an independent reception desk.

The first indication that we were in serious trouble was when we were escorted away from the suite by the neurologist and led into a separate room on the left-hand side of the corridor. I felt that no good news could be coming if we were being brought to a different area of the hospital. I worried that it was a room for delivering difficult news.

After being given maybe ten minutes to settle ourselves, we were told the results of the tests, which had been sent to Glasgow. Ava's epilepsy wasn't a generalised form, nor was it hereditary. Paul initially thought that this was very good news; however, the neurologist said, 'No, it's not.' She was sorry to break the news to us, but the results showed that Ava had a mutated gene and, more specifically, she had a type of epilepsy known as Dravet syndrome.

I asked, 'What does that mean?'

The neurologist frowned. 'Well, it's a very rare form of intractable, drug-resistant epilepsy. It is also known as severe myoclonic epilepsy in infancy.'

'What does that mean?' I again asked.

The neurologist was blunt. 'It means that your daughter's outlook for the future is that she will never walk, she will never talk, she will be in a wheelchair and you will have to accept that she will be in residential care for the rest of her life. However, it is unlikely she will live beyond the age of three, as the mortality rate for Dravet syndrome is very high.'

I hate swearing. I always feel guilty afterwards and think I should have made greater use of my vocabulary. My father drove that point home when I was young. That day in the hospital I don't even remember what I said, but the neurologist later described it as a most unusual reaction. I started to say, 'No, no, no, fuck, fuck', etc. This is not the normal way that I react to bad news, but this was worse than my worst nightmares.

The neurologist went on to explain that there were only a limited number of drugs available to treat Ava's seizures, as many of the drugs used to treat generalised epilepsy were contraindicated (unsuitable for treatment, as they may worsen rather than ease seizures) in the case of Dravet syndrome. This resulted in Ava's options being restricted, the neurologist admitted; however, she would do her best with what was available and would see us every three months to monitor Ava's progress.

Shell-shocked, we asked if there was any information available on the condition and were given three photocopied sheets that had been printed from the Internet, titled, 'Dravet Syndrome for Dummies'. I kid you not! That's all we got, nothing more.

The meeting finished and that was it. We weren't offered counselling or any other form of help. With the meeting over, the reality of the situation hit me with renewed force. I had to be lifted out of the chair and half carried down the corridor. We were escorted out via a side door into the car park. I was obviously hysterical. I was not offended by this being done, as it was as much for my benefit as anyone else's and it avoided upsetting other people. I guess it was a vivid example of pure shock.

I was really angered by how little information we had been

given, particularly when I later googled 'Dravet syndrome' and discovered that the Dravet syndrome UK website was massively informative. It had an abundance of articles and was linked to a Facebook page filled with parents going through the same hell. Why hadn't I been given literature from here, rather than one meant for 'Dummies'?

Day had been turned into the darkest night. Our beautiful little girl's future was changed forever. According to those with a medical background there was no hope for Ava, which offended me to the core. If Ava's future was mapped out to be as depressingly short and pain-ridden as suggested, then we would have to accept it, but what Paul and I would never, ever do was give up without even trying. These people were telling us all about when she would die and what she wouldn't achieve. Well, they could say what they liked, but in my mind I said, 'Let's get to work and see if we can prove these boyos wrong.'

At least we had a diagnosis now. Don't get me wrong, no parent wants to hear that their child has a rare and serious condition, but for the purpose of maintaining your sanity and on the practical level of conducting research, having a specific diagnosis is very beneficial. At least when you have a name your ability to research is made easier, allowing you to approach groups, and later other parents who have children with the same illness. This gives you room to learn and hopefully help and protect your child into the future.

***

What is Dravet syndrome? Put simply, it is an incurable, rare, very severe type of epilepsy. It was first identified by Charlotte

Dravet, and can be very difficult to treat due to the high frequency of the seizures, their unpredictable nature and the fact that the seizures are resistant to many anti-epileptic medications. A wide variety of seizure types may be experienced. The syndrome is often caused by a mutation in a gene that produces a protein involved in the electrical signalling between nerve cells. This electric signalling normally allows the cells to communicate, but the mutation instead causes a disfunction in the electrical activity in the brain, which then leads to seizures.

Dravet syndrome can be catastrophic to the mental development of young children. Seizure by seizure their potential and personality is taken away. Without your mind, you don't live; you simply exist. Gradually, the epilepsy was going to take Ava away from us. You can't believe it, then you hope to God it can be treated. Epilepsy, even something as serious as Dravet syndrome, sure there must be drugs to treat that, right?

Children commonly suffer their first seizure from the age of five to eight months. By the second year, delays in mental and physical development become increasingly apparent. There can also be numerous associated challenges, including disruption of the systems controlling body functions such as body temperature and sweating; chronic infections; difficulties with sleeping and speaking; nutrition issues; and problems with balance.

People suffering from Dravet syndrome have a much higher incidence of sudden unexplained death in epilepsy (SUDEP). SUDEP involves a sudden, unexpected death without any cause detected post-mortem. Some of the proposed mechanisms of SUDEP include seizure-induced cardiac and respiratory arrests. The random terror of SUDEP is never far from my mind, due to the severity and number of Ava's seizures.

There are many 'triggers' which can initiate a seizure. Something as mundane as the bath being a little too warm, a hot summer's day or an ear infection can lead to seizures. Then again, on other occasions, the attacks come without any obvious trigger. The child is constantly walking on a thin, wobbly tightrope, waiting for something to knock them off.

Often it is found that the seizures cannot be completely stopped and the best that can be achieved for the child is a reduction in their number and severity. An uneasy balance is maintained between minimising the damage the Dravet syndrome is causing, the number of drugs being administered, and the often undesirable side effects of many of the available medications. In addition, support with speech and language therapy is very important, so as to give the child every assistance in achieving their potential.

I think it's fair to say that a diagnosis of Dravet syndrome is something you'll never want to hear. Aside from the enormous impact on the child's health, caring for someone with Dravet syndrome will present you with challenges you can't even begin to imagine, not that you'd ever want to.

***

After being sent home from the diagnosis with what I felt was little or no guidance, I initially began to reach out and try to obtain information and help from the organisations in Ireland that deal with epilepsy. I rang the Cork office of the Epilepsy Association of Ireland. The person I spoke to seemed really nice and offered to meet. However, when I invited them to come to my house, they said that wasn't possible. I wondered if it had something to do with health and safety. They then offered to meet me in Macroom for a coffee and said that if I wanted to talk and cry, I could do so there. I recall saying, 'You want to meet me in Macroom, where I can cry in a café?' This was somewhere I might run into one of my neighbours or someone who knew me by sight. Also there was the fact that, with the amount of seizures Ava was having, it was extremely difficult for me to leave the house for any length of time, so the suggestion simply wasn't practical. 'Thanks, but no thanks,' I replied.

Paul and I did get a chance to attend a support group meeting organised by Epilepsy Ireland one evening. There was a circle of chairs around the edges of the room. The people in attendance each gave their names and a short outline of their situation. At the time, we were dealing with, maybe, six to eight big seizures on a bad day, and as we listened to the other parents there it dawned on us that we weren't at the right meeting at all. The other parents had kids who were having one or two seizures every couple of months. For several parents the child's epilepsy was stable, but the drugs were producing side effects, like mood swings or severe drowsiness. Some of the older parents had children who had been seizure free for several years but still came to share their experience with other parents in similar situations. And that was the problem – none of the other parents had kids with intractable, drug-resistant epilepsy. Paul and I listened and looked around, then back at each other, and we both knew what the other was thinking: 'My God, if Ava only had three or four seizures in six months we would feel like we were living the dream.'

These people had no experience of how bad Ava's epilepsy was. Don't get me wrong, the support groups are great for a lot of people in obtaining information, but it doesn't help to hear how much better absolutely everyone else's child is doing compared to yours. It drove home how desperate Ava's situation was, given the fact that even the epilepsy support group was divorced from her reality. I came to see that, realistically, we could only gain the necessary understanding of Ava's plight from people in a similar situation. As those around me reached out to hug each other, I squirmed, not wanting to hug anyone, especially a stranger. We left as soon as we could.

I've never learned of any formal support group for children like Ava; you have to make or find your own. Over time, you get to meet and know the parents of other very sick children and develop a loose, informal support network. On the drive home that night from the epilepsy support group, I looked out the passenger window into the darkness. As the rain ran down the window, the tears ran down my face. It was unbearable to be so different and so alone.

3

Living with Dravet

'If you're going through hell, keep going.'
– Winston Churchill

The handing over of the 'Dravet Syndrome for Dummies' literature may have been the spark that ignited the fury that has kept me going all of these years. Being told that Ava would never walk or talk by doctors who seemed to me to have no hope for her future prospects infuriated me. Their apparent negativity became my starting point. It forced me to go away and make something better than nothing happen, to try as hard as possible to give Ava a chance.

I said to myself that she would walk and she would talk. I believed it then and continued to believe it throughout the most difficult times. I thought, 'Okay if they're right, they're right, but we are going to put our heart and soul into keeping her out of a wheelchair and getting her to speak.' That was our goal. I would never give in to someone else's reading of Ava's potential without trying everything I could to make it better.

This period of time was extremely difficult. Our joys and plans for the future were replaced with me launching myself at the Internet in order to find out everything I could about Dravet syndrome. What I found was not a comforting reality. There was no Dravet syndrome Ireland organisation, which is logical, because the number of cases diagnosed in Ireland is small. At the time Ava was diagnosed, we were told we had the only child in the country with the syndrome; however, we discovered maybe a year later that another beautiful girl in Dublin also had it.

After we went home with the first set of medication, phenobarbital, we set to work making sure that we gave the correct dose at the exact time specified. Paul and I had no inkling that there was a possibility that the medicine wouldn't work, despite the fact that the doctors had said with perfect clarity that the syndrome was drug-resistant. I suppose you naturally trick yourself into thinking that any illness can be quickly and easily treated. It was an epilepsy medicine and Ava had epilepsy, so it had to help her, right? That's what we kept saying to ourselves, anyway.

However, over the coming weeks, it became very clear that our hope for an early success in treating the condition was unfounded. It rapidly became apparent that the phenobarbital wasn't working. Phenobarbital is one of the most commonly used medications for treating seizures in children, but the reported side effects are many: it is highly addictive and withdrawal can trigger even more severe seizures; it can also result in a decreased level of consciousness; a decreased effort to breathe; dizziness; and depression and suicidal ideation. Thankfully, Ava exhibited few obvious side effects, but it was really disturbing having to use a drug like this on her.

The months after Ava's diagnosis were filled with fear – of when the next seizure would occur, of how severe it would be. Emergency trips to hospital became the norm, often occurring on a weekly basis. Amid the panic of the seizures and having to frantically phone for the ambulance, over time it was a strange sort of reassurance to know the questions that were coming. 'Yes, she is breathing. Yes, she has a history of epilepsy. Yes, all the lights are on in the house. No problem, of course we can take the car out to the end of the lane to meet you.'

After a while, we often didn't need to park the car at the end of the lane, especially when the crew came from Macroom as opposed to the city. Sadly, the minute they heard the name 'Ava', they said, 'Grand job, we know well where Ava lives.' It's not the sort of name recognition that anyone ever wants to acquire.

We were in a much better situation when the ambulance came from Macroom, as it was only fifteen minutes away; unfortunately many times the Macroom or city ambulances were unavailable and so an ambulance had to come all the way from Midleton, which is a good forty-minute drive away. Ava would often be in a seizure the entire time that this longer wait occurred and then she'd have the drive into CUH. It sometimes got worse and we'd find out that the crew from Killarney, about an hour's drive away, had been dispatched. The worst case I can recollect was an ambulance being sent from Kilkenny, which we were completely incredulous about at the time. It must have been a good two-hour drive. By the time they got to us, Ava was out of the seizure, but she could have died in our arms, or in the car on the way into hospital if things had gotten so bad that we decided to transport her ourselves.

***

We spent so much of our time on the Ladybird ward in CUH over the following months that we grew to know the staff quite well. We met some of the kindest people and most amazing nurses you could hope to meet. An exchange of a glance, or the kind mention of your name, was enough to know that the following hours would be as good as they could be, all things considered.

In time, I began to see for myself that these nurses were the medical professionals holding up the whole hospital. Their ability to placate the parents of sick children was their particular magic skill. We grew to love the nurses, who you'd be well aware were reassuring you despite the fact that they were grey with tiredness, run off their feet, but still there, hanging on and doing the best they could. They didn't forget about Ava and when they could they'd come back with what was needed. It is awfully sad to see wonderfully professional nurses run off their feet, hurrying back and forth in order to care for their patients. It's no good for anyone to have a nurse caring for too many patients.

There were many times, when Ava's seizures were really bad, that the nurses couldn't have been more helpful. We remain grateful beyond belief for their compassion and experience. Often it was the nurses who had to use their compassion and social skills to pick up the pieces after a visit from a consultant, who, with a blank, emotionless face, would deliver some devastating news and then turn around and walk out the door, leaving you looking on, wondering, 'Why to God did I allow that person to speak to me like that?' The nurses actually talked to us and did so even though their backlog of work only continued to pile up as they comforted us.

The Ladybird ward was a long corridor with the patients' rooms off to the side. When you entered via the double doors the wave of heat, as in most hospitals, was overpowering, if – at least initially – somewhat reassuring. However, as we became more frequent visitors, the absence of cold led to an anxiety that the stifling heat may be a breeding ground for infections, particularly for kids like Ava, who had an ever-declining immune system.

I'm aware that a baby doesn't take up much space in a cot in the hospital room; however, I don't agree that because your child is small and only a few months old that the size of the room should also be very small. Room size should not be based upon the child's size. The type of room that Ava was given on her first day, and on subsequent admissions, was the most claustrophobic I've ever encountered. These rooms had the size and feel of a cell, being about as wide as they are long. There is just enough room for the bed on one side and a reclining chair and wash basin on the other. When the child, parents and medical professionals are all present, they would become unbearable, particularly with the heat. The hard chairs were like all the other hard chairs I've sat on in hospitals over the years, in that they prevent you from ever establishing a comfortable position. Parent after parent I've spoken to would say, 'Oh my God, those chairs!'

A stay of several days could become exhausting, what with the stress of Ava's illness, the lack of sleep, the heat and the constant worry. However, it did become something of a common currency between the parents who were spending long periods of time in hospital, often leading to the beginnings of a friendship, which usually resulted in you sitting and grumbling together about the whole set-up. These conversations usually happened in the parents' rooms, a little oasis of normality where the sofa, telly and a cup of tea allow you to take a short break from the vigil at your sick child's side.

So, this was how we began to make contact with other parents struggling with sick kids, some of whom we might only meet once, while there were other mums and dads whom we'd meet again and again. It was pretty easy to bump into myself and Paul on the Ladybird ward at that time, after all, as we began to spend increasing amounts of time there with Ava.

***

After several months, the anti-epilepsy drug Topamax was introduced to Ava's regime. With all the frequent ambulance trips, we were just so glad to have another option prescribed alongside phenobarbital. Paul and I felt like, okay, it probably wasn't realistic that the first drug would work immediately, but now we had two, and two is better than one, right?

What we gradually discovered was that two also meant twice the potential negative side effects. Often these were almost as upsetting as the seizures. Some of the reported side effects of Topamax include dizziness, disturbed balance, mental impairment and damage to eyesight – as well as a long list of other potential adverse effects.

Some of the drugs given to Ava looked and smelled unpalatable and I have no doubt they also tasted that way. When medicines were prescribed, we were never adequately advised about how to actually get a child to take a distasteful liquid or tablet. Fortunately, Ava was very good at taking her medication. We were fierce lucky in this regard, as many children find it incredibly difficult to swallow them. I guess she was on the drugs from such a young age that she knew nothing else, and so we encountered none of the distress many parents experience when children can't or won't swallow their medicines.

When Topamax was introduced to the treatment regime, we were advised that we would have to gradually reach the therapeutic level based on Ava's bodyweight, so we began on a low dose and over the course of a number of months this dosage was increased to the maximum level. Occasionally, there might be a day or two free of attacks and these would get our hopes up; however, these were invariably followed by a week of daily, near-constant seizures. It was very upsetting to see the seizures continuing despite all the medication.

As time went on, it became more and more apparent that when a new medication was added one of two things would happen: either the medication wouldn't work at all, or it would bring a week or two of reduced seizure activity, and then, as sure as night follows day, the seizures returned with a renewed vengeance after those couple of weeks had elapsed. Dravet syndrome always broke through the latest pharmaceutical drug administered to Ava.

As the two initial medications didn't work, the ambulance continued to make weekly visits to our home. The visits became so frequent that the neighbours began to comment, saying, 'Oh God, they're going down for Ava again.'

We were busy all the time, monitoring Ava, watching for the next episode, never having a moment to think about anything other than protecting her from the seizure she was having and hoping that each new medication would be the one to stop the endless cycle of agony.

And it did seem endless. In any one day there could be many different types of seizure, such as tonic-clonic seizures, absence seizures, myoclonic jerks. There could easily be hundreds of actual seizures each day, but it was the violent tonic-clonic seizures that resulted in the urgent calls for an ambulance. Most people have an idea of what the stereotypical seizure looks like (i.e. falling to the ground and violent muscle spasms), but are unfamiliar with the wide variety of other types that can manifest themselves. In particular, the absence seizures, where it looked like Ava was daydreaming or staring into space, could rapidly come and go, and often there were too many to make an accurate count.

Ava is sensitive to patterns, and stripes in particular triggered seizures. Too much excitement or noise, a very restless night, a long journey or unusual surroundings could also trigger an episode. Like many sufferers of Dravet syndrome, she's also very temperature sensitive. Once a body temperature of thirty-seven degrees Celsius was reached, she was in immediate danger of a seizure, so Calpol or Nurofen was required.

Over time we realised what a challenge it was having a sick child with a rare condition. We saw what the word 'challenge' really meant. Every single time we arrived at the hospital, for example, we would meet doctors who would not be able to answer our questions. They couldn't help us as they didn't know enough about Dravet syndrome. There was a protocol in the hospital for the staff to try to stop seizures, but for Dravet that went out the window, as this standard procedure could exacerbate the seizures rather than ease them.

For a long time, the A&E staff lacked a protocol to follow when we were admitted. Often, in the early days, we had the misfortune of knowing more about the appropriate medications to administer than the staff. We would have to tell the doctors that the regular medications that they were suggesting would not work. Some appeared to take exception to us telling them what was medically appropriate. It was difficult for us because we knew what we were talking about, but we had trouble being taken seriously.

On many nights when we were in the hospital, the doctors would have tried all of the medication to stop the seizures without success. What would eventually happen is that the seizures would stop, either from Ava being completely exhausted, or more likely from the seizures just coming to their own conclusion. We would then be admitted and the same routine of questions would bombard us: 'Did you record the seizure on video? What was it like? What part of the body was in spasm?' I never had time, then, to video Ava's seizures, as I was always rushing to get the rescue medication to try to stop them when they happened at home. It was more important to try to protect her, after all, than to be taking videos.

This was our life from the time of Ava's first attack. Over time, the admissions to the hospital became more and more frequent and more and more fraught. Again and again we were presented with the same list of questions in A&E. On top of this was the unbelievable frustration felt by us over the fact that none of the medication was working. I began to ask myself whether these people had a coherent plan.

Often when we got there we found that Ava's file was not immediately available. It was either on its way or not available at all, as the office where the files were kept was closed at the weekends. All of these factors provided us with a reputation in CUH for being difficult, which was disclosed to me about that time. Apparently, when news would get out that Ava was coming, the word would go around: 'The Barrys are back', said as if we were trouble.

Well, we didn't care; they could say whatever they wanted so long as Ava was okay. We were minding our daughter and were going to do everything we could to get the best for her, no matter how many times she was admitted.

***

Time moved along, weeks building into months, but the effects of the epilepsy on Ava's development became more and more apparent, as one milestone after another was missed. Her peers were happily experiencing the delights of childhood, while Ava was suspended in a life of pain. We had so much to contend with as a family that when friends or relations called we could never really relax. We were always on edge, waiting for the next attack.

I continued to seek out any source of advice and assistance. At one point, I found the epilepsy nurse in Killarney. Although Paul and I had learned an awful lot about Dravet syndrome by the time we met her, and she didn't have any new information, she was a godsend as she was so kind and full of compassion, and she gave us guidance on caring for a child with severe epilepsy. People's compassion can mean a lot during the difficult times. In her case, even though we were outside her work area, she still called us a number of times and posted a lovely book to Ava which made the sounds of cats, dogs, sheep and other animals. I just thought she was wonderful. The book in particular was a lovely, practical gesture. Even though the seizures kept coming, we constantly kept trying to engage Ava and bring her on.

The Dravet syndrome UK website and its Facebook page were also a constant godsend during this period. They provided the detailed information we were sorely lacking for Ava's diagnosis and the website was filled with facts and forthrightness. It didn't paint a rosy picture for the future, but instead spoke of a spectrum of severity. If Ava was on the more severe end we would know soon enough.

The society does wonderful things to help struggling families, like organising yearly camps away. They also give great guidance on how to deal with other family members. Each sibling's birthday must be acknowledged, not just that of the sick child. It is crucial to consider the other children in any family and to allow time to make them feel special, important and loved. This is vital when their sick sibling gets so much attention.

The Facebook page was filled with mothers and fathers trying to deal with what life had thrown at them. There were lots of pictures of little kids, in and out of hospital, most showing the good times, with happy faces and smiles during their all too brief periods without seizures. There were fewer articles and pictures showing the inevitable bad times. A lot of the talk and messaging related to the medication that the children were on. Some patients did experience varying degrees of reduction in the number of seizures through using various combinations of drugs, which was great to hear; however, many others experienced no benefits from the drugs they were given and, to compound matters, often reported horrendous side effects.

Around this time, I looked beyond the UK to the Facebook pages of American parents of children with Dravet. This is where I started to see postings on cannabis. I was really taken aback. At the time, I wondered why people were discussing it on Facebook pages for epilepsy patients.

I hadn't much knowledge of cannabis at the time, only knowing that some people smoked it to get a temporary 'high'.

But it quickly became clear to me that what was being discussed on the US Facebook pages was something quite different. There were videos of children who were visibly in a tonic-clonic seizure receiving a small amount of medicinal cannabis under their tongue and, incredibly, this treatment appeared to calm the seizure down.

I wasn't quite sure what to make of it at first. I contacted the mothers on the Facebook pages and over time got to know their stories. They were not 'out there' kind of people, as I'd first worried, and they were not against pharmaceutical drugs. What they had in common was that the pharmaceutical medication given to them had not worked for their children and so they had been compelled to try what was then considered an 'alternative medicine', namely medicinal cannabis.

At the time I just filed it away in the back of my mind as some interesting-but-unlikely-to-be-useful information. I wasn't at their stage yet; we still had options.

***

Towards the end of 2010, Ava had her first birthday and a new drug was introduced to her treatment. Frisium is a benzo-diazepine (a class of psychoactive drugs that can have an anti-convulsant effect) and the drug is commonly used to treat epilepsy, but it is addictive, with sleepiness, drooling and constipation all commonly reported side effects. After its introduction, Ava became very sedated and, at night, disturbed sleep became a significant difficulty. Her sedated state also seemed to hinder her learning to walk, as she had trouble standing or confidently taking a step.

I had convinced myself around this time that, while she had been diagnosed with Dravet syndrome, this diagnosis in fact wasn't correct at all. She was different to the other children who'd been diagnosed with this condition. Then, after I had prayed and prayed, in December of that year the seizures stopped – well, the big tonic-clonic seizures stopped. She still had the staring episodes and some jerks, but in comparison to the attacks from which she had been previously suffering, she was so much better. I felt like my prayers had been answered.

I considered what had been said about Dravet being a spectrum of severity and figured that even if Ava did have Dravet – though I still felt, deep down, that she didn't – then she must be on the milder end of the spectrum. This period was one of a weird kind of quasi-relief, where Ava wasn't getting the big tonic-clonic seizures but was still very vulnerable. A fall off a chair or hitting her head against a hard surface was always a scary possibility. Thankfully, we had avoided any falls or bad bangs, mostly because she was only ever a few feet away from me.

Life seemed to have stabilised and things appeared so good that in February 2011 we went to Spain for a week's family holiday. Paul and I had loved going on little breaks before we got married and now that Ava's condition appeared to have improved we thought that we could all go on a holiday together. Like any normal family.

As the holiday approached, however, I grew terrified that we were putting Ava under too much pressure by taking her abroad. What would happen if a seizure took place on the plane? Paul and I reassured ourselves by reminding each other that the medication was working and by repeating endlessly how the holiday was, in fact, a good idea.

First, it was necessary to obtain a letter from our doctor for Ava's medication. This was to avoid any difficulty in travelling with it on the plane. The next thing we had to do was to make sure that there was a hospital in the locality. Before I booked the flight, I ensured that there was an English-speaking medical centre in the area.

At the time we flew over, I was expecting our second child and was back to foreseeing a wonderful future for my family. We had had a bad run with Ava, but life was going to improve. Later in the year our second baby would be born and Ava's seizures were under control. Having epilepsy, with the seizures under control, wasn't going to be so bad; many families have much worse to deal with.

Despite my apprehension, the flight and travel passed off without incident. We were lucky in that Ava slept for a lot of the journey. In Spain, however, I never felt able to let my guard down and relax. We maintained the routine with the medicines, but dealing with plastic bags filled with the various tablets and liquids was so different to having it all organised at home. The apartment's hard, tiled floor and numerous steps were all hazards for Ava. It was unfamiliar terrain and there was the danger of a fall. The different environment and constantly having to follow her around, to pre-empt any accidents, was exhausting. At home we could organise our environment to try to accommodate Ava's vulnerabilities, but this isn't as feasible when away from home. The weather was wonderfully sunny, but blaring in my head was the worrying fact that warmer conditions could drive up Ava's temperature and induce an attack.

It felt like a relief, really, when we finally returned home.

It is very difficult to accept that your family circumstances are different to those around you. While we left with such high hopes, after that trip to Spain I felt it would be a long time before we would go anywhere again.

Now the thing about it was that the doctors didn't think that there was a miracle of any sort when it came to Ava's apparent recovery. They told us that this was a very predictable stage in the progression of Dravet. At around the age of thirteen months, the development of the brain changes and for a time there can be a break or temporary easing in the seizure activity.

Never mind what other people had experienced, I knew that they were wrong. Ava was getting better. The seizures just couldn't come back; the medicine was working now. By now I was five months pregnant and could hardly walk with the sciatica, but sure who cared, the seizures were gone. Nature can be very cruel in the way it raises and just as quickly dashes your hopes.

Sophia Maria arrived in June 2011 to our huge delight and joy. However, God help us all, the doctors were right and the joy was brutally and abruptly cut short when Ava's seizures returned towards the end of the summer.

Bang, Bang, Bang, Bang.

The nightmare had restarted with renewed terror. I thought I'd simply go mad with the horror. I had begun to get used to Ava being seizure free, and it was the biggest mistake I ever made. All my prayers and positive thinking were dashed as the hospital visits began again. Ava was seizing every day, but, if anything, things were worse now as we had a brand new baby. How could this be happening?

***

You can know someone for a lot of your life and realise, over time, that you don't know them at all. When Ava got sick I thought I knew who I could depend on. In that assumption, I was sadly mistaken. I was so very shocked by one person who said, 'Ah sure, Vera, it's only epilepsy.' This was two or three years into Ava's illness, when they knew very well that Ava spent weeks on end in hospital. I can remember the humiliation I felt as this opinion was expressed.

I saw my mother's face close down across the table, so as not to contradict a guest in the house. I felt so small, as Ava's illness was described as something so trivial. As if my upset, fear and worry were unjustified. I wondered at the lack of understanding: did this person know Ava at all? I've never forgotten that comment. Some people can be strange and, I think, imagine that I'm looking for sympathy or exaggerating the facts so as to garner attention or pity. I never craved attention for its own sake, or pity, and I certainly didn't expect this reaction from a visitor to our home.

A medical professional told me once that I should get an au pair to look after Ava. As they talked, it seemed to me that they were basically suggesting I should just get over it and move on. I thanked this person for their advice and told them that instead of getting over it, I would be getting over them!

Another incident involved a good friend who called one day and saw Ava having a seizure. I ran to her, but after administering the rescue drug Buccolam to Ava, I nearly had to run to him as well. I had my hand out in case he collapsed; the colour had drained from his face. I sat him down and got him a drink, he was so badly shaken. The irony is that it wasn't even a bad seizure. Following this incident, his visits spaced out and gradually dwindled away. We missed him a lot. A long time after, he said to me that he couldn't call any more because he got such a fright. I told him, 'Sure, you don't have to do anything. I'm always there to do it', but the fear was too much and so Dravet syndrome robbed us of a dear friend.

But this distancing wasn't limited to him. To some extent, it happens to many parents with a child who has special needs, but I really wish that it didn't. Don't pass by because there's a sick child in the house, call in. Nobody expects you to cure the child's illness; they only want you to see them as you always did. They are still the same old friend, except now with a lot extra on their plate.

As well as those who grew distant, there was another group of friends and acquaintances who believed Ava would grow out of her seizures. They had perhaps heard this, or had some personal experience of a relative who had grown out of seizures and imagined Ava would have the same experience. For Ava, however, this isn't the case. With a genetic malformation of her system to contend with, that isn't possible. Explaining that to someone who thinks they are 'on the money' is tricky. They sometimes think you're wrong and that you simply don't want to accept that Ava will grow out of it. My God, I can think of nothing I want more. They believe you're badly informed because it's happened to another child. I have found myself on many occasions saving other people's feelings by nodding away, while inside I'm thinking, 'Why am I agreeing with this? Why don't they understand that Dravet is different?' But, I suppose, how can you expect people to grasp something completely beyond their experience?

In contrast, the friends we met during Ava's hospital

admissions were in an altogether different category. Parents like us can pick each other out a mile away. We are a sort of club of our own, one you never want to join. There is a hunted look in the eyes. We look a little bit edgy, maybe a bit drawn and pale. More often than not, we are trying, and failing, to hide it. Our attention can be a million miles away, thinking about our child and trying to solve the unsolvable riddle of their illness and treatment.

The other interesting thing about parents who have kids with rare conditions is the dramatic intake of breath when you meet someone else in the same boat. The questions that follow tend to be incisive, knowing: 'Oh, your little boy has Lennox-Gastaut syndrome. How is he? Who are you under? Are you? We are under her, too. How are ye getting on?' Then it's on to the medicines that you've tried. That conversation can go on as long as a piece of string. 'We tried that too, it was useless.' 'Was it? It worked for us for a while but then stopped.' Then there's the joy of talking to them because, oh my God, the relief in not having to explain from the beginning what Ava's condition means. To have somebody who is not going to get bored of listening, or someone trying so hard to understand, but they are so scared of the seizures that they can't deal with being around you any more. Instead, having someone to talk to who knows what twenty seizures a day is like and someone who is as glad to offload onto you as you are to offload onto them, is priceless.

It's a giving kind of neighbourhood that you begin to be drawn into. In this neighbourhood, everyone is at different stages. You may learn a lot from one family and then encounter another wandering around in circles like you were yourself once. It's only kindness, only decent, to talk and give help to anyone who wants it. Then, let them work away themselves. Often, we have the information we need right there in front of us, but it takes time to know what to do with it.

We kept in touch with many of these parents on Facebook and found that they had a level of understanding of our situation that some of our other friends didn't. If you didn't get back to them for a while there was patience and empathy. They knew that we were dealing with a new, very serious reality. When you could talk, you talked; if you couldn't, you weren't going to be asked questions as to why. Their children may have had different conditions, but the pressure and the all-consuming nature of looking after the kids were similar. Friendships based on your child's illness were unusual; often you knew very little else about them. Talking about medications or seizures passed the time when you got a chance to go to the parents' room. Speaking to people going through the same ordeal left you somehow feeling not so alone – although, on the whole, we felt very alone most of the time.

Of course, we also found out which of our friends would stick around and be there for us through thick and thin. God, did we appreciate them. They'd say, 'God, Vera, you must be so stressed.' I never knew how to react to this. Yes, I suppose I am – tiredness, worry and stress had become my constant companions after Ava's diagnosis – but when your child is so ill all the time you really don't have time to quantify it. Our best days with Ava were worse than the very worst days most people would ever experience with their children. As a result, stress is just there with you; you haul it around.

The people who remain by your side when the going is tough and you feel suffocated by the illness are the very best friends you can hope for. When trying to navigate such stormy seas, the fair-weather friends drop away, and you are left with the staunchest, most unbreakable friendships. I'd thank them for calling and they'd say, 'Sure, I'm doing nothing by calling.'

In reality, nothing could be further from the truth; their friendship is very special. For maybe twenty minutes or half an hour I could almost imagine that things were normal. My mother wasn't any different; she was still the clever, witty, wonderful lady she'd always been. I was the same old girl, too; the only difference was that my mother had a sick granddaughter and I had a sick daughter.

Visits gave us a break. We got a chance to talk about something else for a change. Hear a funny story or a bit of gossip. The people who don't pass by the end of the lane are special. Paul and I have some great friends who have been there from the start and with whom our friendship is as strong as ever. Likewise, the friends made over the course of Ava's illness are a godsend. Meeting up, or even just a short chat over the phone, can be a real tonic.

***

You genuinely descend into a living nightmare when your child has drug-resistant epilepsy. With constant exposure to the health system, you get to really see its shortcomings. It can be simple things, like wards not being as clean as they should be – which is usually due to overcrowding and staff shortages. The disgusting vision of a pool of vomit that I witnessed one night in the corner of the children's waiting area has never left my mind. This was in a unit with sick children who had compromised immune systems. I can clearly remember being asked to wait in that cramped space, with the nauseating smell wafting around the room. I refused point blank.

We would endlessly wait for the neurology teams to arrive on their rounds. The cycle of doctors on placement from other parts of the country to Cork for three to four months would come and go. Student doctor after student doctor would file into the room and ask questions for their studies. You'd be happy to help, at first, but we eventually tired of the experience. Some of them would stand next to you and discuss Ava's condition. They'd give their diagnosis and prospects all within earshot. They must think the parents are deaf and stupid. They may have used medical jargon, but I can assure you that I knew how dire their diagnoses were. In my opinion student doctors should not discuss their views on the condition of the sick child in front of the parents. After just a couple of minutes in the room, they aren't qualified to do so. Besides, I'd already had those upsetting discussions about Ava's health with her established medical clinicians.

The introduction of a fourth drug, Keppra, helped to control Ava's incredibly frequent absence seizures and myoclonic jerks, but had no impact upon the tonic-clonic seizures, which could occur several times a day. The admissions to hospital had become a weekly event, with Ava spending at least two weeks of each month in the ward. It was decided to introduce a fifth drug, Epilim, to try to control the tonic-clonic attacks. It was a worry to read that one of the serious potential side effects of this drug was liver problems. Ava's little body was dealing with a lot of medication. Unfortunately, the Epilim had no observable effect and the seizures continued unabated.

I can recall how, even as the side effects of the pharmaceutical medicines became more pronounced, Ava started to verbalise and babble away a little with a few words. By the time she was about two and a half she was beginning to walk. This was a major milestone in her development. I had known she could do it and I told her how proud we were and what a great girl she was. I knew she had so much potential in her. That inside my beautiful little girl there was so much more waiting to burst out. She had already proved the doctors wrong by walking, after all, so now it was just a case of helping her to survive and prove what she could achieve, rather than what they had expected her not to achieve.

She then suffered from five fairly big seizures that resulted in another long stay in hospital and her being administered a new drug, stiripentol. The seizures were spiralling out of control and it was hoped that this drug might control the tonic-clonic seizures. Devastatingly, however, during this hospital stay, Ava went into a coma for six days. The grave faces on the doctors and nurses who treated her made it clear how serious the situation was.

She wasn't expected to survive. Paul and I sat by her bed, looking at the grey, still shadow of our daughter. Nothing seemed real and time simply evaporated as Ava clung to life. Who can you talk to about your daughter's life-threatening coma? No one. So you sit there, hoping and praying that she'll turn the corner and pull through. When she finally came out of the coma, she had lost the ability to walk; she couldn't support her head unaided and all her clothes were hanging off her because she had lost so much weight. The victories that had been won with such unimaginable effort were snatched away in an instant. It took another twelve months to build back up her weight and get her back physically to where she had been.

That was the first time, but not the last, that she nearly died.

As the stiripentol made no obvious difference, Paul and I felt that it should be withdrawn from Ava's treatment programme and it was reluctantly removed by the neurologist, with Ava being weaned off over a period of six weeks as she recovered in the hospital. We also looked for at least one of the other failed medications to be gradually phased out.

You lose one, you gain one. The drug rufinamide was given to Ava then, in an attempt to control the tonic-clonics. We didn't see any improvement in seizure control, nor were there any visible side effects. It was becoming really worrying to see drug after drug failing. You don't give up, though; you keep trying to find the magic combination.

Later, another benzodiazepine, Rivotril, was introduced. With this drug there was some initial reduction in the incidence of tonic-clonics. However, the side effects were alarming. Ava became very sedated and withdrawn, and she had to wear a bib due to the constant drooling as she rocked back and forth. You'd have to change the bib several times each day. My daughter just couldn't get a break, because over time the seizures returned to their former severity, while the drooling and sedation remained. In addition, Ava's sleep remained very disturbed.

We were very wary of the side effects of any new drugs, but were even more desperate to help Ava, so when Zonegran was suggested to try to control the seizures, we again administered it to Ava. Thankfully, she didn't seem to experience any of the reported side effects, such as dizziness, agitation, mental confusion or memory impairment. The reduction in seizures we saw at the beginning of the treatment tailed off, however, and they returned again, as bad as ever.

After trying a number of drugs, we began looking at the potential side effects of the next drug being proposed, as much as the possible benefits. Often the side effects were more costly to Ava's development than the limited amount of seizures they may have prevented. In total, Ava tried eleven different pharmaceutical drugs: the benzodiazepines Frisium and Rivotril, phenobarbital, Keppra, Topamax, stiripentol, Zonegran, rufinamide, Epilim, lorazepam and phenytoin. On one occasion, when Ava went into cardiac arrest after suffering seventeen tonic-clonic seizures in eight hours, she was given multiple doses of rescue medication, but the lorazepam, phenytoin and other medication didn't work and put further strain on an already fragile and stressed body. We felt that this terrible state was partially due to the prescribed medications, which were failing to stop the seizures and also had catastrophic side effects.

Ava had a very painful, confused and stress-filled life. One seizure after another. On and on and on. During really bad days she hardly had time to recover from one before the next one struck. Every seizure is upsetting, but the bad ones are really frightening. I'd try to comfort her as she went through it and attempt to keep her safe. Each had the potential to cause permanent brain damage and because of their length, which varied from a couple of minutes to over an hour, they were life-threatening. Her heart was under tremendous pressure. Her life was in imminent danger, every day of the week. After each and every one of these seizures she'd fight back, reach out and hold on, until she had recovered somewhat and was with us again. I think the physical contact comforted her greatly, letting her know that she wasn't alone.

The seizures led to profound developmental delays as the years passed. They tore away any normality she might have had. She could only manage a few words when her peers were talking. Her understanding was limited. Her balance and walking were very poor. Often she had trouble sleeping and could be in constant pain. She'd be in a bad, bad way after a big episode. Observing her every move was a constant necessity, so as to get to her as quickly as possible. Any small bit of progress was hard won and often taken away by the next cluster of seizures or the side effects of the drugs. And yet, between the seizures, just by being herself, she could provide such joy. When the epilepsy allowed, we could see that she was a placid, funny, determined little girl, who enjoyed watching *Peppa Pig* and playing with LEGO as much as other children do.

Meanwhile, while all this turmoil was happening with Ava, we were still trying to raise Sophia with as much normality as possible. This continued over the years, as Michael joined the family in September 2012 and Elvera-Mae was born in January 2015. Calm and sleep-ins became a distant memory as, on all fronts, ours had become an action-packed house. But the younger children have been great for Ava and ourselves. Their play and interaction help to bring her along and are a constant source of amusement and joy in what would otherwise be a much more difficult environment.

I always thought the next drug would be the one to ease things, but the seizures continued unabated. As the years passed, I couldn't help but think more and more about the fabulous stories of families in America administering cannabis oil to their sick children, often with very positive results. I looked for more evidence of its use, researching the topic in depth. The more research I did the more it seemed to offer potential respite and hope. I still didn't think it was an option for Ava, however, if for no other reason than the fact that cannabis oil medication wasn't available in Ireland.

We did try numerous alternative treatments during this difficult time. Over the years, Paul and I brought Ava to everything we could find within a safe travelling distance. Craniosacral therapy, energy therapy, music therapy, aromatherapy oils, a healing priest, a mystic healer, a dietitian. You name it, we unsuccessfully tried it.

We tried to provide as much private speech therapy as we could manage, but it was expensive and a financial strain. From day one, the services provided regarding speech and language and occupational therapy had been hopelessly inadequate. It was always just a flat, dead response: 'Sorry but the services are cut back. We only have so many hours to share among everyone.' If a child with a condition as serious as Ava's didn't qualify for adequate help, what hope was there for other, less needy children?

As well as the day-to-day struggle of dealing with Ava's illness, we had to go through the endless struggle for what were essentially basic rights. The endless form filling, with long unacceptable delays in any response. Be it for the medical card, DCA payments, assessments, speech and language or occupational therapy appointments. It became a training ground in persistence. All these applications leave parents frustrated and often humiliated, when unhelpful staff speak to you from some distant office, protected by their anonymity and one's inability to meet them face to face. I'm sure it's a struggle with which many other families with disabled children in Ireland are familiar.

Some of these treatments, once attained, proved beneficial.

Perhaps the most uplifting treatment was equine therapy, which involved supervised riding and interaction with horses. We saw a gradual improvement in Ava's core muscles from this therapy, which was amazing. On the first day, her body was so limp that she leaned really far back and needed constant support. Week by week, however, Ava improved and eventually was able to be led around with her feet in the stirrups.

It was emotional to watch: I hadn't realised how floppy she had been, how poor her muscle tone was. For once, we had found something that we could see with our own eyes was providing an improvement. Sadly, because the seizures kept on coming, Ava missed so many sessions that she lost her place to another child on the long waiting list. The cost of the therapy was again frustratingly an impediment, but the progress she had undoubtedly made was a badly needed emotional boost. I'll never forget her circling the arena on horseback, a big smile on her face from the pure enjoyment of it all. Ava has had too few days like that.

Personally, I kept up the prayers and did the novenas as much as I could. Sometimes I'd not get to the end of them because of another rush to the hospital. I believed good would come, that we were building up a bank of prayers that would allow us to overcome this horror. We also had a lot of family and friends praying to God, Allah, the trees and flowers, and whatever else might help.

In October 2015, when Ava was nearly six years of age, it seemed like our prayers were going to go unanswered. That month the doctors informed myself and Paul that there were no new drugs available to try. Ava had tried them all. We were told, 'Take her home and make her comfortable.' What we felt they meant, though they hadn't the guts to say it, was that we were to bring her home and watch her die.

People tell you it'll get better, it'll get easier. The reality is things can get a lot worse. Paul and I were at the end of our tether when we were told that all the options with pharmaceutical drugs had been expended. That road had reached its conclusion. Now we had to find a new road to take, and if we couldn't find one, we'd have to build it ourselves.

It was then, while at our lowest point, that we realised that we had to start advocating for Ava to be given access to treatment with medicinal cannabis.

4

Make it Medicine

'There are two primary choices in life: to accept conditions as
they exist, or accept the responsibility for changing them.'
– Denis Waitley

Ava's private neurologist, whose opinion I always valued, listened
to our suggestion of medicinal cannabis as a possible treatment
option for Ava and seemed on board, but was unable to help
due to cannabis not being considered a medicine. Incredible as
it seems, it appeared that we were expected to just accept Ava's
constant seizures without exploring this alternative medicine.
But there was no way I was meekly accepting that, or the advice
just to 'Take her home and make her comfortable' – not when
some children, in America and elsewhere, were being successfully
treated with cannabis oil.

I knew that something had to be done. If the medical
professionals couldn't help, I'd have to appeal directly to the
public and the minister for health. This would involve telling
people how serious Ava's condition was and how urgent her
need for this treatment was. The publicity this would entail
troubled me greatly, as our daughter's privacy was of the utmost
importance; however, Paul and I both felt that the reality was
that if we didn't get help for Ava, it was looking more and more

likely that we wouldn't have her in our lives for much longer. I had to come up with something and it had to happen quickly. If not, it was going to be too late.

After a lot of soul-searching, late-night discussions around the kitchen table and personal reflection, going public seemed to be Ava's only chance. As a result, we started an online petition, called 'CBD for Ava', on Change.org in October 2015.

Before this I had never been a public person. I never told our business to anybody, really, or told people how bad Ava was. I had to change all of that. Due to its unavailability in Ireland for treating epilepsy, I had to drum up public support for Ava to gain access to cannabis oil. I was just trying to save her life. I thought that if I got an opportunity to put Ava's case to the minister for health, she would receive that help. It was so obvious, I felt; there were no other options. I hadn't the faintest idea of the struggles lying ahead.

Bang, Bang, Bang, Bang.

In November 2015 Ava had eighteen seizures in eight hours, resulting in a heart attack. It was like some sort of horrific blur, watching all of this happen. I was frozen in terror, unable to do anything to help her and aghast to watch as all the medical professionals surrounding her were unable to do much more. It was like an out-of-body experience, completely surreal. I realised that unless things changed, she was not going to survive. The pressure on her little body was becoming too much. Paul and I were really frantic, with a constant and profound worry that Ava was slipping away. I felt drained and desperate, terrified that we were reaching the end of the line.

The petition was a slow burner, but by March 2016 it had passed the one thousand signatures mark. There was no target

for Ava

number; I just wanted to get as many signatures as possible. I hoped the petition would put pressure on the politicians and show the level of public support behind Ava receiving medicinal cannabis. We had no indication that the oil would work for her, of course, but when you're being told that all the other options are gone, what do you do? This was her last chance and we had to try.

Once the petition was started I canvassed everywhere and everyone I possibly could. Friends, neighbours, family, Facebook groups such as Dravet UK, local councillors, politicians. It was so hard to put Ava's plight and ill health out there on the petition and share it on Facebook. You really have to bare your soul and show your child's illness to the world, which is a very difficult thing to do. Paul and I didn't want her lovely smile out in the public, and people associating it with such upsetting circumstances, but her need was greater. Our anxiety about this exposure had to be kept under control. We desperately hoped it would all be worth it and that the medicinal cannabis would ultimately work.

***

Cannabis has been used as a medicine for thousands of years in cultures as diverse as China, Egypt, Greece and Rome. Ironically, it was an Irishman, William O'Shaughnessy, who first brought the medicinal qualities of the cannabis plant to the notice of western medicine.

The cannabis plant contains a large number of compounds called cannabinoids, many of which have been found to have medical benefits. You're going to be reading a fair bit about some of these cannabinoids, moving forward, so a brief explanation is in order. Cannabinoids have been found to be effective because many of them resemble chemicals that the body itself produces. The chemicals produced by the body are called 'endocannabinoids' and are part of the body's endocannabinoid system. This seldom-mentioned system is involved in regulating several vital body functions, such as pain, neuroexcitation, anxiety, stress and memory.

Cannabinoids can attach to receptors located in the various body organs and the effect depends on which receptor the particular cannabinoid attaches to. The psychoactive cannabinoid THC, for example, can attach to receptors in the brain and has been found to relieve pain and spasticity.

Studies and real-life examples have demonstrated the anti-convulsant activity of several cannabinoids. Epileptic seizures are thought to be most effectively controlled by the cannabinoids CBD (cannabidiol), CBN (cannabinol), CBDV (cannabidivarin) and THC. CBN is thought to be partially responsible for the sedative effects of cannabis. Several cannabinoids, including CBD, exert anti-inflammatory and antioxidant effects. CBD can interact with other cannabinoids, such as THC, in an 'entourage effect', and may benefit the user together more than they would in isolation.

There have been numerous studies, and real-life examples, showing how cannabinoids can be effective in treating a number of illnesses, including epilepsy, multiple sclerosis (MS) and chronic pain, amongst others. Whole plant cannabis is cheaper than many pharmaceutical drugs, has few reported side effects and can be as, if not more, effective for certain illnesses.

Despite all this, products containing THC above 0.2 per cent were illegal in Ireland during this time, coming under the Misuse of Drugs Act. This was because Ireland, like many countries, had adopted the regressive stance of the United States government concerning medicinal cannabis. There, the National Institute on Drug Abuse (NIDA) has blocked almost all meaningful studies on cannabis for several decades. Cannabis's 'schedule 1' status as an illegal drug makes obtaining a licence to conduct research very difficult. Cynically, the US government actually has a patent (No. 6630507) titled 'Cannabinoids as antioxidants and neuroprotectants', basically staking a claim on using them as a specific type of medication. The UK government deny cannabis has any medical use, yet the UK is one of the world's biggest exporters of medicinal cannabis. How is that for a contradiction? However, like a beautifully resilient weed, cannabis has emerged as a medicine in spite of all this repression. Why? Because it can work, and desperate parents have pushed and pushed for access for their sick children.

Colorado would be known as one of the most progressive locations for the use of medicinal cannabis. There are numerous cases of children suffering from severe seizures going there to receive treatment, often as a last, desperate hope. For many of them, the results have been spectacularly successful. Almost as important for families worn out from dealing with the often-severe side effects of pharmaceutical drugs, was that the reported side effects were mild – namely, sleepiness, fatigue and diarrhoea – and are easily manageable.

Seizure control isn't the only potential benefit of medicinal cannabis. Its main medical use is probably in pain management. An online survey of over 1,300 fibromyalgia patients, carried out by the National Pain Foundation in the United States, found medicinal cannabis to be a far more effective pain management treatment than the three main prescribed drugs approved by the Food and Drug Administration (FDA).

Furthermore, it's been reported that in the American states that have legalised medicinal cannabis, there has been a reduction in opioid overdoses, while in the same period in the other states the deaths from opioid overdoses have shown a massive increase. Literally tens of thousands of people die from opioid overdoses in America each year (over 70,000 Americans fatally overdosed in 2017), mostly from prescription medication. If anything, medicinal cannabis is an exit drug, not an entry drug, helping to free people from dangerous opioid addictions.

My good friend Tom Curran, who is a tireless advocate for medicinal cannabis, saw for himself the benefits his late wife, Marie, obtained from cannabis. Marie suffered from MS and the only thing that gave some relief from the constant neurological pain was cannabis. As Tom described it at a public meeting, 'It was like a burning pain all over her body and when we increased the pain medication she was almost comatose. Pretty soon she was taking the maximum dose and it wasn't controlling her pain.' Her experience with medicinal cannabis was different, however: 'Within twenty seconds of taking the medicine, her constant pain subsided and her body relaxed completely. You'd have to see the extent to believe it. It really lifted her spirits and made her feel alive again.'

The American television personality Montel Williams is another MS sufferer to benefit from medicinal cannabis. As he's publicly stated, 'When I was diagnosed with MS, my doctor told me I'd be in a wheelchair in four years and dead by fifty-six. The only reason I'm even able to write this today is because my doctor, a world class neurologist, recommended medicinal cannabis.'

At the symposium on medicinal cannabis which was held in Dublin by the People Before Profit party, an Irish cancer patient spoke of being diagnosed with cancer. She had chemotherapy and radiotherapy but ended up in 'excruciating' pain, because they irradiated the whole bone rather than just the tumour in her spine and hip. None of the usual medication helped, because the bone was so inflamed. As she said, 'I had no choice but to explore medicinal cannabis. I had my life in my hands. The day after I took it for the first time I couldn't believe the difference. The pain had completely dissipated.'

Clearly medicinal cannabis had made a difference in these people's lives; now I was determined to see if it could make a difference for Ava.

***

In 2016 my public campaigning intensified. Tentatively, I began to contact the local radio stations and try to raise awareness. It was around this time that I came in contact with Neil Prenderville and Red FM radio station. I didn't realise it at the time, but it was a real coup to meet such great people. Over the coming years they really couldn't have done more, facilitating interview after interview. They gave me the priceless opportunity to raise desperately needed awareness.

I also made contact with the television stations TV3 and RTÉ. Disappointingly, RTÉ gave little response and appeared essentially uninterested in Ava's story. It was Paul Byrne of *TV3 News* who took call after call, and *TV3 News* in general which covered Ava's story repeatedly, highlighting my daughter's situation all over the country. Crucially, Paul also offered me advice, and I was blessed to have such experience there to assist us, as well as such consistent support.

In the beginning, I was incredibly nervous to come out and speak on the radio and television. I worried that I'd say the wrong thing and wouldn't get my point across. I was concerned about what other people might think about me coming out in public about my daughter's illness. But, whenever I had thoughts about being nervous, I said to myself, 'Pull yourself together and get over it, because if we don't get something sorted for Ava, she's going to die.'

It was that simple. It didn't matter whether I was shy or often nervous. I had to do something, because Ava needed me to do something. We were lucky to still have her with us after the cardiac arrest. It was time to 'woman up'.

So, I started talking to and meeting some of the people working in Irish media. There were cameras set up in the kitchen and TV3 microphones up on the table. I experienced the discomfort and horror of hearing my voice on the news. I don't really sound like that, do I? Do I really have such a high-pitched, pronounced accent? I never seemed to be able to complete a sentence without a 'like' or 'you know', which is a common Cork trait. We grabbed on to something to laugh at; it just happened to be my early media performances.

I started contacting newspapers, to see if they would cover Ava's story. My initial contact was with the *Irish Examiner*, which has a strong readership in Cork. They published a number of articles about Ava, as did the *Evening Echo*, the *Lee Valley* and the *Cork Independent*.

After Ava's story appeared on the television, I reached out to other radio stations, like Newstalk, hoping that they might be convinced that Ava's story was newsworthy. Contacting Jonathan Healy on Newstalk was another major breakthrough as he had me on his programme on several occasions.

Then, on top of all this, there was the public speaking. The first time I was asked to speak at an event concerning medicinal cannabis was in early 2016 to Wexford cannabis club. I know, I didn't realise such clubs existed either. I was eager to attend, as much to learn from people more experienced in medicinal cannabis than I was, as to tell people about my petition and daughter. I'd been researching all the studies and websites, but nothing really beats sitting down with knowledgeable people who are willing to share what they know.

I was quickly put at ease by the warm welcome that I received. 'Vera, just tell them about Ava, her story and what she needs. That's what people are interested in hearing.' So that's what I did.

This meeting was my introduction to the addiction specialist Gareth McGovern, who works in treating various addictions. He's seen it all and has vast experience and expertise, both in dealing with patients who need help and with the Department of Health and the HSE. Gareth felt strongly that medicinal cannabis should be available for doctors to prescribe in their treatment programmes. I've been fortunate to have him stay in contact and offer his experience over the years.

A young man, apparently in the prime of life, approached me that day after my speech. It was the same old story: he'd suffered from chronic pain for years and obtained no relief from the prescribed pharmaceutical drugs. Moreover, they'd left him feeling constantly sick. He'd missed a lot of events as a result over the years, and had been worried about what the future held.

'Medicinal cannabis has changed my life, Vera; I've much less pain. It's amazing. I'm sleeping much better and haven't taken a sleeping tablet in weeks.' You could hear a tremendous optimism in his voice. The fact he felt compelled to self-medicate with an illegal medicine was of little consequence to him because of its life-changing effects. That young man was the first person I'd actually met in the flesh who'd benefited from using medicinal THC and CBD. The first, but not the last.

In early March, Ava suffered fourteen seizures in twenty-four hours. I poured out my heart on Facebook: 'This is the only hope that Ava now has. I don't want to be forced out of Ireland with my family to get treatment. All we are pleading for is a little common sense. If medicinal cannabis can help my daughter, why can't she be allowed to benefit from it in her own country? She doesn't have any alternatives.'

I had recently read a testimonial from an American family whose son was having up to 500 seizures per day. He had been prescribed twenty-two pharmaceutical pills daily, without success. Medicinal cannabis stopped his seizures and he gradually came off the other drugs. Such stories were incredibly powerful for a parent in my position. I decided that I wouldn't let myself be fobbed off by any politician or doctor telling me that medicinal cannabis wasn't an option. Ava had to have that option; I just hoped she wouldn't have to go abroad, to somewhere like Colorado, to receive it.

I also read about a young American girl during this time. She had intractable epilepsy and had moved to another state, as a medical exile, to obtain better access to medicinal cannabis. She had already tried twenty-three pharmaceutical medications, but had only improved when she started using THC oil. Sadly, in

March she went to sleep and never woke up. In the same month, four other children with Dravet syndrome also died. The Dravet syndrome community is small but strong; however, that was a tough, heartbreaking time. One moment your child is fine, the next they're having a seizure. Any seizure could be their last.

Early in the morning on 2 April 2016 Ava had three long seizures. I spent the next few hours watching her sleep on the baby monitor placed in her room. It allowed me to see her without disturbing her sleep by entering the room. I was waiting to see if she had any more; if she did, an ambulance would probably have to be called, with another stay in hospital. Worst-case scenario, we could lose our daughter. It was that serious.

The seizures also risked setting her development back. Skills she'd learned could be lost. As I said at the time, 'She can pick up words, have a seizure and they would be lost again. One of her first words was "Nice", she said it a couple of times, then suffered a cluster of seizures and didn't say it again for another two years.'

At the time, we were receiving some help from a night nurse during the week, but even with this welcome assistance life was completely draining. Neither Paul nor I had had a proper, stress-free night's sleep since before Ava was diagnosed.

***

Amid all this gloom and upset there was one incident which still makes me laugh. An appointment had been arranged in a Dublin hospital, but Ava was too sick to travel by car. Enter the amazing charity, BUMBLEance. This is an ambulance kitted out especially for children who need to visit a hospital, but are too poorly to travel by more conventional means. It's a simple, practical solution to a problem faced by families all over Ireland who are caring for seriously ill children.

The BUMBLEance is set up with the child in mind. Its brightly coloured interior creates a warm and friendly space, while the DVD player, iPad and books make the journey as pleasant and relaxed for the child as possible. Behind the child-friendly approach lies the real beauty of the service, in that Ava had immediate access to trained paramedics and medical equipment, should it be needed.

It was long after the scheduled time of five o'clock in the evening when the BUMBLEance finally drove into the yard. They had travelled down from Dublin and the two medics appeared mightily relieved to have arrived. Smiling, the driver said, 'Jaysus, we thought we'd never get here, we've been driving around for ages. I think we got a bit lost.'

My mother said, 'My God, did ye get lost, where did you go?'

'Ah Jaysus, we did, we were lost for sure. We ended up on the side of some mountain and the roads just got narrower and narrower; it was just sheep, bogs and trees. If we'd met a lorry we'd have been in real trouble, like real trouble. You know something, you're really out in the countryside here.'

We do live out in the countryside, there's no doubt about it. Jokingly, my mother told them, 'By the sounds of it, you were up around Mushera mountain. You were lucky to make it down alive. Those sheep are pure wild and very unpredictable.'

They must have spent most of their time in the city because later one of the medics exclaimed, 'Jayney, it's really dark here, I mean it's really dark.' I remember saying to him, 'Sure, doesn't it get dark in Dublin too?'

'Yeah, no, ah no, it's not dark like this. We have lights on the roads. I mean here it's pitch dark, yis can't see a thing.'

I looked out the window and yeah, I suppose, if you're used to street lights it would appear pretty dark. He went on, 'And another thing, it's very quiet, there's no traffic noise or anything really. It's too quiet, my missus wouldn't like this at all, no, the dark and silence would freak her out, she wouldn't be able to sleep at all.'

'Jeez,' I said, 'I wouldn't be able to sleep with the noise and street lights shining in the windows.'

Laughing, we came to the conclusion that we had better stay living where we were, it was much more agreeable all round. They kept up the friendly banter over the duration of the trip. With their watchful, attentive eye, Ava couldn't have been in better hands on the drive up to Dublin and down again. Their jovial nature made an otherwise stressful experience much more manageable.

***

In early 2016 I felt like I was getting quite the run-around from the people I contacted in the Department of Health. My efforts were being dealt with by shifting my enquiries from one person to the next, none of whom would take responsibility for looking into doing anything for Ava. These are people who were supposed to be working for the Irish public, so I felt that they should have been more supportive of my efforts to help my very sick child.

In May 2016 there was a cabinet reshuffle and someone new, young and apparently a breath of fresh air entered the role of minister for health. We were very eager to obtain a meeting with the man who talked about all the dazzling changes he was going to make in the department. That person was Simon Harris.

By this stage the online petition had garnered several thousand signatures in support of Ava and so I sent repeated emails to the minister for health's office requesting a meeting. I also began to ring Dáil Éireann, in Leinster House, directly, to get in contact with his parliamentary office to ask him when he'd meet me to discuss helping my daughter.

I believe it was through an interview on Jonathan Healy's programme on Newstalk in late May that I obtained my first meeting with Minister Harris. Jonathan interviewed me, and I told him that I'd spent several months trying to get a meeting with the minister for health, but, despite all my endeavours, had met with no success. I told Jonathan that I just had to get a meeting about Ava, and if I had to get a train up to Dublin and stand outside the gates of Leinster House until he walked out of them, then that's what I was prepared to do. I implored Minister Harris to help us. People needed to realise that Paul and I had exhausted all the reasonable and more conventional options, I explained, long before we had resorted to direct action.

My phone rang later that evening. I was coming out of the Dunnes Stores supermarket in Macroom, where I'd run in for some soya milk for Ava. As I was struggling with three cartons of it in my arms, the phone rang. I managed to get the phone out and a familiar voice spoke and asked, 'Is this Vera?'

'Hello, yes it is.' I stopped for a moment and stared at the ground.

'This is Simon Harris.'

The minister for health had finally responded and made contact.

I thought, 'This could only happen to me. I've waited several months for this phone call and now that it's taking place I'm totally unprepared.' That's how we started our first conversation: me walking across the car park, soya milk in one hand, car keys in the other, and the phone balanced precariously between my ear and shoulder.

'Hi, Simon, my goodness I've been a long time trying to get to speak to the minister for health, and now I have you I don't know what to say.' There was a momentary 'Ha, ha' on the other end of the line and I proceeded, 'Except, I must ask you Simon, when are you going to meet us?'

'We can arrange a meeting via the office; we would be glad to meet you.'

And with that the arrangements for the first meeting with Simon Harris were set in motion.

Despite the cursory acknowledgements of my previous emails and phone calls, and the lack of action to date, I felt this first short discussion with the new minister was hopeful. He had actually seemed to agree or at least empathise with what we were trying to achieve. However, I knew that being nice wouldn't be enough, not when people's lives are in danger, or constant chronic pain is destroying their quality of life. It would take a strong minister to overcome the institutional inertia and vested pharmaceutical interests in the area of health. I desperately hoped he would be able to achieve this.

That May, as I watched Ava playing in the garden with Sophia, I smiled and thought about how much courage she had in order to endure her illness, day in, day out. She's a complete and utter warrior. She's not even aware that she's the bravest of girls, because this life of struggle is all she's ever known. I wondered if the government had an ounce of her courage and would embrace Ava's story and really listen.

Once, while speaking on the phone to a politician, I was advised about 'how complicated matters can be'. Perhaps he was trying to convince me that it was all too complicated for a little woman from the 'sticks' to understand and that I should give up. But every issue can be made to appear complicated until you resolve to sit down and achieve a solution.

Towards the end of May, Ava had sixteen seizures and an admission to hospital. It was a frightening few days. While Ava is in hospital normal life gets put on hold. Paul and I had to stay with her all the time, leaving my mother and my friends minding the kids at home. Really, without my mother's incredible help we'd have been lost.

That month Paul and I also travelled up to Leinster House for our first eagerly anticipated meeting with Simon Harris. We both had a lot of hope that the new minister would be open to listening and prepared to provide assistance.

We brought along a photo to show him Ava and let him see the very sick girl who lay at the heart of our meeting. We also provided him with a print-out of the petition, and the many thousands of signatures contained therein. Simon and his officials were pleasant enough as they outlined the government's current position on medicinal cannabis; however, it was all very general statements and soothing words. There was nothing being said to provide any hope of real, substantial progress. As a result, I left the meeting feeling deflated.

This trip was also the first occasion where I met Gino Kenny, who is a TD for the Irish Solidarity–People Before Profit party. Gino had a deep interest in the whole issue surrounding medicinal cannabis and the need for legislative change. He's subsequently recounted how when 'Vera explained her situation with Ava, I was struck by her desperation. That she wanted to get this medicine for Ava. As soon as I got out of that door, I knew something had to be done. So Bríd Smith and I put the "Cannabis for Medicinal Use Regulation Bill 2016" forward in the Dáil, on the last day of July. Its main goal was for patients to be able to receive a legal, secure supply of medicinal cannabis, which was safe and effective. The public response was overwhelmingly positive and still to this day it's been overwhelmingly positive. It's set off a debate which is long overdue.'

Gino had already been approached by a family in Clondalkin who had a little girl with Dravet syndrome, so he had an understanding of what the condition meant and how cruel it could be. He had promised the girl's mother and granddad that, if he got elected to the Dáil, he'd try to do something positive regarding medicinal cannabis. Now, here he was meeting another family who had a child with the same condition. Dravet syndrome is so rare that I've always thought this to be an extraordinary coincidence. It must have been written in the stars that our paths would cross, as Gino's been a constant, unwavering source of support since that day, patiently taking call after call and providing sound advice and motivation.

I was thrilled that the bill was put forward. If it was eventually enacted, it offered hope to Ava and all the other children with intractable epilepsy, as well as people with chronic pain, MS and cancer patients.

The effort to gain access to medicinal cannabis for Ava was taking up more and more of my spare time, day and night. I was constantly asking for people's support, for them to contact their local political representatives, TDs and councillors, or the minister for health directly. It was a lot of work on top of everything else.

It's probably best that I didn't know that I was still only in the foothills of the campaign. The loftier mountains were still up ahead, unseen, but ready to present tremendous challenges.

***

Our second meeting with Simon Harris and his officials took place in June. Paul and I travelled up to Dublin again. We still had some hope that, if Ava's case was put across better, we might make some progress. As I passed the gates of Leinster House, however, it felt like we were entering with nothing and in all likelihood would leave with the same.

Two nights earlier, Micheál Martin, the leader of the Fianna Fáil party, had rung, asking could he sit in on the meeting. As a former minister for health I was happy to have him there and heartened to receive the phone call. I had also hoped that my local Fine Gael political representative, Michael Creed, then minister for agriculture, could attend the meeting and help in moving things forward. While waiting in Buswells Hotel, however, Michael Creed's assistant came in and told us that Michael probably couldn't make it, but he'd attend in his place.

Later, as we sat in the meeting room, waiting for it to start, there was a 'tap, tap' on the door and Micheál Martin stuck his head in and said, 'Hello, is it okay if I join you?'

Surprisingly, several minutes later, Michael Creed did arrive and, a short time later, Simon Harris and his officials entered the room.

for Ava

The crux of the meeting was trying to find someone to oversee Ava's care on medicinal cannabis. Due to the illegal status of medicinal cannabis, it appeared to us that the public neurologist in CUH was unable to do so. The private neurologist was also unable to because of issues with indemnity insurance, again due to the illegal nature of cannabis. Micheál Martin suggested that the indemnity be removed from the private neurologist and hospital and instead be covered by the state. This meant, in essence, that the state would act as the insurer. Simon said this wasn't possible; however, as a former minister for health, Micheál said it had been done in other health cases. When Simon and his officials remained adamant that it couldn't be done, Micheál retorted, 'Yes, it can be done. The minister sanctioned it. I should know, I was that minister.'

This put Simon and his officials in an awkward position and they said they'd look into it. It was then suggested by Simon and a department official that a GP could apply for the licence. This was great news because I knew of two GPs who were prepared to make an application. Shortly thereafter, our forty-minute time slot elapsed and Simon and his officials said they had other meetings to attend.

Afterwards, I was glad with how the meeting had gone overall, but also concerned that nothing might come of the suggestions. For me, it was also telling that at no time did Simon or anyone on the government side of the table enquire as to how Ava was doing, which to me, after all, was the most important question.

Within a week we learned that the private neurologist and hospital could not be moved on the indemnification, but we still had the hope of the GP applying for a licence to prescribe the medicinal cannabis. We were obviously excited and motivated by this news and after some discussions one of the doctors agreed to make the application. He spent over two months overcoming the obstacles placed in front of him, while putting the application together, and after it was submitted I felt hopeful that the application would be looked on favourably.

***

Tears were a common feature of life in 2016. With three younger, boisterous children, as well as Ava's very serious and demanding illness, I felt like I was reaching my emotional and physical breaking point. The one hour a day of home help we got from the HSE had come to an end. Even with the huge amount of support I received from Paul and my mother, it was very tough. To see the impact Ava's epilepsy had on all the children was upsetting. When Ava has a seizure, we had to wait for a short period to see if it passed of its own accord, before giving her rescue medication. If Michael or Sophia were with her they'd automatically start counting to sixty, trying to copy what they'd seen the adults do. Counting helped them to show their love for Ava. They were only three and four years of age; that's no experience for such young children to have to live with.

There were also, thankfully, some uplifting events. A 'Fight for Ava' boxing tournament took place that summer in the Tower Hotel in Waterford city, and over 400 people signed the petition that night, while in July there was an open day at the 'Hydro Farm' near Blarney in aid of Ava. These two events spanned the entire spectrum of Irish society and showed that ordinary Irish people supported Ava.

One morning in early August brought the awful news that a beautiful little American girl had died after courageously battling Dravet syndrome. She was five years old. We hoped and prayed that we could obtain treatment for Ava, so we wouldn't have to suffer the terrible loss her family were dealing with. I asked people on Facebook to 'Please pray for sense to be brought to bear in this country. Our children deserve the chance to try medicinal cannabis, surrounded by the love of their families. Please sign Ava's petition, but most important of all today, think of that brave little girl, her mum, dad and family.'

It felt horrendous that morning, to be standing there in the kitchen looking at Ava, asking myself, 'What else are you going to do?' I was trying to do everything that I could, but I knew there was more that could be done to help her, if only the government stopped blocking her path to medicinal cannabis. If she was a little girl living in Colorado or the Netherlands, she could receive treatment with medicinal cannabis, but just because she was from Ireland, she couldn't receive the medication she needed. It galls me that people have to suffer needlessly.

Dravet syndrome stole another child's life on 19 August.

It was unbearable to see the constant notices of deaths, all the while living with the possibility that my daughter could be next. I was feeling particularly raw at the news of another child's death because the day before Ava had suffered sixteen seizures. This period was one of the most emotionally painful and negative. I felt myself sinking into a dark depression and those black, heavy clouds were a constant companion. So many children with Dravet syndrome were dying and I felt that we were not far away from being the next family to suffer the loss of their child. People telling you to 'pull yourself together' is all well and good, but it's hard to pull yourself up after so many knocks. It takes a lot of doing.

At the time, the Dravet was winning in a big way. The seizures just kept on coming, piling on, one after another. Bang, Bang, Bang, Bang. The length of an attack could vary, anywhere from two minutes up to ninety minutes. I really feared that they would result in lasting and profound brain damage. I stood as nurses rushed back and forth while Ava was still seizing, and all I could do was pray. Our responses felt so inadequate when compared to the magnitude of her suffering. It was overwhelming.

By September, the petition 'CBD for Ava' had garnered almost 12,000 signatures. I posed the question on Facebook: 'How many do you think I need to get for Simon Harris? Will it be 15,000 or more? How many newspapers need to share her picture and tell how hard she's fighting Dravet syndrome every day?'

At the time Ava was spending another night just about holding on. She was so sick that Paul and I were taking turns spending the night with her, to be there when she had the inevitable seizures. It was a very long, dark period.

Around the end of September, Ava suffered twenty seizures in one day. It took the whole life out of her for several days. It was a slow, painful process for her to claw her way back to us. After that many attacks in a day, you'd be wondering would she still be able to speak? Would her legs still work?

The seizures were out of control. It was really, really frightening. Something had to change.

5

Roadblock after Roadblock

'We may encounter many defeats,
but we must not be defeated.'

– Maya Angelou

Cannabis CBD oil became available in Ireland, as a food supplement, in September 2016. I went to the Hemp shop in Dublin, and by chance met Joel Stanley, one of the Stanley brothers, who are based in Colorado and manufacture the CBD oil known as Charlotte's Web. Speaking to Joel was a tipping point for me; his caring attitude and experience solidified my confidence that I was doing the right thing in giving Ava the CBD oil. Charlotte's Web is a CBD oil in its purest form, a whole plant extract, containing no pharmaceutical additives. It was developed when an American mother pleaded with the Stanley brothers to create an oil for her then five-year-old daughter, Charlotte Figi, who suffered from Dravet syndrome.

We were unable to get a neurologist in Ireland to prescribe the oil as it was not licensed for medical use in Ireland. There was also the problem that few of them considered medicinal cannabis to have any proven medical benefits. But I took comfort in the fact that there were extremely well-respected doctors

Roadblock after Roadblock

in Colorado, Israel, The Netherlands and Canada who did. We knew it was working for kids suffering from Dravet elsewhere.

There was very little advice out there in Ireland, but I discussed possible dosages with the Stanley brothers and with one of Ava's neurologists. This was the first occasion where the lack of knowledge about cannabis oil within the Irish medical community made itself felt. We had a battle on our hands and you know something – we were still afraid. We were wondering if we were doing the right thing. After all, it was a major leap into the unknown; however, when you have an inferno at your back, the only option is to jump.

At the end of September 2016, Ava had twenty-three seizures in thirty-six hours. The seizures were as bad as they'd ever been. Following on from this we began giving her a small dose of the Charlotte's Web 'Everyday Plus Hemp Oil' in the morning and again at night. This was it, possibly her last chance.

Unbelievably, the results were almost instantaneous, with an abrupt reduction in the number of seizures. Paul and I would look at each other in disbelief during those first days. Was this real? Had the seizures really reduced? You learn not to hope too much when every previous drug has ended in failure, but with the CBD oil the effects were unmistakable, undeniable. There was a big reduction.

I waited until 9 October before tentatively announcing the improvement on Facebook: 'Okay, a deep breath, I'm letting people know the wonderful news that our darling Ava has experienced eight days seizure free. Yes, eight days. There has been no tonic-clonic, no absences, drop seizures or myoclonic jerks. There has been no change to Ava's routine or medications [she was also still taking Zonegran and vitamin B6 at the time], other than the introduction of Charlotte's Web. She appears brighter and even more engaged than previously. I'm almost afraid to speak of this magnificent news in case she has a turn tomorrow, but I had to let people know.'

In addition to the huge reduction in the number of seizures, there were a number of side effects from the CBD oil. However, in contrast to the side effects from the pharmaceutical drugs, the side effects of the CBD oil were beneficial. Ava had an increased appetite, which was great because she needed to put on weight. Her sleep was still very disturbed and despite appearing extremely tired it could take a long time, each evening, to get her off to sleep. This was getting slightly better now, however, and she even exhibited less pain when standing. She was smiling more, was brighter and, while still largely non-verbal, her teachers said that she was engaging more with her peers. It was a revelation, life-changing. We were getting to see a whole new side to our child.

Keep in mind that all of this had been carried out by ourselves with no ongoing active involvement by medical professionals. Of course, this was a completely unsatisfactory situation. Ava should have had a prescription for the medicine. A paediatric neurologist should have been in a position to prescribe it and oversee her care.

By late October I could report, 'Charlotte's Web has had a fantastic impact. She went eleven days with no seizures, then she had two on the thirteenth and has now gone five days without one. That mightn't sound like much, given she'd two seizures, but she had hundreds in September. People have no idea; to be able to put on her uniform and send her to school, she's not wrecked-looking any more, she's talking more and she's brighter every day. I can tell you now that it works. Before, it was just me trusting others, but my child has changed for the better. Beforehand, we were wondering whether we would be dealing with wheelchairs, brain damage and paralysis.'

Over the course of the next few weeks we were able to gauge more clearly the impact of the CBD oil. There was a major reduction in the number of seizures – we estimated by eighty to ninety per cent. She had seven in the whole of October, nine in November and only three in December. Only three! A few months previously Ava had been having more than that every day.

As we well knew, however, every seizure is potentially life-threatening. One is one too many. There were still moments of real danger, when Ava's life hung in the balance. That all-pervading fear still lingered in the background, no matter how much her condition had improved since taking the CBD oil. We were also concerned that the effectiveness of the CBD oil would wear off over time. From our research and the stories emerging out of some states in America, I could see that other children with Dravet were especially benefiting when the cannabinoid THC was added to their treatment with CBD oil. I became convinced that Ava deserved the chance to combine the THC oil with CBD oil.

BLUE HAZE

When we first decided to go public with Ava's illness Michael Creed of Fine Gael had been the first politician we approached. I can remember him calling to our home and taking details. But this was around the time of an election, so when I heard nothing back I presumed it was because he was busy in his new role as minister for agriculture. It was to be a while before I had another opportunity to speak to him.

I first approached Michael because, for as long as I could remember, there was no uncertainty about political affiliation in our house. It was very simple: we always voted Fine Gael. My father had been a party member and after his death that membership had been passed on to me, the next generation of 'blue shirt'. I had naively thought that never in good conscience would I be able to tick any other box on the ballot paper. They were the good ones, weren't they?

That was all before the 'blue haze' subsided and I realised that even though generations of my family had supported them, when the chips were down and we needed help, in my eyes the party failed to help us. In spite of Paul saying over and over again, 'They aren't going to help Ava, how much more proof do you need?', I just couldn't believe that Fine Gael would do so little.

It must have been around late October 2016 when a Fine Gael meeting was held in Millstreet, because the question on my mind was how Michael Creed was going to vote on the 'Cannabis for Medicinal Use Regulation Bill 2016' when it came before the Dáil in December of that year. Paul and I decided to attend the meeting and ask Michael what his intentions were. I was new to quizzing politicians and a little unsure of myself. I was going to be standing up, asking questions and looking for answers. My neighbours and friends would be in attendance and a lot of them were staunch supporters of Fine Gael. I didn't want to upset or fall out with anyone, but resolved to overcome any fear or reticence. Ava's well-being was too important not to gather up the courage to act.

As we entered the meeting room, the energy and excitement were palpable. Young men gathered together in small groups of three or four, leaning forward, earnestly discussing various topics.

Already sitting were the older generation, men like my father, who had worked hard all their lives and showed the signs in their walk of a hip that had been replaced or that badly needed to be. Again, as with my father, these were the sure signs of decades of backbreaking work.

Thank goodness that there were a couple of women also in attendance, as it made me feel a little less like 'the odd woman out'. As we all started to sit down I felt very alone, even though Paul was beside me. The publicity surrounding my advocacy of Ava receiving cannabis oil must have attracted some negative local attention, as I got a few hard-looking glances and disapproving frowns from some of the attendees. I was a little scared, but I soon toughened up again. It's the waiting to speak or act which is often the hardest part.

The meeting commenced and I saw one woman actually begin to weep with pride and joy that Michael had been given the job of minister for agriculture. Tears were wiped away from her face amid the clapping and cheering. In fact, it was akin to the reaction of the local team winning the county, or maybe the All-Ireland, final. I looked around as the people in the surrounding seats looked on with pride at the local Fine Gael man made good. It was always good to see a Cork man get into some position in the government, so on that note I was hopeful that he'd help some local people, perhaps even Ava.

The meeting progressed and at the questions section, I stood up and said, 'Michael, hello, my name is Vera Twomey.' I had seen him already take note of our presence. During the meeting, his gaze had passed along the seats of attendees, and as his gaze passed over me, it had momentarily stopped and come back to me for a second look. I thought that was good for Ava. If he recognised me from our previous meetings – including that meeting with Simon Harris – then he must remember and recognise Ava's plight.

I asked him what he would do to help Ava get the medication she needed and how he was going to vote in the upcoming debate. This wasn't an easily answered question and there was a pause as he formulated his answer. A good neighbour of ours shouted out, 'These people have been very patient; I wouldn't have been as patient. It's a child, Michael. What are you going to do for the child?'

Michael answered that he didn't know yet how he was going to vote in the debate.

I said, 'Michael, that's just not good enough at all, we need your support to help our daughter.'

More of my neighbours chimed in, agreeing, asking what was to be done. Michael made a few more general comments about needing to talk to a consultant and that was it.

When the meeting was over I walked over to him with fire in my belly, especially after hearing the support of our neighbours. I quizzed him again as to what he was going to do to help. He asked, 'What can be done?'

'Michael,' I said, 'what could be done is you could help us find a way out of this for Ava.'

His final remark to me that night was an enquiry after my mother's health. I told him, 'Do you know what, Michael, her health would be a hell of a lot better if her granddaughter had access to medical cannabis to help her seizures. You still have time to help us.'

I left it at that.

Paul and I went to the bar for a cup of tea to relax after the meeting, but that didn't work out as the looks we got from some of those who came in afterwards were not conducive to relaxation or good digestion. People looked over at us, then back to each other, muttering away. We looked at each other with raised eyebrows and decided we'd go for a bag of chips instead. At that stage of dealing with Ava's illness, for us being out of the house with a bag of chips was like a week in Lanzarote, so we sat there, eating and chatting away.

The carry-on at the meeting and afterwards was sad. Why were some of these people looking at us like we had done something wrong? All we wanted was a chance for Ava to receive this medication. How was it that after asking a politician for help, we were made to feel so unwelcome inside the doors of a hotel not a dozen miles from home? But then I suppose Ireland has always had an unattractive tradition of trying to marginalise people who speak out about injustices. Heaven forbid that the 'powers that be' are made to feel in any way uncomfortable.

***

On 1 November Ava had a really bad seizure. She had an ear infection and a high temperature at the time, and that is probably what triggered the attack. The seizure lifted her up off the bed with the power of it. After witnessing the terrible power of that seizure I knew something had to be done: not planned for, not in the future, not under review. No, it had to be now, before it was too late, before the next barrage of seizures ended her life. That's when I had the idea of walking to the Irish parliament in Dublin to protest.

We'd been waiting twelve months at this stage. The HSE and minister told us they were trying, but the progress they had made was totally inadequate. I was tremendously frustrated by the continuous efforts needed to try to get updates. Ava couldn't wait another six months. She had to gain access to the THC oil, which could potentially work to treat her epilepsy even more successfully than the CBD oil on its own. I didn't know what was ahead of us, but I knew Ava needed that medicine. I'd tried Facebook, phoning and emailing them. Other people had tried getting in contact with them. The petition had thousands of signatures by this point. I had tried everything imaginable. Walking seemed like the final, desperate option.

I heard the voice of my father in my head, saying, 'If the mountain won't come to Mohammed, then Mohammed must go to the mountain.' If he'd still been alive, he'd have fought. I began to realise that we'd have to stand up and fight harder.

I really didn't want to walk to the Irish parliament in Leinster House. I had no idea how I was going to manage what I thought must amount to almost 200 miles. When I told Paul he thought I'd lost my mind and asked me to sit down and have a cup of tea. After a few minutes, though, Paul agreed that something had to be done. He asked, 'Do you think you can do it?'

'I will do it, there's people who'll help, I'm sure of it,' I replied.

We'd both walk over hot coals for Ava, and now was the time to prove it. We'd been patient, respectful and given the HSE and Minister Harris space. They told us that they'd do everything to help us. I believed Simon when I met him in June, so what I deemed to be the subsequent inaction over the last four months was inexcusable. For me it was simple: the minister needed to sponsor the bill and get the legislation which was drawn up moving forward.

I started at about 9.30 a.m. the following morning, 2 November, leaving the house and heading for Dublin. Other than announcing my intentions on Facebook and contacting some of the media, I hadn't prepared at all and didn't know how I was going to get there, as neither the route nor accommodation were planned, but as I optimistically said at the time, 'Sure, I'll find somewhere to put my head.' Paul Byrne of TV3 came out to film my departure and conduct an interview. Looking back, I can see how I was completely unprepared for such an undertaking. My supplies consisted of, 'My coat, my phone, a bottle of water and a couple of pears.' Not a very comprehensive list!

There was a great outpouring of support as I walked the road towards Mallow. Just before 'Crean's cross', a neighbour stopped his car, leaned out and asked, 'Vera, do you need a spin?'

'No thanks,' I said, 'I'm walking to Dublin to protest for Ava.'

His eyes widened and jaw dropped as I explained my predicament. He drove off, saying, 'This is the worst carry-on I've ever heard.'

As the miles passed, I started to find that people were joining me. Word had spread via Facebook and my interviews with the media. Timmy O'Sullivan walked twenty-one miles with me. A man in Bweeng invited us in for soup and was full of support and enthusiasm. Others came out with water and sandwiches. They, too, were full of support, but equally angry that I felt driven to walking. People who knew me realised that I wouldn't have walked unless I'd run out of alternatives. I get very emotional running through the memories forged on the roads of central Cork. Alan and Theresa from Mallow walked with me, as did several of my neighbours. I thought I was on my own, but soon began to realise that there were so many people out there supporting Ava. That gave me a tremendous boost.

Colm O'Sullivan of Red FM brought me along some food and a phone charger, compliments of the Vodaphone shop in Cork city, and we held an interview near Drommahane village. I told Colm, 'I'd be delighted if there's anyone around to walk a mile with us. I didn't give much notice [of the walk taking place], it kind of happened quickly. Walking a few miles is not even close to the suffering Ava goes through. If we don't get legislation shortly to help Ava, I really feel we won't have her for much longer.'

After finishing up the interview with Colm we continued onwards. We had walked about twenty miles at this point and it was about six o'clock in the evening when I got as far as Mallow. It was here that Simon Harris rang and asked me to stop the protest walk. He said, 'Well Vera, I'm not comfortable that you are doing this, that you are walking all the ways up to Dublin. You don't have to do this.'

I replied, 'I'm not comfortable having to walk either, Simon, but what am I going to do? What are you going to do?'

He was adamant that he was going to help Ava. He promised to sit down with me and a formal meeting was arranged. He gave his word that he'd sort out this situation that our family and others in Ireland were being put through.

As I said, I really didn't want to be walking the roads, not when Ava was so poorly, so I gladly took up his offer. I had been advised that, if I started, I had to be willing to see it through to the end, which I was, but a meeting at least held out some hope of a resolution. It would have been remiss to not take him up on the offer.

I went home to my family, hoping that it wasn't in vain. The minister later released a statement announcing a review of Ireland's policy on medicinal cannabis. The Health Products Regulatory Authority (HPRA) were asked to provide him with their expert scientific advice on the issue.

After he gave this statement I briefly hoped that progress had been made. However, I spoke to one journalist shortly afterwards and she told me that it could take a whole twelve months to produce a report. That was a blow, as Ava couldn't wait twelve weeks, never mind twelve months. I needed to get a reasonable time frame, one which recognised Ava's fragile condition, at the planned meeting. If that happened then we could wait, but if the length of time was too long then we would be forced to peacefully protest for a quicker solution. If it came to it, I was determined that I'd go out walking again. And this time I wouldn't stop until I reached Dublin.

The Dravet syndrome community is relatively small and I had gotten to know a lot of people via the Facebook support pages. On 5 November, I learned that another American family had lost their young son when he didn't come out of a seizure and passed away. He was just eight years old.

We met Simon Harris and department officials on 9 November. The minister said at the meeting that he had asked his officials to complete the review by January. He also took the opportunity to update us on the policy review. The HPRA would provide him with advice on recent developments in cannabis, its use for medical purposes and an overview of related products that had been authorised in other jurisdictions. He said he also asked for an overview of the 'wider ongoing and emerging clinical research' on the efficacy of medicinal cannabis and the different regulatory regimes that were in place in jurisdictions which allow it.

What I had learned by this stage, however, was that politicians could talk all day about reports and reviews as if they were a solution that we should be grateful for. Well, we weren't grateful. Ava needed action, not a review to action.

I interjected, 'Let's park it there about the HPRA report for now and let's get back to talking about Ava. We only have a certain amount of time, Simon, so let's not waste it.'

This suggestion elicited a response of furrowed brows and what seemed to me to be poorly disguised expressions of displeasure. I also felt that I saw some confusion in the officials' faces. It seemed that they were taken aback that I hadn't meekly accepted them dictating events. Clearly, they weren't used to parents speaking up for their children's rights. Neither Paul nor I were verbally abusive, so we couldn't be demeaned for that. We also understood the subject and could argue away the irrelevant points that they constantly raised. We knew what had been said at the previous meetings and in the phone calls and we weren't in awe of the civil servants or the minister. Frankly, we weren't going to give up, quieten down and go away. They seemed to be missing the point that this wasn't some abstract issue for us; this was our daughter's life that hung in the balance. We were prepared to do *whatever* it took.

Simon Harris told us that the HPRA would be able to advise him on any legislative changes required. He would move forward with any legislative changes based upon the HPRA report and advice from the Oireachtas Health Committee. He appealed for Paul and me to be patient, that the review couldn't be done any quicker. It all sounded good, but ultimately vague, with no firm indication of when, or if, Ava would receive the medicine she needed.

At the end of the meeting I told the minister that if he didn't resolve the situation for Ava, I'd have to recommence my walk from Mallow and that hundreds of people had contacted me; it would no longer just be myself that would be walking.

THE NIGHT THAT FLOR CALLED

Late one evening, the doorbell rang. It was 10.20 p.m., so getting into 'someone calling with bad news' territory. Paul still hadn't arrived home from work and my mother had gone to bed. I wasn't expecting any visitors and so got a bit of a fright. It had been an uneventful day. I had just put another load of washing on and all the kids were in bed asleep. I could hear Ava breathing away on the monitor. Who could be calling unannounced at such a late hour?

Cautiously, I went to the front door and could see the outline of a tall figure in the glass. I slowly eased the door open and pulled it back more fully once I recognised the surprise visitor; it was Flor, one of the local guards.

I invited him in and my first thought was that he had bad news. Happily, I could quickly tell from his demeanour that this wasn't the case. He told me he had been passing and decided to call about the gun. Now, my father, being a farmer, used to own a shotgun, but it was a long time since we had one. There was no real need and I was uncomfortable having one in the house with the children.

Anyway, it wouldn't be usual to call so late to inquire about a firearm licence. I immediately suspected why the call had been made. I had been campaigning about medicinal cannabis for a long time now, so word must have eventually reached the gardaí, and perhaps now they were curious about this local 'drugs activist'.

Now, Flor is an affable man and as I turned on the kettle to make the tea, I decided we had better cut to the chase, so as I took down two mugs I also reached over for the bottle of cannabis oil. I poured Flor his tea and, as I offered him a biscuit, said, 'This is it, now, Flor, this is the cannabis oil. Would you like to see it?'

'I would,' he said, so I handed over the bottle and explained how Ava took a couple of drops twice a day. I also went into some detail about CBD oil and its current status in Ireland as a food supplement.

Flor was taking it all in, but played his cards very close to his chest. He had taken his hat off and placed it on the table. I didn't know if this was good or bad news. I couldn't discern what direction the night was going in. We kept talking, me explaining about Stanley Brothers, Charlotte Figi and the Hemp store, while Flor silently drank his tea with the occasional nod in my direction.

After two cups of tea Flor leaned forward and said he was delighted that Ava was doing so well. To lighten the mood, I jokingly asked if he would like to try the Charlotte's Web, but with a wry smile my offer was politely declined. By the end of our conversation, Flor seemed happy. I was just slightly bemused by such an unusual house call. My recollection is that no one has ever enquired about us having a gun licence since then.

But, for whatever purpose the visit was made, it didn't result in any subsequent action. We'd continue to occasionally see Flor passing by in the garda car, up until his retirement. Hopefully, the conversation we had put his mind to rest that Aghabullogue was not home to some nefarious activities, and he now had a good impression of medicinal cannabis.

***

On 24 November, I spoke before the Oireachtas Committee on Health. It was felt that my family's experience would provide a real-life example of how medicinal cannabis can benefit people. I told them of all the pharmaceutical medications that Ava had unsuccessfully tried and said, 'It's the nature of Dravet that it breaks through the medication.' I detailed Ava's incredible improvement on the Charlotte's Web and how we wanted the government to move forward and help us make this a medicine that doctors in Ireland could prescribe. I was convinced that if our doctor could prescribe it, they'd then become more involved in the process.

It was a long day, but it was an opportunity to change people's perceptions and minds. I was not naive enough to expect hard hearts to soften, but you have to try, so I asked people on Facebook, 'Please, if you pray, say one that will soften their hearts today and make them all see how much we need this medicine. If not a prayer, send us some good wishes.'

Soon after, on 30 November, I was invited to speak at a medical cannabis event in the European Union Parliament, in Brussels. Luke 'Ming' Flanagan, MEP, and his team looked after us during the stay. Arriving in the parliament was extraordinary as it was absolutely enormous and quite imposing. Security was tight, with regular checks of your bags and coat as you moved around the complex. The technology in the building was impressive, with TV hubs to do interviews and so much more. It was fascinating to watch the media, running here and hurrying there, trying to get their stories completed.

A wide variety of people attended the event and provided a broad overview of the situation regarding medicinal cannabis in the European Union and elsewhere. There were speakers from Israel, Spain, Germany and several other countries, who detailed the ongoing research and the use of medicinal cannabis in cancer care, pain treatment and other illnesses. I listened intently as speaker after speaker passionately put forward the case for medicinal cannabis and the reasons for moving forward with it, for the benefit of every country and community.

It was incredible to be asked to speak amidst people with such a vast knowledge. They spoke with such authority – what was I doing there? I suppose I was able to describe the reality of using it with a sick child. You can't understand that from reading it in a book or report; you have to actually live it to appreciate it. I gave an outline of Ava's medical history and told them, 'My daughter's life was completely and utterly overtaken and controlled by seizures' and 'We're being introduced to a new person since she started this medication.'

I got a real sense of reassurance that I was doing the right thing for Ava, in spite of the negativity at home concerning medicinal cannabis. It gave me a broader overview of the situation outside of Ireland. This wasn't just Aghabullogue, this was Europe and people were saying, yes, yes, yes. I could only feel saddened that this positive attitude hadn't reached Ireland's medical community or government.

While I was over in Brussels, an Irish journalist gave me the surprising, but splendid, news that the Fine Gael-led government wouldn't oppose the 'Cannabis for Medicinal Use Regulation Bill', thereby allowing it to pass the first stage in the Dáil.

Gino Kenny's bill, which aimed to regulate the use of cannabis for medical purposes, was debated on 1 December and passed the first stage of the legislative process unopposed. In the Dáil chamber, the support of the majority of the political representatives was a heartening sign. I felt confident that any of the niggling concerns held by some of the politicians, such as rescheduling cannabis to make it legal for medicinal use and establishing a cannabis regulatory authority, could be worked out and resolved at the amendment stage. It felt, at the time, that progress was being made. We were all cautiously hopeful that the bill would progress quickly. The momentum seemed to be shifting and an *Irish Times* poll at the time found that eighty-one per cent of people surveyed supported legalising medicinal cannabis.

What a difference a year makes. In late 2015, Ava had suffered a cardiac arrest after having sixteen seizures. Between October and December of that year, she was in hospital continuously, bar five or six days. A year on, we hadn't seen the inside of a hospital since September. Before, it was worry, worry, worry, every single moment. Obviously, we were still concerned and monitored her carefully, but it was definitely a much better standard of life for her.

For the first week in December, Ava managed to attend school every single day. On the Thursday, she turned and said, 'Bye, bye, Nana.' She was happier, in less pain and sleeping better. It felt like we'd struck gold because we'd never had this before: the smile, the couple of words and the way she looked at us. We had spent nearly seven years trying to tackle her seizures, without any real success. Now, we felt like a curtain was opening before our eyes. I said on Facebook, 'She's an amazing kid, who just needs a chance in life. We know there's no cure, but if medicinal cannabis can help her, then why not prescribe it for her? They said she'd never walk or talk. She does both. We just want her to live as good a life as is possible.'

On 21 December I received some very upsetting news and, in response, I asked people in a Facebook post to send love and peace to a wonderful lady and dear friend, Mairead. She had lost her beautiful son, Bobby, that morning to seizures. We think of Mairead and Bobby often, and were so saddened by his passing.

In stark contrast, that Christmas was the best one that the family had yet experienced with Ava. Life was so different compared to every other year, when she'd spent most if not all of the holiday in hospital. There were no frantic calls for an ambulance, no prolonged stay in hospital – it was incredible. There had been no seizure for nearly two weeks. She even managed to remain seizure free while she recovered from a cold during the middle of the month. That felt like a significant development. We even got to visit Santa with all the other children.

Just before Christmas Day, while driving to Macroom, Ava shouted out 'Merry Christmas'. Paul nearly drove the car into the ditch with delighted surprise. Even that small trip, that small piece of normality, was wonderful. It was better than we had ever imagined it could be and we started to allow ourselves to hope a little bit.

6

Confronting Simon

'As much as I searched, I could not find a documented case of
death from marijuana [cannabis] overdose.'
— Dr Sanjay Gupta, chief medical correspondent, CNN

A meeting to raise awareness of medicinal cannabis, the proposed legislation and Ava's plight was held in the Castle Hotel
in Macroom on 10 January 2017. As the day approached,
it started to occupy my every spare thought. It was so local,
after all; it would mainly be people from Macroom and the
surrounding areas in attendance. Friends and neighbours
would be there. I was nervous, but determined. I would try to
make people understand why this legislation was so desperately
needed.

I made up a poster, had copies printed and started to put
them up in prominent locations: shop noticeboards, Cremins
bar, the pubs in Rylane and Donoughamore, and several other
establishments. The event was shared and shared on Facebook
and, to my delight, the politicians Gino Kenny and Jonathan
O'Brien said they were going to attend.

The night of the meeting arrived, and as Paul and I drove
into town, my heart was in my mouth. I said a silent prayer that
more than a few people would turn up. Approaching the hotel,

I received a welcome reassurance that I'd not be disappointed. There were cars parked all around the Castle Hotel.

Entering the meeting room, we saw people already occupying most of the chairs. The room was humming with conversation. I'd see a familiar face and greet them with a nod of the head and an upbeat hello. More and more people continued to arrive, and not only from the local area. Such was the interest in the event that people had travelled from Dublin and Galway.

As the start time approached, hotel staff brought in more chairs to accommodate the unexpectedly large throng. I could see neighbour after neighbour and several friends and family in the crowd. Things had undoubtedly been tough with Ava's illness, but we were blessed with their support. That night was one of the most revitalising experiences I've ever had – this was our community and our friends coming out to support us. Sometimes I find it hardest to express my gratitude to those friends I know best. They'll never know how much they energised us and lifted our spirits. It helped myself and Paul to continue the fight.

By the time we kicked off the meeting, latecomers were standing at the back. Jonathan O'Brien was stunned and after his speech said, 'My God, Vera, that was some crowd, you'd hardly get that in town [Cork city].' I had to smile at the comment, saying, 'Sure, Jonathan, this is local.' It was a long way for Gino to travel from Dublin, but he did a great job of explaining the bill he had put to the Dáil. He was equally blown away by the crowd, both its size and enthusiasm.

Tom Curran gave a powerful, personal testimony of caring for his late wife, Marie, and how much she benefited from medicinal cannabis in terms of alleviating her chronic pain. The crowd went very quiet as they listened to him. Much like my family, Tom was a person with first-hand experience. You can't beat that account of personal experience, as it's then that the reality of medicinal cannabis's benefits becomes undeniable.

Afterwards, as the meeting wound down, a lot of time was spent talking to the many attendees who had come seeking information. I did my best to tell them what I knew and, if I couldn't answer their questions, where they might go for additional advice. A lot of my friends and family stayed to chat, some of whom I hadn't seen in so long. It was late by the time we made our way home, delighted and relieved at such a successful evening.

***

The next day we travelled up to Dublin for another meeting with officials from the HPRA. At this meeting I was told that Minister Harris had the ability to authorise a ministerial exemption for the use of medicinal cannabis. It became evident that Paul and I needed to have immediate correspondence with the minister. Because I was already in Dublin, I decided to stand outside the gates of Leinster House waiting for him. I was totally unprepared and had no placards, supplies or supporters. No preparations had been made, it was just me.

That was a very difficult day. It was very humiliating to be left standing outside the gates from 1.45 p.m. until 7.15 p.m. That was when Gino Kenny came and pulled me away. He said I had to leave because I was frozen with the cold. Earlier in the day Gino had been attending a symposium about the case for medical cannabis in Ireland. A panel of people spoke who have been campaigning for legalisation on this topic. The speakers included Professor Mike Barnes of Newcastle University, who had published the 'Barnes Report' on the case for medicinal cannabis. It was an event I'd have loved to attend, but been unable to, due to my meeting and impromptu protest.

That night, I realised that I needed to take more effective action. If I couldn't get an official meeting with the minister, I felt I had no option but to make it my business to force such a meeting. A Fine Gael politician whom I had spoken to at the gates during the protest had informed me that Harris was scheduled to attend the official opening of the injury unit at Mallow general hospital the next day. I resolved to confront him there.

***

I was exhausted from the previous day's protest outside Leinster House and all the travelling that had been involved in getting to and from Dublin. It takes a good seven hours to travel by car up and down. I was becoming increasingly distressed at the treatment my family had received. Ava deserved much better. I was at my wits' end, driving over in the pouring rain to Mallow.

Waiting near the hospital entrance, I had a whole myriad of emotions: fear for Ava's health, mortification about confronting Simon Harris in public, anger at the official inaction, as well as a feeling of just being tired at having to endlessly fight for what Ava so desperately needed.

A lady working in the hospital recognised and approached us. She asked again and again if I'd be more comfortable going inside to a room. Only after repeatedly telling her, 'No thanks, I'm fine here, but I appreciate your concern', did she relent with a disappointed expression.

The black ministerial car drove into the car park and Minister Harris and the accompanying officials emerged, walking over to the entrance. As he entered, Paul and I approached and confronted him in the packed corridor. 'Simon,' I asked, 'what are you going to do to help my daughter Ava?'

We were quickly surrounded by the media, with cameras flashing and microphones outstretched. The minister's handlers appeared perturbed, with furrowed brows and worried looks on their faces. This was not the type of media exposure they had planned. They tried to steer us away from the cameras and media, but I wasn't in any mood to move.

Simon Harris leaned in towards me. He wrapped his arm around me, but I wasn't having any of it. I said, 'You're putting your hand out to me, you're putting your hand on me now. But you didn't put your hand out to me since before last Christmas. And I had respect for you. I've been a member of and voted Fine Gael for the last twenty years of my life and you've betrayed us. You were able to give a statement to TV3 to tell them what the current position of the government was regarding medicinal cannabis, but you didn't have the common decency to come down and tell me what was going on.'

The minister then tried to steer me away from the view of the cameras, but I wasn't for moving. He maintained that he was doing his best and that we were being kept in the loop with regards to developments. That he had initiated the policy review by the HPRA on the use of medicinal cannabis and expected it to be completed by the end of the month. He said, 'If it sees a benefit to the availability of medicinal cannabis, I can act on that immediately.'

His words did not have the desired effect. As I said at the

time, 'If he respected me, he wouldn't have left me standing outside the Dáil, the way I was last night, without some bit of compassion to send someone down to talk to me. I've always done everything I possibly can to be respectful and reasonable to them and every time they're pushing us and pushing us to this point where we have to do something like this to get their attention.'

Paul and I disputed the assertion that his department had not received an application from a doctor to obtain a licence to prescribe medicinal cannabis for Ava. Minister Harris was certain that such an application had not been made. He said, 'If a doctor puts in an application for your daughter to have medicinal cannabis that will be expedited, but there has been no application.'

Paul argued that we had done everything asked of us, even sourcing a wholesale pharmacist to import the prescribed oil. Each time the Department of Health came back with further requirements. They sought the names of reputable companies that we were planning to use to import the medicine. We had done that, with representatives of the companies travelling to Ireland to meet department officials, but we were still unable to obtain a licence for Ava. As Paul said, 'We are met with roadblock after roadblock.'

A lot of politicians have told me that the situation was very complicated, but I was afraid that if Ava suffered more seizures she would have another heart attack and be gone. Four or five children with Dravet syndrome had already passed away since the start of the year. This was the only chance that Ava now had. All we were asking for was a little common sense and urgency. It was heartbreaking to take Ava to the emergency department, despite knowing that there was nothing they could do for her.

We wanted Ava to have some chance of a normal life; surely, every Irish child had that right?

I think it's fair to say that we had a heated and emotional discussion. It wasn't how you'd want to hold a discussion, though, with members of the public, staff and the media looking on. But it had become necessary.

At one point I broke down and had to be consoled by Paul. With no sign of a satisfactory conclusion to the confrontation, Minister Harris offered to meet with both of us in private once the official opening had concluded.

After the opening, we did have the private meeting for ten minutes or so. He spoke about us 'perhaps going away for treatment. Perhaps that would be easier?'

Easier for whom? There's nothing easy about going into medical exile, but isn't that the traditional Irish way – export the difficult problems. Out of sight is out of mind. I just thought to myself, 'You're some "boyo". Go where? How?'

We were just as much in the dark after that meeting. We didn't see an obvious way forward and the minister had once again provided no real clarity. He did, however, tell us he'd recommence contact and in the general discussion said that his department had signed a licence for another Irish person to receive medicinal cannabis. So that gave us some hope; if he could sign a licence for another Irish person, then surely he could do the same for Ava?

***

The eagerly awaited report was released by the HPRA on 31 January. After reading it, myself and most other advocates for medicinal cannabis were disappointed by its very limited scope and ambition.

No mention was made of many of the conditions which medicinal cannabis can help. There was even no mention of chronic pain, which was an incredible omission. It only recommended medicinal cannabis be made available for patients with: spasticity associated with MS that was resistant to all standard therapies and interventions; those suffering from intractable nausea and vomiting associated with chemotherapy, despite the use of standard anti-emetic regimes; and patients with severe treatment-resistant epilepsy who have failed to respond to standard anti-convulsant medications.

Three very restricted options. And, to be eligible, you had to spend an indeterminate amount of time trying all the existing pharmaceutical drugs. That could take several years.

Furthermore, no account had been taken of the side effects of the existing drugs, such as benzodiazepines, which Ava had tried, and opioids, which were used for treating chronic pain. Both have very serious side effects, including overdose deaths and drug dependency. Medicinal cannabis can be effective at treating severe epilepsies, chronic pain and other conditions, and has far more benign side effects. Why in God's name would anybody try a highly addictive opioid, with a high potential for abuse and overdosing, before a non-addictive cannabis oil, which it's impossible to overdose on? It rings hollow to claim concern for safety, while at the same time ignoring the greater dangers of the drugs that are currently being used.

If ever there was a false dawn, the announcement by Simon Harris of the compassionate access scheme on 10 February was it. It followed on from the recommendations of the HPRA report and, initially, we greeted the scheme with great hope. Surely Ava would benefit from the inclusion of severe treatment-resistant epilepsy on the list of conditions that the patient had to be suffering from in order to access medicinal cannabis?

The previous night had been gruelling, one of the worst since she went on the CBD oil, with Ava suffering three major seizures. She was worn out; we were all worn out. The scheme seemed to offer some hope.

Boy oh boy, were we in for a rude awakening. We quickly found out, from talking to friends in the medical profession, that no medicinal cannabis containing THC oil was even being considered for inclusion in the scheme. The only drug being considered was Epidiolex, a pharmaceutically produced oil containing CBD. And the kick for seriously ill patients was that this drug wasn't even licensed yet, which meant that even in the best-case scenario, patients would be waiting a long, long time before they'd be able to access it. That's the 'compassionate' access scheme that Simon Harris proudly announced: one that was not operational.

The crunch meeting with Harris and officials from the Department of Health and HPRA took place on 23 February. Paul and I were given the news that Ava's application for a licence to use medical cannabis was being turned down. We had previously been told a doctor could make the application, but now the goalposts were once again changing.

While Simon did a fair amount of talking, I felt the direction and outcome of the meeting was largely orchestrated by the department officials sitting to either side of him. They said they could not accept our application because it had not been submitted by a consultant. They weren't rejecting it, they clarified; they just weren't accepting it. They couldn't have been more Jesuitical in their language.

We were now being told that for an application to have any chance of success, a consultant paediatric neurologist needed to sign off and submit the application. We had previously spoken to Ava's neurologists, who felt that for them to be able to submit a licence application, the legislation surrounding medicinal cannabis needed to be changed. Basically, they felt unable to apply for an illegal substance.

I felt very powerless. However, I had no intention of going away. For me, the answer lay in the 'Cannabis for Medicinal Use Regulation Bill 2016', which would legalise THC oil and help in making it a recognised medicine. It lay within the power of the government to fast-track this bill.

So in order to protest at the impasse and raise awareness of Ava's plight, I decided to resume my walk to Dublin.

7

The Rocky Road
to Dublin

'Don't wait. The time will never be just right.'

– Napoleon Hill

I refused to let Ava's health and future be thrown on the scrap heap. I came away from that meeting feeling like Ava and I had received a slap in the face of the cruellest nature. It appeared that I was expected to meekly accept this refusal and go home. I can recall thinking that I'd been left with no choice but to continue my protest walk from Mallow up to Leinster House. I didn't care about how many miles it was or how arduous it would be, I was going to do it. I wasn't going to stay at home to watch my daughter die.

Straight after the meeting, I was already thinking about the walk: which roads to take to Dublin, how I wouldn't be able to walk along the motorway, that a new coat was needed to combat the worst of the Irish weather and that I'd have to contact Neil Prenderville at Red FM and tell him I was being forced to restart the walk. Other than that, I had no plans for accommodation or support, but, as with the previous walk, I optimistically thought, 'Sure, I'll find somewhere to put my head.'

As Paul and I were walking down the corridor to the lobby, I told him I would have to walk again. He replied, supportive but pragmatic, 'I know we have to do something girl, but I don't think you're able for it.'

I couldn't really disagree with his honest assessment. Lack of sleep, stress, worry, constant phone calls, on top of the day-to-day minding of four children had taken their toll and aren't ideal preparation for such a challenging ordeal. However, we both agreed that we'd no choice.

Leaving the building, I looked up at the portrait of the great patriot Michael Collins and thought, 'Michael, I'll be seeing you again shortly. I won't let my daughter be treated like this.'

We made our way over to Gino's office in Agriculture House, which is adjacent to Leinster House. Upon arriving, we told him of what we planned to do. He expressed some disquiet at first, saying, 'You can't, you can't. You can't do that, Vera, it's not possible. It could take a week or more to do that, you're mad.'

He was right. I was mad; in fact, I was seething.

I heard him out and agreed that it did sound impossible, but Paul and I had been dealing with impossible situations for so long, so what was new? I told him I was walking and would start the next day.

'I can and I will walk, Gino. It's the only thing I can do. I gave him my word, that if he let Ava down I'd recommence the walk. Now he's let Ava down and I'm going to keep my word.'

'But you can't, you can't.'

I was going to walk and I told him I'd really appreciate it if he'd support me, but wouldn't hold it against him if he couldn't. (Though I would have, a little!) Realising that I wasn't for turning, he came around to the idea of the walk. 'Okay, Vera,' he said, 'you know I'll support you. If you're going through with this, I'll be there every step of the way.'

Both Gino and Paul were against starting the next day, however. It was too soon, they said; I was totally unprepared. As a compromise, it was agreed to hold off until the following Monday, 27 February.

Gino also explained how he had a prior commitment to campaign for a colleague in Derry city in the next few days. Holding off on the walk would allow him to make it down in time for the start of the walk. To his eternal credit, he was as good as his word. He got a train from Derry city to Dublin and then a one-way train ticket from Dublin to Mallow. Now that's real commitment and a statement of intent. He was going to walk all the way to Leinster House. They must breed them different in Clondalkin!

In the few days between the meeting and the Monday, I learned that another little girl with Dravet syndrome had passed away, further underlining how Ava's life was literally on the line. These awful notifications seem to come most often towards the end of the winter, which makes sense since children with Dravet have compromised immune systems. After fighting infection after infection all winter, accompanied by the inevitable seizure after seizure, they're often so worn out that a final big seizure can kill them. That's the terror that Paul and I were still living with during this time.

***

I decided to restart my walk at the Roundabout Inn, near the train station in Mallow town, which is where I had postponed it on the first occasion. Several good friends came along to support me. I spoke to a number of radio stations that morning to get the word out that I had recommenced the walk. The various radio stations and social media were essential to getting the message out. We were just wrapping up the radio calls and preparing to leave when Brian Mahoney strolled in and said hello. I already knew his wife, Sarah, after talking to her at the meeting in Macroom town. He expressed an interest in supporting me on the walk up to Dublin. Between myself, Gino and Brian, it looked like there'd be at least three people walking the entire way.

Brian later recalled, 'I was driving through Mallow on the way to work and turned on Red FM. I started hearing the words "medicinal cannabis", "walking to Dublin" and knew immediately it was Vera and that she must be continuing her protest walk to Dublin. I'd have walked the last time, but Vera had stopped before I knew she'd started. My wife, Sarah, and I were looking for access to medicinal cannabis for our son Cillian, who also has intractable epilepsy, the same as Vera was for Ava. I thought if Vera has the guts and determination to walk all the way from Cork to Dublin, I'd have to step up, walk with her and support her efforts. She was doing the right thing and deserved people's support. It's hard enough to have to mind a chronically ill child; you shouldn't have to fight for access to medicine as well. Anyway, I detoured to the Roundabout Inn and introduced myself to Vera. Then I phoned work to say I'd be taking the week off and probably most of next week as well.'

Gino later recounted, 'When I went down to Mallow, I thought I may be coming back that night. I had enough [supplies] for a week, at least, but I was thinking I was coming back that evening. Little did I know how long I'd be gone. The experience was incredibly uplifting. The solidarity and support of the ordinary people was incredible. I enjoyed every step of that walk, because it was for the greater good. It's not just about Ava, many people could benefit.'

After leaving Mallow the road gradually climbs out of the Blackwater valley. Off in the far distance I could see the Galtee mountains. They looked a long, long way away. But we'd be well past the Galtees before we were even at the end of the beginning of the walk. They'd be left far behind, far out of sight, before we even got a quarter of the way to Dublin. It was starting to truly dawn on me that this was going to be a major undertaking.

Out on the Dublin road we met up with Neil Prenderville and the Red FM crew, who did an interview as we walked. The road was extremely narrow for such a busy national route. The numerous blind bends and lack of a hard shoulder had the group tightly hugging the ditch to avoid the traffic. Poor Neil was very concerned about our safety as we walked along, chatting. We constantly crossed from one side of the road to the other, in order to have the best line of sight; as well as that, we had to keep checking that traffic wasn't sneaking up behind us unnoticed. Safety-wise, it was definitely the most dangerous day of the walk and a hair-raising experience. I was thankful of my choice of a red rain jacket, and that Brian had decided to wear a high-vis vest.

A little further along the road, I had a picture taken at the painted 'shell house' with Gino. You'd know the house when you see it. It's a treasured photo and shows both of us still full of energy and raring to go. The miles hadn't ground me down yet.

Jim Connell, a colleague of Gino's in the People Before Profit party, drove out from Cork city and met us with sandwiches and tea. I'll tell you they were some of the nicest I've ever had. Several miles of walking was a great sauce and we finished them off in short order. It was a cold, dry day, ideal for walking, but that short rest stop eating sandwiches while we sat on the bonnet of Jim's van was very welcome. It was a very thoughtful gesture.

Considering the short notice given, I was delighted with the support. I had prepared myself mentally to walk alone if needs be; however, I secretly knew that it would have been soul-destroying. I'd have done it, anyway, because the alternative would have been far worse, but the miles roll by much quicker when you have company. They also succeeded in keeping my spirits high and I'll always be grateful for their support. I didn't walk one step alone. Several friends walked for part of the way to Kildorrery and several supporters I had never met walked for the entire day. It seemed like Brian and Gino were prepared to accompany me the entire way to Dublin. It was great to have that constant, familiar support each day.

As we approached Farrahy, a jeep pulled over and the driver beckoned me across. The man told me that he had great admiration for what I was doing. As he shook my hand, he had a twenty euro note in his palm which he tried to give me. Politely protesting, I told him, 'Go way out of that, I can't take that at all.' I didn't need any donations, rather for him to contact his local TDs about Ava's plight and my protest. As he drove off, he smiled and told me, 'Ah now, you're an awful woman', meant in the best possible way.

A short while later, he was back. This time a set of walking poles was produced and handed over. Now, these I did take, jokingly telling him, 'You're an awful man.' I was never so happy to see a walking pole in all my life. I soon realised what a fantastic gift they were. They really helped take a lot of the weight off my legs and the constant tapping of the pole with each step helped me to keep pace.

There was a steep hill for the last mile or so up to the village of Kildorrery. The village itself was a welcome sight. Kildorrery is set on the top of a hill and it was visible from miles away. The telecommunications mast in the village had been beckoning us on for the last few hours. After reaching the village and thanking the people who came out, we called it a day. Day one of the walk was completed and I was still in one piece. A modest start, but at least it was a step in the right direction.

Considering the late start, we completed a lot of miles on the first day. I felt fresh, though the transition from spending most of the day minding four children to walking was a shock to the system. I was sanguine enough about eventually reaching Dublin; I knew it would be tough, but felt we'd get there in the end.

Brian lives only a ten-minute drive from Kildorrery and so he offered myself and Gino beds for the night. It was great to be walking into the warmth and not be searching around for a bed and breakfast. We ended up staying there overnight for the first few nights, as we'd drive up and down from the various starting and finishing points each day. I didn't need to explain anything to Brian or Sarah about Ava, epilepsy, or its impact on family life. They already knew. Only the parents of sick children ever really know what it's like. It's a relief to be in the company of people who 'get it'; in fact, it can be quite emotional.

I'd be mentally and physically exhausted after each day and

it helped to be able just to come back and relax, although you'd never really relax. The phone would be constantly on the go and I'd be doing Facebook posts on the day's progress and what was planned for the following day. I did get to soak my feet in a basin of hot water with Epsom salts, though, and now that really felt good. In the morning, Sarah would prepare breakfast, and she also always had food ready for us on the nights after we returned. It made the logistics of the walk much easier in those early days. Sarah would have loved to walk, too, of course, but she still made a vital, unseen contribution. Like Paul and my mother, someone had to stay at home and mind the kids. Without that family support, after all, I'd never have gotten out the door.

Another big bonus was that their house was close enough for Paul to drive over to meet me each night. It was great for my morale to see him and get his encouragement. He'd be able to tell me how the kids were doing, which allowed me to feel like I was keeping in touch with them. The walk to Dublin was the longest I had ever been away.

That first night was the worst. I really missed the children but didn't want to let on to the lads that I was feeling as bad as I was. I knew they'd be fine with Paul and my mother. Neighbours and friends were also pitching in. It's just that I wanted to be at home and be with them. I had explained to the kids that I was walking to try to get the medicinal cannabis for Ava, and that I had to go to see Simon, if he wouldn't come to see us. While it was tough explaining such an extraordinary situation to the children, they'd lived with Ava's seizures and understood that medicinal cannabis was the answer to a better life for her.

***

I was stiff the next morning, muscles not used to such abuse. A couple of small blisters had formed the first day, but they were not bothering me yet. Give them time. Gino and Brian were in good form and ready to go. They were both fitter than I was and seemed to be taking the walk in their stride.

Previously, I'd heard about this thing called 'Facebook Live'. I'd seen people use it at some of the meetings over the last few months. I conducted my first Facebook Live in Kildorrery, early on the second morning. I asked people, 'Please support Ava. If you can walk a mile of the road with us that'd be great, or send an email to the minister or contact your local TD and ask if they can do something to help.' This platform turned out to be a godsend, as it helped me to update everyone on our progress. It also lifted the spirits to see that people were watching, interested and even expressing horror at the fact that I had been forced back walking.

It was a freezing-cold morning and not one for hanging around. The next couple of miles were to be the only part of the journey where it was only the three of us. From then on we had constant support. Around Glennahulla, a group of very upbeat, smiley women joined us. One of them, Lindsey Graham, was to end up walking the entire way to Dublin with us, which was an amazing gesture. She also felt that a family member of hers, who suffered from chronic pain due to arthritis, could benefit from medicinal cannabis, and wanted her to at least be in a position to try it.

Now there were four permanent walkers!

As we walked further on, small groups of people and individuals started to join us. The local councillor, June Murphy, joined us for the next few hours. A friend of Sarah's, Lucinda, pulled over and produced thermos flasks of tea, sandwiches and biscuits, all of which were really appreciated by the crowd of walkers.

Being out in the cold, wet weather and the constant talking had started to give me a sore throat. It felt like a bout of tonsillitis was coming on, which was a worry, as I'd need my voice as much as my legs on the walk. I began taking antibiotics to try to ward it off.

We got caught by a few torrential showers, and on the outskirts of Mitchelstown it poured out of the heavens. I was doing a radio call at the time, so got into a car to make myself heard. The group showed great patience in waiting outside while the call went on. It was a welcome relief to reach Mitchelstown. There was a large enough crowd with us at the time that we needed to walk down the middle of the road. And why not? Sure, when do you get a chance to walk down the road into town? A lot of people came out of the shops, lined the street and clapped us through the town. The Mitchelstown people really gave us a great welcome, one of the very best.

We took a break in O'Callaghan's café on the main street. Here I had my first experience, the first of many on the walk, of a business refusing to accept payment for a meal. It's a strange and humbling experience to receive such kindness.

My feet were getting sore, which was worrying this early in the journey. They had swelled up from all the walking and my runners were becoming tight. Seeing this, and without my knowledge, a supporter went up the street and bought me a pair of walking shoes! This was much too generous, but she insisted on my taking them. They were to see me on for several miles. I still have them and, even if they become threadbare and the soles wear clean off, I'll keep them so I can remember that kind gesture.

I gave an interview to the *Avondhu* newspaper and the group had a photo taken. Then we continued on our way. Just outside of the town a car pulled over and Kevin O'Keeffe, a TD for Fianna Fáil, got out. He was on his way up to Leinster House, just like us, except he'd be getting there considerably quicker! Again, I outlined my reasons for walking. After a short, amiable chat, he drove and we walked on. As he quickly disappeared from view, I couldn't help but start to appreciate the benefits of a car.

The walk into Kilbeheny was a pleasant stretch of road. The sun had come out, so it was turning into a nice evening, and the scenery was lovely and the chat good. The traffic on the old Dublin road was much lighter because of the nearby motorway and we finally had a fine, wide hard shoulder to use. I arrived into Kilbeheny community centre in a positive frame of mind, although thankful for the rest. My feet were still acting up.

My friend Nuala was there and suggested I try her runners. She was one shoe size bigger and, when I tried them on, the extra room really helped. Those running shoes ended up accompanying me all the way to Dublin and Nuala drove home in her socks! It was a couple of weeks before she was eventually reunited with them, minus a good layer of the soles.

We soon headed onwards for Cahir. This is a long, straight stretch of road, which receded off into the distance. The Galtee mountains rose majestically to the left and Slievenamon Mountain, straight ahead, beckoned us on. The scenery was magnificent, if you had the energy to appreciate it. Cahir town was a welcome sight when we finally turned off.

On the outskirts of the town, some of the local Sinn Féin branch met us and walked us in. It's here that I met the local

Sinn Féin councillor, Martin Browne, who was to prove a huge help in the days ahead. When I started the walk, some of the people who helped the most were strangers whom I'd never met before but, let me tell you, by the end of the walk they were good friends. Martin is one of those good friends. Martin's Sinn Féin colleague, Fachtna Roe, who is a photographer, also started to accompany us and document the walk.

The group took a couple of photos below the castle and then headed up to the Cahir House Hotel to finish for the day. Martin had arranged for refreshments to be laid on. A big thank you to Martin and the hotel, as I think that day's walk was the longest. As Gino said, 'If anyone tells you that there is no community solidarity in Ireland any more, they're completely wrong.'

After the first two days we had got an idea of how fast we were capable of walking while still being able to reach Dublin in one piece. We had to take into account the constant stops to talk to the various media, chatting with the people who came out to walk and the rest breaks, which I really needed. There were no prizes for speed, anyway; it was all about raising awareness and talking to people. We figured it would take nine days in total to reach Leinster House. Getting an idea of where we'd be each day was important for posting our itinerary on Facebook. This gave people a chance to meet up and walk with us, or even just to pop out and wave us on as we passed by.

I was feeling upbeat for the Facebook Live posting that night, saying, 'Thanks for all the support, especially going through Mitchelstown. That was amazing, absolutely phenomenal. I can't begin to tell you how much Paul and I and my mother and our kids appreciate that. It was fantastic. All of the Facebook posts, all of the messages – I'm really trying to answer everybody. If they're short, please forgive me, it's just that there are so many. It's really hard to get to everybody.

'I looked at the responses today in the Dáil. Richard Boyd Barrett, Aindrias Moynihan, Michael Collins and all the other great people who raised questions for the sake of Ava. Enda Kenny said that Simon Harris is not a prescribing minister for medicinal cannabis. Neither Paul, nor I, nor anybody ever said, or assumed, that Simon Harris had the authority to prescribe medicinal cannabis for our daughter. We never asked him to prescribe it.' This was a request we had never made. I believed it was a smoke screen used to try to confuse the people in the Dáil and those listening.

Mine wasn't the only protest taking place at the time. Friends were up in Dublin, protesting outside the gates of Leinster House for the medicine Orkambi to be made available to cystic fibrosis sufferers. I wasn't standing beside them, but I was in total solidarity with their protest. As I said on the Facebook Live posting in Cahir, 'We're thinking of you today and we wish you the very, very best of luck. I hope you get a good outpouring of support.'

***

Paul drove up and walked with us from Cahir to Cashel at the beginning of the third day. It was great to have him there. I got to talk to several radio stations that morning, and with all the starting and stopping the pace was slow. The increased interest from the radio stations was heartening and it seemed like the protest was making an impression on people. A group of over fifty supporters in Mallow town, who couldn't make it to the walk, held an impromptu rally in solidarity. As one gentleman said to me, 'There must be something very wrong with the country, when the mother of a sick child feels she has to walk from Cork to Dublin to protest at the state's failure to provide adequate care.'

Martin had arranged for tea and sandwiches to be available at Ollies bar in New Inn. It was one of those old 1980s-style pubs, a great spot, and we got a lovely welcome from the owner. Big piping hot pots of tea, constant refills and lots of sandwiches. You'd love to stay there for the day, but we had to push on. Still, it undoubtedly helped; you felt like you could walk all day after a welcome and feed like that.

We'd always try to get a photograph of us at the road signs along the way. It showed the people following us where we were and, in the bad weather, it was often the only sheltered spot to do a talk and Facebook posting. Walking from Cahir to Cashel was one such day, as we got soaked just outside Cashel. As Paul said on Facebook Live, 'We're in Cashel today. It's very wet at the moment. We're being blown across the road with the rain and the hailstones. The "powers that be" can stop this. I'd appeal to their better nature, to change the legislation to legalise medicinal cannabis, so we can all go home.' I followed on and told people, 'We're after walking in the rain for the last few miles. People are after coming from Kerry, Cork, Aghabullogue and Tipperary. People passing are beeping in support. The people in Cashel are waiting for us. Thank you very much to the people who protested in solidarity with us in Mallow this morning.'

From Cahir onwards, we were passed by garda cars, at least once, but usually twice, during the day. I'd acknowledge them with a wave and a smile, and encouraged the others to do likewise. Sure everyone's entitled to walk along the side of the road. For the most part, they'd return the greeting. I think they were just checking us out and ensuring that there were no traffic hold-ups when we walked into the towns.

Given the large crowd walking into Cashel, we once again had to walk down the road. It certainly gets people's attention. We got a great welcome in Cashel, with beautiful food in the Brian Boru restaurant and supplies from the SuperValu. The hungry walkers quickly demolished the food. To say the Cashel people did themselves proud is an understatement.

That night I went home with Paul to Aghabullogue to see the children, as I felt it might be the last opportunity to see them and give them a hug before I'd walked too far up the country. I'd explained to the children what I was doing and why I needed to walk, but you couldn't be sure they fully understood. I'd never been away from the lads before for so long and it was one of the hardest things about the walk. The blisters, meanwhile, had grown to the size of euro coins. Even when they were fully taped up, they still stung with each painful stride. My voice was also becoming increasingly raspy from the constant talking and sore throat.

***

On Thursday morning, Ava had another seizure before we left home. Mother had to mind her after I left. That was hard, leaving like that when your daughter is ill. But I felt Ava's best chance was for me to keep going. That morning I asked people to contact their local TDs and tell them to stand up inside the Dáil and just get the children the medicine they need.

A ways out the road from Cashel, a gentleman 'herbalist' produced a tonic which he swore worked wonders on sore muscles. Seemingly, 'It's great on the horses, great for the legs.' I must really have started to look bad! 'Sure, why not,' I thought, and tried it. He was a true gentleman to make the effort and help me. Unfortunately, while I can't say that it did me any harm, from the way my legs declined over the next few days, it certainly wasn't the miracle cure I needed.

The walk attracted a lot of free thinkers. We had a great experience with several of them in the Horse and Jockey Hotel, near Thurles. It was towards the end of the day's walk and we had stopped there for a break. The hotel very kindly gave me a free massage for my legs. The whole leg was starting to hurt me now, not just the blisters. The members of one of Ireland's cannabis clubs walked in support with us that day. Chatting away, they started to extol the benefits of cannabis. One of the members outlined his detailed recipe for cannabis chocolate! I'll never look at an innocent bar of chocolate in the same way again! Another told about how people in England were scattering hemp seeds along motorways and vacant pieces of ground in the hope of it self-seeding. The things you hear! These weren't your stereotypical cannabis smokers, though; they were very articulate and informative people when it came to cannabis. Another lady explained her pagan religious beliefs to Lindsey. They had a great energy to them and were lovely people to talk to. It was a real tonic to sit down and have the chat about the most random and interesting of topics. Lindsey and Brian both agreed it was one of the most entertaining and 'different' conversations they'd ever had! In Horse and Jockey of all places, and sure, I suppose, why not.

There was only a short stretch remaining from Horse and Jockey to Littleton village, where we ended our fourth day of walking. Members of the Thurles Sinn Féin youth branch joined us there, as did Seamus Healy, the independent TD for Tipperary, who wished me every success. It was a heartening end to the day's walk.

But there was still more road ahead of us than behind.

8

One Step at a Time

'I am a slow walker, but I never walk back.'
— Abraham Lincoln

We were just under halfway. At the start of the fifth day, we received an amazing welcome from the pupils, teachers and parents of the primary school before leaving Littleton. The entire school was lined up in the school yard and listened to the headmaster explain to the children what we were doing, the importance of fighting for what's right and helping little Ava. I don't know if they all understood what it was all about, but they were delighted to be out with us in the school yard and cheering us on. It was very moving. I suppose it isn't every day a protest walk to Dublin passes the school.

It was a magnificent morning and really energised us for the day ahead. We needed it, as that day was extremely cold with lots of really bitter showers. The younger children clapped us out of the school yard and the older pupils walked on with us, with flags flying, to the edge of the village. Despite the weather, I think most of them would have gladly continued on, and it seemed to be with great reluctance that many of the students turned back to class. Several of the children were protesters and social activists in the making. It was a start to remember!

My friend Paddy O'Brien drove up from Cork to be with us and expressed concern about me walking in such inclement weather. I was so focused on my goal, it would have taken a hell of a lot worse weather to derail my protest. The cold and the rain I could handle, I felt, although I still needed my legs and voice to keep going. Unfortunately, my knees were acting up now, as I continued to wear them out with the huge undertaking, and my throat felt increasingly raw and inflamed. Saying that, every good wish and beep of the horn from the passing traffic gave me strength and hope. It's surprising how people beeping their car horn in support can lift the spirits. While they weren't able to physically walk with me, they were sending me a message of moral support.

The old Dublin road that we were following was fairly quiet, but it was a long slog of a walk, with the road stretching off to the horizon. It was a very rural landscape with occasional areas of bog and forest. Thankfully, the road was level for the most part. We were leaving Tipperary that day and I have to say that the support we received in the county was just massive. The people had really gotten behind us and that encouragement pushed us on.

Approaching Urlingford town there was a fierce pull up the hill and, just at the hardest part of the day, we got soaked by a heavy shower. It poured on us, blown by a driving wind. The abilities of everybody's rain gear was really put to the test. As we crested the hill, the town below us was a really welcome sight. We planned to take a rest stop there. The last mile went on forever, though, as we could see the goal but it didn't seem to get any closer. Let me tell you, anyone who says that Ireland is a small country has never walked across it.

People had some soup, sandwiches and other refreshments in

Butler's Inn as their soaked clothes steamed in the welcome heat. It took several minutes to thaw out. It's a beautiful sensation to feel the warmth slowly spread out in the hands and legs and to regain the feeling in numb fingers.

I met the Fianna Fáil TDs Bobby Aylward and John McGuinness there. As two senior Fianna Fáil figures and, like Gino, legislators in the Dáil, it was great to have the opportunity to explain Ava's situation to them. These were the people who could help make the necessary changes. Luke 'Ming' Flanagan and Diarmuid O'Flynn of the 'Ballyhea says No' protest group also walked with us this day as far as Johnstown. They were both staunch supporters of what I was doing.

In Johnstown that evening, Luke, Gino and I spoke to the crowd. Luke was his eloquent self: 'We're here with Vera halfway to Dublin, on her walk that should never have had to be done in the first place. But it's being done. What can you say, superb solidarity is being shown. Politicians need people like alcoholics need alcohol. It's quite simple: you [politicians] need these people. Everyone is on this woman's side, except for the very people we need on our side. We need Fine Gael to do what the rest of the people are doing: join this woman and let her end this walk. She shouldn't have to walk to Dublin, but if she does, she's going to do it because every now and then in a battle, you come up against someone who doesn't give up. That is what we've met here in Vera Twomey.'

Gino followed on from Luke: 'The last four days have been absolutely phenomenal. We should not be on this walk. If we have to go all the way to Leinster House, we will. We won't go back empty-handed. It's not just about Ava and Vera, it's about the countless other people around Ireland who could benefit.'

I was very tired after the day's walk. With the bad weather, it had been tough. The antibiotics hadn't alleviated my sore throat, which at this stage likely was tonsillitis as it was becoming painful to talk. One knee was acting up with a constant throbbing pain. Anytime I got an opportunity to sit down, I'd try to raise the leg, to take some of the pressure off the knee.

When it was my turn to speak to the crowd, I said, 'Today we walked in the hail and the rain and the wind and we're still walking. We're in Johnstown and still no contact. That's okay because we're going to keep walking again tomorrow. If we have to keep walking till Tuesday, then we'll keep walking. Ava needs her medicinal cannabis and she has to get it. There have been politicians here today who were confused and uncertain about what we were looking for. Simon, they're not confused any more. They know that Ava can't get the medicinal cannabis that she needs via the compassionate access scheme as it stands, and that there are two paediatric neurologists back in Cork waiting to help us. They know that the legislation needs to be brought in to change the law and to allow Ava to get access to the medicine she needs.'

***

On Saturday morning, we had arranged to meet up with any supporters in Cullahill, the next village after Johnstown. It was a cloudy, cold morning. It's hard to get motivated in that weather, but at least the cold encouraged us to keep walking. What happened to the warmer, sunny weather we'd had over the previous few weeks, I often wondered. The walk seemed to coincide with the last sting of winter.

for Ava

I kept the talk brief at this meeting: 'There's been no contact from Simon Harris. No contact from the HSE. We're on our way. Thanks for all the support. We're going to Dublin for Ava and Cillian and all the other people. They need it badly.' Lindsey, who had been walking for a few days at this stage and had by this point become a good friend, said, 'I joined just outside Kildorrery. As a mother, I can't imagine what she's going through. She's so strong.'

We trekked on, eventually stopping at the Castle Arms Hotel in Durrow town. I needed to rest my knee for a while and it gave us a chance to meet people who had come out to support us but weren't able to walk. Some of the ladies there had very kind words, saying, 'On behalf of all the community in Durrow we want to wish Vera huge support, one hundred percent support, on her journey and her fight for poor little Ava.'

I spoke to the crowd gathered outside the hotel: 'Simon, we're after coming through Durrow now so we're a little bit closer to Dublin. You're the man with the power at the moment. I'd say you're making a big mistake by not helping out a little child here, because an awful lot of people are very upset with you above there for not moving forward. You'd be well advised to do something to help this child and people like her. You have to legislate. There is no point in having meetings regarding the HPRA report. I'm telling you, I was told recommendations could take a couple more months, then it's sent back for review. Simon, that's not good enough. We're looking for progress since October 2015 and you're going to have to come to the party now, at this time. We're going to be getting up and standing outside the Dáil and when the walk ends, then it begins for real. Please help Ava, Cillian and all the other people who are looking for access to medicinal cannabis.'

With it being a Saturday, a lot of the people supporting us, but who were not able walk with us, attended a number of protest rallies under the 'Stand up for Ava' initiative. These were held in Sydney, Quebec, Wellington, Gorey, Cork city, Coachford, Dripsey, Spain, Mitchelstown, Midleton, Ballyhooly, Mallow, Macroom, Rylane, Ballincollig, Grenagh and Aghabullogue. The hundreds of people who came out showed real solidarity with myself and Ava. They showed that while they couldn't physically be with me on the walk, they were with me in spirit.

I had slowed up pretty badly by this stage. The pain in the knee had become intense. It felt like the sort of damage that only rest would heal and there'd be none of that for a while yet. Over the course of the day, the crowd became strung out, with the fresher walkers surging off ahead and myself and a few others bringing up the rear.

We were moving through a part of the country that I had only ever seen out the window of a car, where it can be a bit of a blur. With my slow pace I really got to see it that day. It was good farmland, with well managed fields, thick ditches and the occasional woodland.

That evening, we stopped in the Abbeyleix Manor Hotel. A big thanks to Martin and the management. Dinner in the hotel was an absolute feast; there was no spare room on the plates they served up.

Most of the supporters headed home after the hotel, while the rest of us strolled up the street to Morrissey's pub. Morrissey's is fabulous, with lots of character, and is largely unchanged since it first opened as a grocery shop in 1775. We sat into one of the snugs and unwound after a long day. We wouldn't be heading back to Brian's house in Cork from here on; we had gone too far for that to be practical. The Maldron 'Midway' Hotel in Portlaoise let Gino, Brian and me stay that night, compliments of the hotel. Fair play to them.

That night I had no less than two physiotherapists treating my knee. Their work really helped to ease the pain and allowed me to sleep that night. I had compression straps placed on both my legs to try to control the swelling. Other than to keep on taking the antibiotics, there was little more I could do to ease my tonsillitis. With the cold weather, physical deterioration and missing the kids, it was a struggle, but people's kindness helped to keep me focused and resolute.

***

The weather was good the following day, with a fresh breeze and lovely spring sunshine. A large crowd was gathered in Market Square to greet us at the start of the walk. The countless radio and newspaper interviews and Facebook posts had made an impact, and people were coming out in large numbers. I was feeling pretty angry and gave vent to my feelings:

'I'm not going home to Aghabullogue with promises, recommendations, meetings or reports. I'm going to stay up in Dublin. This is very, very hard. Away from my children and away from my home, but we haven't been treated fairly and it's not right and we can't put up with it. I had tonsillitis on the second day. I've been on antibiotics since. I've had physiotherapy on my knee last night because after walking ninety-nine miles up to Durrow it swelled up to three times its size. We have to come up to Dublin and be treated fairly and get what we need for a little girl. Then we can go home and live our lives. It's just been tremendously hard, very, very difficult. Simon Harris didn't have to do this to us, but I have to do this now and I'm coming up to see you on Tuesday. I hope you'll be out to meet me because if you don't come out Tuesday, I'll be there on Wednesday and Thursday and Friday and every other day until we get this issue resolved.'

I succumbed to the crutches that day. I so wanted to walk unaided the entire way; however, it just wasn't possible. Even with the crutches it was very painful and I had slowed to a crawl. Brian had sourced a wheelchair in Portlaoise. A lovely lady, Liz, loaned it to us. It was very seldom used and belonged to her mother. Liz reckoned that we'd be finished the walk and have it back to her before her mother noticed its absence! While Brian was pushing it empty, I had an ominous feeling that it would be occupied tomorrow. He had told me repeatedly that I could go in the wheelchair, but I didn't want to. It felt like letting the side down. Later in the day, we all took a break in Tracey's Bar and Restaurant on the Heath. The soup, cakes and other food were fabulous; unfortunately, I had to spend most of the time being treated by another physiotherapist.

We received a really big welcome from the people in Ballybrittas. For a small village, it was a great crowd. Most people from the village must have come out to support us! The support I received surpassed my wildest expectations.

Brian recounts, 'Compared to Gino and Vera, I had an easy time of it. I only had to walk and occasionally help carry Vera's bag. Both Gino and Vera seemed to spend most of their time with the phone attached to their ear, talking with the media, trying to reach politicians, as well as talking with members of the public, attempting to get their message across. Vera's voice became completely worn out from the talking. It was as big a mental and emotional challenge for them, as it was a physical effort. I think Gino was also dealing with other constituency issues much of the time. Vera was never in a rush to leave people, I noticed; she'd spend longer talking to a supporter along the road than to one of the politicians on the phone.'

Paul drove up with all the kids so they could walk the last few miles into Monasterevin with me. Ava had quickly recovered from a small seizure that morning, so had been able to join the rest of the family for the trip. It really lifted the spirits to have them see what the walk was all about. I think that by walking for a little bit they felt they were helping Ava and taking part.

I felt energised walking into the town, even though I was on crutches. At the end of the day's walk I said to our supporters, 'We're here in Monasterevin and there's a massive crowd of us here. They're here from all parts of the country actually, supporting my daughter Ava. I'm on crutches now at the moment, but we'll keep going, keep walking, because Ava needs this medication. She had another seizure this morning and it just goes to show that we need THC, Simon. We need it really badly. You just have to do something. We can't go away now, the seizures won't go away without it.'

The closer we got to Dublin the more energised Gino became. He was blown away by the support in Ballybrittas, saying, 'I don't know what to say after today. The welcome in Ballybrittas was incredible. Fair play to everyone in Ballybrittas and Monasterevin. The response so far has been absolutely phenomenal from all the ordinary people of Ireland. A mother like Vera should not be walking the roads of Ireland to get medical justice for her daughter. It's immoral that a mother has to do this. The government has to listen. We're not going to let her down, we're going to keep walking to Leinster House. So, make it medicine, make it happen.'

Deborah, a friend of Sarah's, had arranged for some food to be laid on in The Venice of Ireland pub, and we stayed there most of the evening. It was a real energy boost to spend time with Paul and the kids. A little bit of normality in the middle of a hectic, mad week.

After they headed back to Cork, Gino and Brian and I drove over to Sarah's sister, Gillian, to stay for the night. It was great solidarity to have people open their house to you without even having to be asked. That evening Brian told me that he found my relationship with Gino to be quite amusing. He told me, 'You and Gino are the proverbial odd couple. Gino is a socialist Dubliner, with a background in politics and activism, and you're the mother of a sick girl, from a sleepy village in a very rural part of County Cork. You couldn't get two more different Irelands and yet you work really well together. Your different personalities complement each other. Gino is always very thoughtful and considered before speaking in his understated manner. You, on the other hand, are full of drive and a fierce determination. You've fire in your blood.'

***

The end was almost in sight. In Kildare town the next morning, I could see the Wicklow and Dublin mountains off in the distance. We had come a long way and were nearly there. It was a bright morning and I hoped that we'd have good weather.

Unfortunately, my legs were failing. The previous day, I'd

thought I'd be able to manage on crutches, but that was too optimistic. It looked like I'd be in a wheelchair for the rest of the journey. I never imagined it would be so difficult, or that I'd be reduced to a wheelchair. My knee was still on fire. I tried to walk, but was told not to because of the way my leg was looking. So, by Monday morning, the only option was a wheelchair. My legs may have been gone and my voice was rapidly going, but my heart was still strong. Brian said, 'Vera's legs have packed it in, but we're going to push her; we'll be her legs for today and tomorrow.'

I made one of my morning Facebook Live posts in Kildare town square saying, 'This is what I've been reduced to [tapping the wheelchair]. What has happened to me and my family after a year and a half of trying to communicate with the HSE and Simon Harris? Out walking, out in the cold, out in public, begging for the people of Ireland to help us. Grateful beyond belief that they do care about my little child. Having to depend on friends to push me now as far as the Dáil, to maybe or maybe not, meet Simon Harris and get what Ava needs and deserves. I can't go home without a resolution.'

I learned that Simon Harris had issued a press release. I'd been walking since last Monday and it was only at the eleventh hour that he released it. I'd say he held off as long as possible, hoping I'd have stopped long ago and it was only when it looked like I'd make it to Dublin that he issued the statement. I found that quite insulting. The press release just reiterated the same old line. Excuses for inaction and delay. Its only positive point was that he'd be available to meet myself and Paul when I arrived in Dublin tomorrow.

We had a rest stop in Newbridge. When we headed back

out of the town towards Naas, however, we had one of the most extraordinary events of the entire walk. After crossing the bridge over the Liffey, we saw the pupils from the local Patrician school lined out on both sides of the road, forming a guard of honour. It was the most amazing sight.

Zara King from TV3 interviewed me with the school band playing in the background; to be honest, I found the experience quite overwhelming. I had a bit of a cry, I was so emotional. The thoughtfulness of that school in showing their support will be remembered by me forever. When Gino was asked by the media if he expected positive progress when Vera arrived at the Dáil, he said that he wasn't too hopeful and accused the government of playing 'mind games' on the issue.

With Monday being a work day, the support was down on the previous day, and the weather became a bit misty and dreary towards the end. I also found it very hard to keep warm in the wheelchair. Without any movement I wasn't able to generate any heat. My feet were like icicles and my throat was terribly sore. When you're not fighting the pain of walking on all the blisters and the sore knee you have more time to think. I thought it was a terrible indictment of the government that I had been reduced to this. It was one of those afternoons when there was nothing for it but to keep driving forward. One of the people walking put a very positive spin on events, however, which I've never forgotten. 'Vera,' he said, 'the further you have to go, the smaller Simon looks. By the time you reach Dublin, he'll look very small indeed.'

So many times during the walk people came up to me and told me how they found that self-medicating, with illegally obtained cannabis, was really great in helping to alleviate their chronic pain and other illnesses. That they'd been able to ditch the strong painkillers with the nasty side effects. They'd say, 'Why don't you just do the same for Ava?' Isn't that an Irish solution to an Irish problem, though? Let the politicians off the hook and allow them to continue to bury their heads in the sand. Ava needed to have a medicinal cannabis oil like those available in so many other countries and she needed it to be under medical supervision. I couldn't risk other routes. No, this had to be done above board, I felt; the politicians needed to be dragged into the twenty-first century.

In Naas, I met the Fianna Fáil TD James Lawless. James listened to me for a long time and later issued a press release: 'I was delighted to invite Vera Twomey into my office today as she was passing through Naas. Having spoken to Vera it is clear that this form of treatment would make a huge difference in her daughter's daily life. The minister needs to address the barriers and access issues as soon as possible to allow Ava and others to benefit from the pain relief and therapy that this drug could offer. Well done to Vera and a safe onward journey.'

As a lifelong Fine Gael member, I found it very disappointing that not one TD from the party made an effort to support Ava. That really hit home. As I said to the *Leinster Leader* newspaper, 'What would you do if it was your child and if there was a solution out there that could ease your child's suffering? What would you do to go and get it?'

That night, Gino, Brian, Lindsey and I stayed with Rita Koenig, a friend of Brian's mother. She was a terribly nice lady and went out of her way to look after us and make us dinner. She was funny, as she thought that half a litre of milk would see us through. At the rate we drank tea, though, it wouldn't last the night, never mind the breakfast. Brian popped out to the shop to get supplies. After she was decent enough to give us a roof over our heads, we didn't want to eat her out of house and home as well.

I was a bit nervous that night. After all, we were almost finished walking and only then would the real battle begin. I didn't know what tomorrow would bring, would the support be there? I made a final call out. 'We're going to be above in Dublin tomorrow. We'll arrive at the Dáil around 1.30 p.m. I don't know what is going to happen. We've had no contact from Fine Gael, any Fine Gael TDs even. I'd say the people who came out to support us would have been People Before Profit and Sinn Féin first, Fianna Fáil next, then Independents and Labour.

'I very much hope for people's support, as it's scary what's ahead of me. All I know is Ava needs this and doesn't have a chance without it. Say a prayer for us and I hope to see you there. If you're somewhere in the country and it's not realistic to go, that's okay; contact Simon Harris by email, or phone your local politician. Ask for them to stand up for us, they need to push this issue to the front of the queue. There's people in chronic pain, people with seizures, MS, cancer. So many out there need this. We have to do our very best and continue to be as strong as we possibly can.'

9

Up in Dublin

'The ultimate measure of a person is not where they stand in moments of comfort or convenience, but where they stand in times of challenge and controversy.'

– Martin Luther King

The weather on the final day of the walk was cold and dry. Ideal conditions for walking, but not so good when you're sitting outside in a wheelchair. I put out a call on Facebook for anyone who could to bring a blanket to lay over my lap. I didn't want a repeat of the unbearable cold I'd already experienced. Our itinerary was to meet up with supporters in Rathcoole and Newlands Cross as we made our way to Leinster House. We would also pass through Clondalkin, where I'd never been, and have the opportunity to see all of Gino's supporters. Gino was really looking forward to getting back to his home base; I suppose he'd been away a long time.

During my morning Facebook Live posting I said, 'This is a dignified way we're going about this. I don't want any aggression, any cursing, any swearing or vulgar posters. We don't need that. All we need is a peaceful protest to get Ava what she needs, what other people need. We've got right on our side. I'll be outside [Leinster House] waiting on a small bit of justice. For this long road to be over and a bit of sense to prevail. I'm really anxious that there's no aggression. I hope Mum is watching and gets to see this at some stage. I really love you and all the children.'

There was a large crowd in Rathcoole to meet and walk with us into the city centre. Someone lent me a 'throw blanket' to keep warm. Thank God! The roads this close to Dublin were very busy with traffic, so we kept to the footpaths and hard shoulders.

From the main street we headed across the overpass and down onto the Naas road. As the main road into Dublin from the south-west, this was very busy with a continuous stream of traffic whizzing by. Moving along the edge of the hard shoulder we started to get tremendous support from the passing traffic. There was an almost continuous beeping of car horns and of the louder truck horns. The van and truck drivers were especially vocal; perhaps they had heard me speaking on one of the radio stations and were keeping track of my progress. People knew what this odd group of walkers, and what appeared to be a decrepit old lady being pushed in a wheelchair, were doing. It really lifted the spirits and showed that whatever about the government's deafness, the people in Ireland sympathised with what I was trying to achieve. I felt immensely relieved that people felt what was being done to Ava was wrong. The tears came fairly frequently and I tried to hide them as best I could.

We slowly made our way towards Dublin city, the surroundings changing to a more suburban landscape and business parks. The land sloped off to the east and we got our first views of the city, spread out before us and visible now all the way to the sea. The pigeon house chimney stacks and Howth hill could be seen off in the far distance. We were almost there!

One of the main threats was from all the broken glass and

pieces of stone and metal along the road edge. A punctured tyre would have been a disaster. With a little bit of manoeuvring, though, we managed to avoid the worst patches and continued on unscathed.

We kept taking photographs at the road signs and posting them on Facebook to let people know we were close. Throughout the whole journey a lot of people probably had their doubts about me making it, but today, everyone knew it was going to happen. If need be, Brian, Lindsey and Gino would have carried me that last day. At this stage, they had almost as much emotional energy invested in me finishing as I had.

After several miles we could see the interchange at Kingswood Cross. Large banners were draped across the bridge by a group of supporters. I could see the signs from a long ways off, but couldn't make them out. Gradually, as I got closer, I started to make out 'Clondalkin supports Ava', 'Make it Medicine' and 'Lucan supports Ava' amongst others. These were Gino's constituents.

We took the off ramp to meet them and have a short break. A big crowd from Clondalkin and the surrounding area had come out to welcome us. They gave us a super reception and with a typically Dublin, wry sense of humour, couldn't resist having a laugh at my Cork accent. 'Jaysus, I don't know what you're saying, where did you say you're from?' Gino was in his element, finally on home turf.

From the bridge we took a slip road down onto the Green Isle road, which was quiet enough that we could talk without having to shout over the traffic. This led on to Newlands Cross, where another big crowd of well-wishers welcomed us. Several radio and television stations were waiting for interviews. My voice was pretty bad by this stage, making it hard to be heard.

All the talking, the tonsillitis and the cold air had taken their toll. I did the best I could with what voice I'd left and thanked people for coming out.

The support was quickly building and a large crowd set off towards the Red Cow roundabout. There was a very convoluted route to get past this busy junction. With all the bridges and road crossings Brian got a good workout from pushing the wheelchair that day. On our own we might have struggled, but there was no fear of getting lost with all the local people who accompanied us.

About halfway down the Naas road, I saw people approaching with banners leaving no doubt as to their origins. There was 'Rylane supports Ava' and a 'Grenagh supports Ava'. My local friends and relations had arrived. The culchies had landed, after travelling by bus and train to meet us and walk in to Leinster House. It was great to see all the familiar faces. We had made slow, steady progress each day, but you could feel the build-up of emotional energy as we neared the end. It was a tonic and it felt like the pain in my leg was lessened by all the positivity and good wishes.

Continuing down along Tyrconnell Road, the pupils from a primary school lined the school fence and clapped us as we passed. The same support was shown by the pupils of another school soon after, when we turned onto Emmet Road. We were deep into the real authentic Dublin and the people were the salt of the earth, they couldn't do enough for you. Several women insisted on pushing the wheelchair. One lovely Polish lady, Barbara, pushed it for a good stretch. They showed a real solidarity and supportive spirit.

A rest stop was organised at Saint Michael's community centre. We'd been on the go since about eight o'clock, so a stretch of the legs was badly needed. I don't think they were expecting the number who arrived, but they rose to the occasion and no one was left wanting. Realising that we were on the very final leg of the journey, and it was unlikely I'd get much of a break from here on in, I tried to enjoy the tea and sandwiches laid on for us, but I just couldn't appreciate them as much as normal. The impending arrival at Leinster House loomed larger and larger in my mind. It felt good to get out of the wheelchair and get the blood moving in the legs, even if I was only capable of hobbling along. I was glad of the chance to warm up the feet.

After 'recharging the batteries', we set off towards Old Kilmainham. We had succeeded in keeping off the road until that stage, but with the large crowd it wasn't possible from here on in. I hated to do it – you never want to annoy the average person going about their business – but we moved out onto the road and slowly walked on towards James Street. Several marshals had been organised to keep people on one side of the road and allow traffic to keep moving as much possible. I had no part in organising them, so I guess it was done by Gino and the People Before Profit party. They really helped in making that last stretch of the journey go smoothly.

Around the junction of Steevens Lane and James Street we met more supporters. There must have been several hundred people walking at this stage. When I looked back all I could see was a forest of banners and placards. The builders working on the new children's hospital at St James's took their break to coincide with us passing, and they roared and shouted their support as we passed. A large group of school children clapped on the other side. Builders on one side, school children on the other. I was blown away by the spectacle.

The comedian Des Bishop popped over from wherever he had been working to say hello. (Tommy Tiernan also posted his support for Ava on Facebook. Comedians must have an affinity for Ava's story.) The owner of a local chipper came over with a pizza and insisted on me having a slice. It was all getting a bit surreal really. Paul, Sarah and more friends had joined the crowd and suddenly appeared beside us. Brian had seen Paul walking along having a grand chat and decided that he'd be better employed pushing his wife, so Paul got to wheel me those last few miles.

As we approached Christchurch, people started to take up the chant 'Make it Medicine, Make it Happen'. Some onlookers had no idea what we were doing and looked quizzically at us as we passed by. One guard drove past in a squad car and gave us an absolutely filthy look. An unauthorised protest, now that would never do! Well, we were doing it.

A lot of people clapped as we passed by. They knew what it was all about. It felt really strange to be the centre of such attention. It was a long way from the first day, quietly leaving Mallow. The awareness I had been working towards had transpired. The walk had become something far greater than I had thought possible. It had definitely succeeded in raising awareness of the need to legalise medicinal cannabis and of Ava's plight.

We turned off College Green and onto Nassau Street. We were nearly there. The noise of the crowd was deafening: 'Make it Medicine, Make it Happen'. We slowly made our way to Kildare Street. Turning the corner I was greeted by the most amazing sight. About two hundred metres ahead of us, a large crowd was gathered with banners and placards at the front gate of Leinster House. They had heard our chanting for the last several minutes and as they saw us round the corner they let out a big cheer, which was returned by an even bigger cheer by the people surrounding me. The chants of 'Make it Medicine, Make it Happen' increased in volume. About halfway between both groups were the media, both photographers and journalists, lined across the road. What a sight! It was like something out of a movie.

As we approached the media, they started snapping away. The walk had been completely ignored by RTÉ, the national broadcaster. It wasn't that they were unaware of it; a lot of people had contacted them looking for them to highlight why I was walking. I was later told that they made an 'editorial decision' not to cover it. They were the only media outlet to adopt this approach and it was a bit of an eye-opener about how things happen in Ireland. Well, here we were only one hundred metres from the finish and who was at the forefront of the media, only RTÉ! It was a brave move because everyone had noted their neglect of the story and many felt aggrieved.

Voices, obviously Dubliners, yelled, 'Where were yis before now, yis doorty shower?' Meanwhile, the Cork contingent called out, 'Get away out of that, boy, where were ye for the last week? You're a useless shower of langers.' The animosity was justified, as if we'd been reliant on RTÉ for coverage, Ava's plight would have gone unreported, but the comments were water off a duck's back for the RTÉ cameraman.

I was happy to oblige the other media with photographs and interviews.

My cousin later told me that the crowd stretched from the gates of Leinster House back as far as Trinity corner, which must have put the support at well over one thousand people. I could physically feel the swell of energy and support of the people.

Sitting in the wheelchair, all the noise and movement engulfed me, making it far more overwhelming than if I'd been on my feet. I remember looking back and reaching up for Paul's hand. Looking at him, I knew it was okay. He had tears of pride in his eyes and as I squeezed his hand, he just smiled and said, 'Alright girl?' Nothing more needed to be said.

Happily, the people who had most supported me on the journey were beside me. Through the rain and the hail and the cold mornings we had made it together. Gino had walked every step of the way; he could have kept on going for days, I'd say. He had a big smile on his face going up the street. I think the atmosphere and support shown that day far surpassed his expectations.

Paul was right behind me, too, and Brian, Lindsey and Sarah were all nearby. I could see my friends Martin Browne, Deirdre Kennedy and Mick Barry, TD, in the crowd. Seamus Healy, TD, who I'd last seen in Littleton, came up and shook my hand. Several neighbours, friends and relations from Cork came over and gave me a hug. My father's first cousin was there, which was as close as I'd get to Dad being present himself. That'd be worth a thousand miles of walking. I really wanted to get out of the chair and stand. Using the crutches, I hobbled over to the gates. I had made it! Now the real battle would begin.

With the large crowd pressing in on me from all sides it felt claustrophobic. The reporters and media appeared to tussle amongst themselves for the best position or angle to take a photograph. A lot of microphones were thrust towards my face as they literally pushed each other out of the way to get a comment. Thankfully, Gino took control and said we'd be saying a few words to the crowd and were happy to speak to the media.

We briefly spoke to the crowd of supporters. Things had been so hectic that I had nothing prepared. My voice was fairly croaky and weak and I had to swallow to get the words out. I felt disappointed that I didn't sound stronger, but I thanked everyone and said, 'We've done it, we have made it. Simon will have to face us now.'

The gates were locked when we arrived. When the news filtered through the crowd that the gates were closed, some people voiced their annoyance. I think the gardaí were just being cautious and avoiding any spill-over of the large gathering into the car park in front of Leinster House. After the brief interlude of meeting the supporters and talking to the media, the Dáil ushers and gardaí let Gino and myself in the gates. Looking back, it was much too short a time to spend with the people outside the gates. There were a lot of people whom I never got a chance to thank.

I could see groups of politicians looking on, some with supportive smiles, others slightly more detached. Inside, I could barely make it down the corridors due to being stopped for handshakes. I really hoped that the TDs wouldn't leave it at handshakes and that they'd go on to legislate for medicinal cannabis. Token gestures don't cut it when you're dealing with people's health.

Looking up in the main foyer, I could see the large painting of the great Irish leader, Michael Collins, and wondered what he'd make of this carry-on. How Irish citizens have to fight so hard for basic rights, due to the inaction of his political descendants. I made a little request to the big man in that moment: 'Michael, if you're up there, help us out here and do something. Make them show some humanity.'

I had a short break in the Dáil bar with Gino, who managed to get Paul, Lindsey, Brian and Sarah in to join us and have a cup of tea. Senator David Norris was in the bar and came over to congratulate me, enthusing, 'Why, of course medicinal cannabis should be legalised.' The meeting with the HSE and Minister Harris was later in the afternoon, and I wanted to catch my breath and compose my thoughts.

***

Just before four o'clock, Paul and I were ushered into the appointed meeting room. It was an elegant Georgian room with a high ceiling and fine mahogany table and chairs. To say I was worn out would be a complete understatement and meant that I wasn't able to contribute as much as normal. A lot of the weight of the conversation fell on Paul's shoulders, but with his head for details and past events, he rose to the occasion. Again and again he'd undercut the deliberate repetition of Simon and his staff with the cold, hard facts.

Gino and Richard Boyd Barrett of the People Before Profit party also attended, as did Jonathan O'Brien of Sinn Féin and Billy Kelleher of Fianna Fáil. To my surprise, Michael Creed was there, too. Jonathan had a good working knowledge of what was needed and was up to date on Ava's situation. I believe that he really wanted a resolution, and had faith that Simon was of a similar mindset.

Upon entering the room, Simon wasn't a man who looked at all comfortable. There were a couple of furtive glances around, checking who was present. Pale at the best of times, he looked paler than usual and that was the first time I noticed the flecks of grey in his hair. I think it was a very unwilling minister who met us that evening, accompanied by officials of the HSE and HPRA.

The atmosphere had a certain air of tension. In retrospect, it's clear that as soon as we left our supporters outside the gates, we had entered the proverbial lion's den. The government's objective seemed to be to manage us and send us away with as little as we had before we arrived.

The minister actually congratulated me on my successful arrival, after what he described as an 'arduous journey'.

'You're not wrong there, Simon,' was my reply.

I left it at that and then asked him, 'How are we going to get a licence for medicinal cannabis for Ava, Simon?' He immediately reassured us that 'without a shadow of a doubt' we would resolve this situation.

He began to speak enthusiastically about the HPRA report and the 'compassionate' access programme and would return again and again to discuss them, no matter what questions were asked. He said he would personally arrange for a consultation with Ava's public neurologist in Cork the following Friday, which he did after briefly leaving the room. This tied in with two of the treatment options, one of which was to bring the public neurologist on board and the other was to get them to sign off on the treatment abroad scheme, so Ava could be funded to go abroad for treatment. This was of concern to Paul and me, however, as we already knew that our public neurologist was 'not for turning' on supporting treatment with the current legal position of THC; the neurologist was also unwilling to sign off on the treatment abroad scheme as medicinal cannabis was seen as an 'experimental treatment'.

Option three was to contact Ava's private neurologist, who was supportive, but due to the previously mentioned issues with indemnity insurance, could not support a licence application for a treatment that was illegal in Ireland. Simon calmly told us he was going to sort out the indemnity issue and left the room for several minutes. I don't know why he left, though, because when we subsequently met Ava's private neurologist, we were told that nothing had changed concerning the indemnity insurance issue.

We were also assured during the meeting that great progress was being made on the fourth option, the 'compassionate' access programme. They said it would be rolled out in October. Even if we believed them, this was simply too far away and, besides, it was of no real use to Ava as it did not include access to THC oil. Ava needed a far more urgent response. (Little did I imagine that the programme would still not be operational as I write this in early 2019.)

Option five was the proposed legislation, the 'Cannabis for Medicinal Use Regulation Bill 2016', which over the five hours of the meeting was probably given two per cent of their attention. Simon said this was being taken very seriously and would be rushed through the Dáil. Frustratingly, Fine Gael later tried to delay its progress.

The HPRA staff also told us about the 'significant' report they had produced. When asked, 'Who were the people who contributed to the report?', they replied, '... numerous experts had been approached and made valuable contributions to the document'.

'What experts in the area of cannabinoids?' was our next query.

'In the area of cannabinoids?'

'Yes,' we said. 'What experts in the area of medicinal cannabis have you approached from Holland, from America, from Canada? What doctors from these countries have you approached?'

After this persistent questioning they answered, 'None.'

So it turned out that no consultants with expertise in prescribing medicinal cannabis were approached at all. They declared that the consultants and doctors approached were experts in their field, and no doubt they were, but their contribution was of little consequence when they had no experience in dealing with or prescribing cannabinoids.

The HSE officials pondered on the difficulties of obtaining the licence and the ray of hope which the treatment abroad scheme offered. They then promised us that paperwork on the details that we had just discussed, regarding the indemnity insurance, licence, etc., would be ready for us to collect at Leinster House early the following morning. This would help us move forward with the application for the licence.

They knew, as they sat there poker-faced, that they had kept us going around in circles for nearly five hours, while the supporters outside had gone home. Members of the HPRA began to talk about the car park closing. With that, the meeting drew to a close.

***

Directly after the meeting, though, I still held out some hope that the government would come through for Ava. Very late that night I outlined my thoughts on Facebook Live: 'I'm back at my cousin's house. I can barely speak. We got on well enough, we think, at the meeting. They gave us five options that we can go through and try to achieve. I hope we can come to a decent conclusion. I hope we did the right thing in coming away from the gates of the Dáil tonight. It was the best meeting we've had in terms of the government trying to find a solution. There's no doubt that is because of all of you out there. Because of what we all did together for Ava. This last week, I can't even begin to tell you what it was like coming through Dublin today, meeting everybody. I won't ever in my life forget it.

'We'll give them a fortnight and we've some meetings arranged with the neurologists. We'll see how we go. If we don't get what Ava needs we'll be back again. If more obstacles are put in our way, we'll have to come back and bed down outside the Dáil. There were many witnesses to the guarantees given tonight. We'll take the advice Gino Kenny gave us. He said that we should look into these options.'

Gino was cautiously optimistic after the meeting, saying, 'It's not a done deal by any means, but we'd be quite positive of an outcome now. A mother shouldn't have to walk for nine days to get medicine for her child. There's going to be more clarity given to consultants and GPs over what can be done. We hope to have something solid in place within two weeks.'

My initial optimism was unjustified, though, as things rapidly went downhill the next day. Paul and I went into Leinster House to collect the paperwork that had been promised, which would provide clarity to the neurologists treating Ava regarding applying for a licence, as well as the indemnification insurance obstacle for the private neurologist. This was vital if several of the options were to have any possibility of succeeding.

We arrived around about 9.30 a.m. and waited for someone to contact us. They said it would take a couple of hours. We made repeated attempts to find out the time when the documents would be produced. After being away from the kids for so long I was desperate to get home.

There was no sign of anything being produced, however, until pressure was placed on the HSE by some TDs. Incredibly, these documents – with sensitive private information, no less – were left with a security guard in Hawkins House (the Department of Health head office), where Paul had to go to retrieve them and then return to Leinster House.

Upon opening the documents our hopes were dashed when we realised they were not relevant to the neurologist and offered no clarity in helping to treat Ava. What we were given instead was simply a copy of how to apply for a licence and a copy of how to apply for the treatment abroad scheme. They were not what we needed for progress to be made and not what had been promised at the meeting. It was truly disgraceful.

The following day we made renewed efforts to get the correct documentation. All this achieved, however, was the delivery of the exact same useless documentation. The cynical lack of assistance left us in a tremendously difficult position. It appeared that the Department of Health representatives were unable to send what the neurologists needed. This failure cast a black cloud over the meeting arranged for the next day with Ava's neurologists. The options so recently provided were rapidly slipping away.

Simon Harris had said at the meeting that he 'wanted to restore my trust'. Our treatment over the next few days did anything but; instead, it opened my eyes. As I said at the time, 'We will now attend the meeting with the neurologists tomorrow without the necessary documents. It is probable that the meeting on Friday will be far more difficult than it would otherwise be.

As I return down the road to Aghabullogue with Paul, the tears are falling and my heart is breaking because of the injustice we are experiencing. Their cruelty will not defeat my efforts to gain access to medicinal cannabis legally in Ireland. I will return to make whatever peaceful, dignified, but determined protest is necessary for my angel.'

***

That Friday Paul and I had a meeting with the public neurologist and later with the private neurologist, to explore some of the suggested options. These didn't go as we had hoped and I left the meetings deeply disappointed. The neurologists still weren't able to move forward to help Ava. We had a pretty long conversation, and in fairness to the neurologists, on a personal level, they empathised with us, but they couldn't help. Due to the legal situation with THC oil, it was still impossible for them to oversee the care for Ava.

It was also said that the compassionate access programme really wasn't a viable option. This meant that anyone hoping to move forward with an application wasn't going to be able to do so, again because of the legal situation standing in the way.

What we came to see after these meetings was that the only possible way to receive treatment would be for patients to leave the state, to move to another country for who knows how long, and it would be a move that they'd have to finance themselves.

Would Ava even be able to take a long flight to another country? I was concerned putting her into the car going to Macroom, which is twenty minutes away, never mind several hours flying on a plane. It just wasn't a viable option, especially for people who have three or four children. Neither could I break up my family and leave half of them behind. Being away for nine days from my children during the walk, and only seeing them twice in that time, had nearly broken my heart. I wasn't willing to spend any more time away from them.

I didn't know what I could do next, only continue battling to make the government and legislators see that all of us who had stood outside the Dáil on Tuesday and all the people who walked were determined to get treatment for their loved ones. Legislation needed to be brought in, so people like the neurologists would be allowed to treat patients with medicinal cannabis.

Gino's bill would have solved all this. However, since passing the first stage of the legislative process, progress on the bill had come to a shuddering halt – it certainly wasn't being rushed through the Dáil. With five stages to pass in the Dáil and the requirement to undertake the same process in the Seanad, any legislation would come far too late for the people currently suffering. It was becoming increasingly clear that people needed to advocate for it to be enacted into law if there was to be any hope of people receiving treatment in the foreseeable future.

I implored people on a Facebook Live post: 'Email TDs, contact Simon Harris, and enact Gino Kenny's legislation now. It's the best option to move forward. Allow medicinal cannabis, like eleven other countries in Europe. It's eleven, let's make it twelve.'

With that, I signed off, utterly spent. In just about two days all the options given to us on Tuesday had been wiped away. My heart was broken.

Ava enjoying the summer sunshine in Aghabullogue. Being out in the sunshine was very significant as high temperatures could trigger seizures.

With Ava as we built her first snowman. Tiny the dog was keeping us company.

Paul and Ava in Blarney. On this day out Ava smiled and enjoyed the warm weather and the lovely garden.

My mother, Katty, with Ava in her arms. Her love and determination have been fundamental in Ava's success.

Holding Ava after a seizure – a true representation of the suffering caused to the child, and the distress and fear felt by the family members caring for them. *Courtesy of John Delea.*

Meeting the Minister for Health, Simon Harris, and confronting him in Mallow Hospital. Our need at this point was utterly desperate. *Courtesy of the Irish Examiner.*

At the walls of Cahir Castle. The feeling of solidarity as we sat together was palpable and it was here that I fully realised I was not going to be alone arriving in Dublin. *Courtesy of Fachtna Roe.*

Leaving Culahill and heading for Durrow. I will be forever grateful to the countless local people who came out in cold, wet weather to support and encourage our walk in any way possible.

This is one of the few photos of the four who walked the whole way from Cork to Dublin: Gino Kenny, TD, me, Brian Mahoney and Lindsey Graham.

In Ballybrittas with local supporters and friends from Mourneabbey, Cork, who travelled all the way up to be with us. *Courtesy of Fachtna Roe.*

Paul and me on Dame Street, Dublin. I said, 'Are you okay?' He said, 'Yeah, I knew you could do it girl!' It was a very special moment for me; our own private moment among all the crowds and noise. *Courtesy of Fachtna Roe.*

There was a power in the air as we approached the Dáil. It was vivid and real; the will to get what Ava needed was overwhelming and beyond anything I had ever experienced. *Courtesy of Gavin Monaghan.*

Arriving at the gates of the Dáil, where the media were all around us looking for me to answer their questions. With no meeting time agreed with Simon Harris, I wondered was there anything inside those gates for Ava. *Courtesy of Fachtna Roe.*

Standing in the square in Macroom, speaking to the massive crowd who came out. To have this local support was one of the most precious things, giving us strength to continue to advocate for Ava. *Courtesy of John Delea.*

At Dublin airport with Luke Flanagan, MEP, and Gino Kenny, TD, when we had just returned from Barcelona with medical THC; the prescription is in my hand. The bottle was seized and I was left feeling dazed and humiliated. *Courtesy of Hot Press.*

Mags O'Sullivan, Sarah Mahoney and me blocking the gates of the Dáil. We were forcibly removed after four and a half hours. Although we asked, Simon Harris would not meet or speak to us. *Courtesy of The Irish Times.*

Ava having a laugh in Haarlem, the Netherlands, one of the most beautiful towns in the country. It was in the Netherlands that Ava started to experience the real benefits of medicinal cannabis.

The joy at Cork airport as we returned with Ava from the Netherlands. To have what she needed to be well and to know we would have Christmas together at home in Aghabullogue made this one of the most precious days we have ever had. *Courtesy of Fachtna Roe.*

The Next Steps

'You never know how strong you are,
until strong is the only choice you have.'

– Bob Marley

I was physically and emotionally exhausted. I had an X-ray taken of my knee, and the pain turned out to be due to inflammation of the tendons. It would be grand, I just had to hobble around for several days. The problem was that, after all that effort, I didn't know what I had achieved. Awareness of the need to legalise medicinal cannabis had greatly increased, I suppose, but Ava was no closer to actually receiving the medicine she needed.

An informal meeting was held in Gino's constituency office, where it was agreed to stage a protest rally outside Leinster House on 29 March. My suggestion of a protest in Cork was supported, too, as it would be on 'home turf' and an opportunity for those unable to travel to Dublin to show their support.

I was invited to speak at both protests. It always made me feel slightly sick to be leaving the children. Of course it was for the best, but it took careful managing and age-appropriate explanations for them to understand why mammy was gone again. Sophia and Michael were becoming very anti-Dublin. It was always pulling mam away for some reason. Similarly, Simon

Harris became known as the 'bold man' in our house around this time and also, I believe, in Aghabullogue national school. The kid's logic was that Mam was going to Dublin to get Ava's medicine, but the bold man wouldn't allow us to have it. I listened to their discussions at the kitchen table one evening, about what should happen to Simon. My five- and six-year-old ultimately decided that he should be put in prison!

All of the artificial complexity surrounding access to medicinal cannabis can be swept away by a child's simple viewpoint. The medicine (CBD oil) was already making Ava better, after all, so she should therefore be allowed whatever else was needed (THC oil). They'd seen Ava's countless seizures for their entire lives and couldn't understand why Simon wouldn't help. I told them that I didn't know why either, but, 'We'll have to try and convince him, won't we?'

Ava had a very bad day on 21 March, suffering a horrendous fifteen-minute seizure. Fortunately, she didn't fall into a tonic-clonic state, but it was still very aggressive and the extended duration was terrifying. Fifteen minutes was the longest she'd experienced for a long time. With the improvements brought on by the CBD oil, Ava was also more aware of the seizures now. So, unfortunately, even though there were fewer of them, her improved awareness meant that she was very distressed when they struck.

I tried to phone Simon Harris's office around this time and also sent an email, requesting a date for another meeting. At first, I was told that my enquiry would be brought to the minister's attention and be dealt with in due course. Later, I received an email from the Department of Health stating, 'Ava's current and future treatment is best managed by her clinicians and therefore a future meeting with the minister would be of no practical use. Any questions you have regarding Ava's treatment are best addressed to her clinical team.'

This is what you have to deal with. While the Irish parliament was debating the dress code of its members, my daughter was lying in bed, wracked with pain.

I had to meet the officials again and move towards a resolution, I knew, because Ava deserved help and I couldn't do it on my own. I couldn't do it without a road map showing a realistic route towards obtaining the THC oil. I was in an awful state that day and so worried about what tomorrow would bring. She could have the 'big one' and be gone.

***

A lot of local people wouldn't be able to get to the rally planned for 29 March in Dublin. People had approached me, wanting to show their support, so my good friends Mags and Owen O'Sullivan organised a march in Macroom on the twenty-fifth of the month. It allowed a lot of friends and supporters in the local area to come out and show their desire for change.

An excellent crowd of several hundred people marched. There were lots of local children walking, which gave it a lovely atmosphere. No child you speak to can understand why the medicine was being denied to Ava. After meeting up in the Dunnes Stores car park, we wound our way up to Market Square, chanting, 'Make it Medicine, Make it Happen'. We were blessed with warm and sunny weather as we marched. It was a real contrast to the harsh conditions experienced on the walk to Dublin. Several speakers addressed the crowd, including

Aindrias Moynihan, TD, Tom Curran, Owen O'Sullivan and myself.

The entire square was thronged with people. As I looked out, I thought, 'Wow, I'm going to be speaking to all these people, in a place I've walked through all my life.' I could clearly recollect walking through it as a child, shopping with Mum, or going to the mart with Dad. Remembering those happy days put me at ease. This day was another happy day, surrounded by great people with their smiles of support and words of encouragement ringing in my ears.

I went up to speak. There was a lot of confusion among the people supporting Ava as to the five options. I explained how the public neurologist wasn't going to support or oversee an application for a licence, due to a 'lack of clinical evidence' about medicinal cannabis's effectiveness and a 'lack of expertise for her to refer to within Ireland'.

I told the people that taking Ava to Canada for a consultant to prescribe medicinal cannabis was impossible. She'd been 'levelled' by a fifteen-minute seizure a couple of days ago. She'd get up for a couple of minutes, then be flattened again and have to go back to bed. Ava's private neurologist had offered the chance of a teleconference consultation with a Canadian neurologist, but the HSE intervened and said we needed a second neurologist to approve this. It was clear that no matter what we did, an obstacle would be put in our way.

The treatment abroad scheme was mentioned, but the public neurologist wouldn't sign off on this scheme either, declaring that medicinal cannabis was an experimental treatment, which therefore excluded it from the scheme. (And the private neurologist was not allowed to sign off on such a scheme.) Those in attendance were astonished that the compassionate access scheme was considered completely unworkable by both of Ava's neurologists, because part of the medicine they'd be administering (the THC oil) was illegal. They felt it wasn't possible to prescribe something that's illegal without them losing their licence.

The only viable solution was Gino Kenny's legislation, which was at the second stage, where the details of the bill were being debated and coming to the Health Committee stage. It had cross party support in December; however, since then opposition had become more prevalent in the Dáil, particularly from the government. Politicians needed to get to grips with the fact that this was the only option for people like my daughter.

The furthest distance we should be travelling to treat our loved ones was into Cork, I explained to the crowd. The government were trying to put the blame squarely at the door of the neurologists, but that was not fair. At least one of Ava's neurologists was desperate to provide any help possible. Once, she said to me, 'I've been thinking about Ava all week. I've been thinking about what I can do to help her, I don't know what I can do.' She came up with options and alternatives, but they had been ignored by the government.

I encouraged people to go to the protest in Dublin the following Wednesday, where we'd peacefully – though maybe loudly – advocate for change. It was down to us to make change happen. Paul and I had been a whole lot of trouble for Simon Harris. The government would like to see the back of us. And, to be honest, I'd like to see the back of them. But I couldn't say goodbye to this situation, for the sake of my daughter.

After the rally I stayed to chat and mingle with the people in the square. Lots and lots of people came up to express their admiration for my walk to Dublin and the ongoing fight for Ava. As one of the supporters said, 'Well, sure, you'd never know, Ava needs help today, but it could be any one of our families down the line.'

As I chatted away, a woman approached, reached over and locked me in an unexpectedly warm embrace. 'Hello, Vera. I've come over from Kerry. I just had to meet and tell you that the pain is gone, it's gone.'

I replied, 'That's marvellous news. Have you tried medicinal cannabis?'

'I'm a teacher, Vera, and I was going to have to give up my job and go on disability. I could hardly stand with the pain, teaching was becoming impossible.'

She recounted how she'd been reading my Facebook posts and saw several articles related to medicinal cannabis's potential for treating chronic pain. The pharmaceutical drugs hadn't alleviated her pain and she felt 'doped out of it all the time'. She did her own additional research, and with nothing to lose decided to start self-medicating by taking medicinal CBD and THC oil.

'Vera, I'm back at work, the pain is gone, and I feel like a new woman. My friends are all big supporters, too; they know how bad I was and can see the improvement with their own eyes. I'm back to the old me, Vera, I never thought I'd see that day again. I just had to come today to support yourself and Ava. People have to learn about the values of cannabis as a medicine.'

I was blown away by her story. I'll never forget the look of enthusiasm in her eyes. She looked the picture of health and nothing like a woman who'd been crippled for years with chronic pain. I was delighted for her and that my posts could have such a positive impact. I had learned so much from the information out there related to medicinal cannabis, and it was heartening to see other people obtain such benefits.

***

The protest rally in Dublin organised by Gino and the People Before Profit party was a peaceful demonstration, aimed at highlighting the urgent need for action surrounding the issue of medicinal cannabis. The bill was shortly due to go before the joint Health Committee. They would examine the bill, section by section, and could make amendments. It was hoped that the demonstration would put pressure on the politicians to stand alongside all the people who were desperate to see medicinal cannabis legalised. Such was the support in Cork that a number of buses were organised to facilitate people attending the event.

As it turned out, the protest was a large, well-attended affair. The interest and momentum generated by the walk were still there. As people started to arrive, we saw workmen erect an anti-riot barrier across the road to prevent any pedestrian access directly in front of the gates of Leinster House. Who else was protesting outside the Dáil that night? What dangerous crowd was about to appear? It quickly dawned on us that the barriers were for our rally. That was ridiculous. What had anyone to fear from advocates of medicinal cannabis? People suffering from chronic illnesses, their carers and family members are the least likely people to cause trouble. All of the protests were peaceful. I think it made the government and Simon Harris look a bit sad and pathetic.

Several speakers addressed the crowd, including Richard Boyd Barrett, Gino, Tom Curran, myself, Pat Buckley of Sinn

Féin and three friends, Rachael, Ciara and Brian. Both Richard and Gino gave an overview of progress of the 'Cannabis for Medicinal Use Regulation Bill 2016' and warned about the government's tactics to delay and obfuscate.

I felt the personal testimonies of Rachael, Ciara and Brian were very powerful and had a strong impact on the crowd. Rachael suffers from fibromyalgia and spoke of her chronic pain and fatigue, symptoms she had to deal with 24/7, and how the recommended pharmaceutical drugs had proven inadequate. She asked people to imagine being told by their doctor, 'There's nothing more we can do.' (I've been there and it's terrifying.) Medicinal cannabis has made a huge improvement in the lives of so many people with fibromyalgia, she added, but it needed to be made legal and available for patients in chronic pain.

Ciara has metastatic cancer, and tried 'every type of conventional medication and suffered astronomical amounts of pain'. Strong opioid-based painkillers or steroidal anti-inflammatories did nothing to alleviate her pain. 'I got my hands on some cannabis oil and my God, the next morning I woke up and felt completely different and the pain has never returned with the same severity.' She has spoken to her oncologist and he has no problem with her decision. As Ciara said, 'They're slowly coming around. They know. We know.'

I spoke about Ava's current condition and my anger and bafflement at the lack of movement on the government's part.

Brian's situation is closest to my own, as his son also has intractable epilepsy. When he spoke he outlined some of the terrible potential side effects of many anti-epileptic medications, including irreversible damage to the peripheral vision, mental regression, severe dizziness, severe drowsiness, chronic constipation and, ironically, seizures. These could be contrasted with the side effects of medicinal cannabis: sleepiness and slight changes in appetite. I totally agreed with Brian when he said, 'It's scary when you read that a drug you're giving can potentially cause irreversible damage to your child's eyesight. But you give it, because you're told it might work. Don't tell me I can't use medicinal cannabis after that. You know, I'll take sleepiness any day of the week over damage to eyesight, severe dizziness or mental regression. I can handle sleepiness.'

Overall, the protest that day in Dublin was a resounding success.

**

Early in April, a very prominent figure in the American medicinal cannabis movement visited Ireland and spoke at a press conference in Dublin: Jesse Stanley, one of the Stanley brothers who produce Charlotte's Web. It's not an exaggeration to say this CBD oil had saved Ava's life. I had previously spoken with his brother Joel, and listening to Jesse at the conference I wasn't surprised to see that he was equally well informed about medicinal cannabis. He considered it 'irresponsible' that the HPRA report found little evidence for its benefits. He was quite measured in his comments, saying that while CBD oil is not a 'silver bullet', it has been proven to help with conditions such as epilepsy, arthritis and autism with medical support.

Jesse had seen it all before. The people in Colorado had fought, and won, the battle to legalise medicinal cannabis, and state after state has followed suit. The battle in Ireland was nothing new to him. The demonisation and fearmongering were due to a history of 'prohibition, lies and miseducation'. There are no recorded cases of overdoses or deaths from cannabis use, a claim many other drugs are unable to make. Jesse claimed that the pharmaceutical industry has a 'vested interest' in ensuring medicinal cannabis isn't legalised, but that legalisation is 'inevitable'. He was very prescient in his comment that, 'If Ireland doesn't address this issue responsibly, people will go abroad to get what they want.'

Jesse later made the very kind gesture of taking the time to travel down to Aghabullogue to see Ava. It was a very human touch and went to show the kind of person he is. We had some great chats, where he'd express his admiration about the increased awareness of medicinal cannabis in Ireland, but most of all his delight at seeing Ava's improvement since going on Charlotte's Web. It was wonderful to have him visit. It must be very gratifying to have a product that your company makes bring about such a profound and positive impact on people's health.

After the press conference, I listened to Professor Barnes and Professor David Finn speaking to the TDs and senators in the AV room of Leinster House about medicinal cannabis. I really hoped it had a positive impact on the politicians who attended. They certainly couldn't say they hadn't been provided with an opportunity to be informed on the subject by two genuine experts.

From Dublin, I travelled by train down to Tralee accompanied by Gino, as we were scheduled to speak at a public meeting arranged by Brian Finucane of the People Before Profit party. People came from all over Kerry to hear about Gino's bill and my experiences. Gino provided an amusing anecdote: 'The amount of people who have stopped me in Clondalkin, over the last three to four weeks. They don't want to talk about anything else, they just want to talk about the walk and cannabis. It's a very human thing, a positive thing that drives me forward.'

After our talks, there was a long question and answers session, which turned into a really good exchange of information. People told of how medicinal cannabis was helping with their chronic pain, arthritis, cancer and fibromyalgia, amongst other things. That so many people are compelled to illegally self-medicate with cannabis is a shocking indictment of the Irish medical system. One very nice gentleman attributed the remission of his cancer and the decrease in the size of the tumours to the medicinal cannabis he was taking. It's just so sensational to meet people like that and hear such powerful personal testimonies.

Soon after, I was heading back up to Dublin for the 'Right-2Water' protest on 8 April. This was by far the largest crowd that I had ever spoken to. Tens of thousands of people from all over the country travelled up to the protest. It was a very colourful event, with chanting, placards and banners galore. I felt very honoured to have been invited to speak at such a prominent event. I believe it was the biggest protest rally in Ireland in the whole of 2017.

Several prominent politicians also spoke, including Mary Lou McDonald, Bríd Smith, Catherine Murphy, Joan Collins and Paul Murphy. I was sick with nerves as I thought about addressing the immense crowd stretching into the distance. The nerves nearly got the better of me that day. After several pats on the back and people reassuring me, 'Sure you'll be grand', I took one final gulp of water and walked onto the stage, muttering to myself, 'You can do this, Vera.'

Something happened that day. I started awkwardly, but the

support from the crowd was palpable; it came in waves that I could almost feel rushing past me. It started to simmer in my soul and I gathered myself and held my nerve, being buoyed up by this support. I worked up into a passionate plea for Ava and everyone else who deserved medical justice.

I told the people, 'The injustice done to us is fundamentally wrong. People all over the world, their lives are being changed by medical cannabis and we have to have it here. It's about every single person who needs it, that are struggling, their lives controlled by seizures. Their families' lives are controlled by their loved one's illnesses.

'Countries all over the world have access to medication that I am not allowed access to for Ava, and you're not allowed access to for your family. The sisters and brothers and mothers and fathers that are looking for this medication, they need it now. A mother's love is unyielding, that's what's kept us going. When we get tired and we get shagged out, we go back to Ava, and she needs this, and we need this. Simon Harris, there'll be no stopping until we get what we need for our family. The legislation is prepared, the bill is there waiting. Sometimes you need to break bad laws to make good laws. Don't you?' There was a load roar of 'Yes' in response. 'Maybe that's what we're going to have to do, break bad laws and bring the good laws in.'

As I left the stage, the crowd loudly chanted, 'Vera, Vera, Vera.'

After the highs, come the lows. I felt very down in the days after the 'Right2Water' protest. I felt that I hadn't done enough to get Ava what she needed. Paul and I had been straight and honest, but it had not been reciprocated. There was still no sign of another meeting with Simon Harris, never mind making progress in terms of getting Ava what she needed. My heart was broken. I wished I'd done more, though I didn't know what more could have been done.

In the days that followed, however, I started to brush myself off and dispense with the negative thoughts. They achieve nothing; focus on positive actions, I told myself. Figure out what can be done next. We'll get there for Ava, because we simply have to.

Sniffer Dogs

'One has a moral responsibility to disobey unjust laws.'

– Martin Luther King

Ava's potential treatment was caught up in a tangled web of highly paid civil servants, HSE staff and politicians in the Fine Gael government. They seemed to be, at worst, trying to complicate the situation as much as possible, or at best, doing as little as possible in the hope that we would eventually quieten down and fade away of our own accord. Ava's needs were pretty straightforward. To access the medication, we needed a neurologist to prescribe it and we needed the licence to use it. We had neither. It was obvious that we had reached a point where a different approach was necessary.

I had hoped that we could avoid leaving Ireland, but it now seemed that we had no other options. Desperately, I began to search abroad for medical centres experienced in treating epilepsy which would be in a position to prescribe medicinal cannabis. A friend, who was using it to treat their cancer, gave me the details of the Kalapa clinic in Barcelona, suggesting that they may be able to help.

At this stage, I knew things were becoming more serious. Even by considering the option of looking abroad for help, our journey was going to change completely. Theoretically, getting a medical professional in Spain to treat Ava would be a major breakthrough, opening up the possibility of receiving a prescription for an appropriate treatment. In an ideal world, this should have been something to fill the family with joy; however, there was nothing ideal about the situation and I was apprehensive about what the authorities would do if I brought the medication back to Ireland.

I contacted the clinic and found them to be very friendly and professional. We organised a consultation over Skype with the doctor. It was a very stress-free experience, with a wide-ranging discussion, and it made me feel comfortable about taking the plunge and travelling over to Barcelona. They had so much experience in terms of dealing with children with epilepsy. They were treating about forty kids from about seventeen different countries, I was informed. Ava didn't even need to accompany me to the clinic as they had already been able to review her medical notes. This made the whole process a great deal easier; saving Ava from having to make the trip avoided the possibility of a seizure while travelling.

I asked Gino and Luke Flanagan were they interested in going. They both said, 'Yes, absolutely, we'll go out and support you.' They both believed in what I was doing. The willingness of both of them to accompany me on the trip was probably one of the most emotional moments in the whole campaign so far. They were putting themselves out for my family and for Ava. It was very special. They both reorganised their busy schedules to make the trip.

I was so happy to have them there, because I was worried and, honestly, a little scared by what I had to do. I had to bring Ava's medication home. And there was every chance I'd be arrested for bringing the medication into the country. After all, I had no intention of hiding what I was doing.

Many people had commended me for my bravery, but up until this point I'd done nothing illegal. However, this journey would lead to me openly flouting the law and was where I had to prove, both to myself and to the many people supporting Ava, that I had the guts to do what needed to be done. Ava had the courage and guts to keep fighting the epilepsy; now I was going to do what I could do to ease her pain.

I travelled up to Dublin on 19 April and stayed with my friend Leah. Gino and I made our way to the airport in the early hours to catch the flight to Barcelona. We met Luke at the airport and, as I saw his smiling face striding towards us, I thought, 'We are all here now, this is it.' Both of them were up at an ungodly hour of the morning, and all to help my little girl and others like her. It's regrettable that there aren't more people willing to stand up and do something, rather than simply sit around thinking about how terrible the situation is.

In Barcelona, we proceeded directly to the Kalapa clinic. I got to have a fantastic and amazingly informative consultation with the doctor there. They were just as professional as I had expected and it was, I felt, a very routine consultation, except that the doctors here happened to accept the medical benefits of medicinal cannabis and considered it a realistic option. They were as measured as any doctor should be, considering the fact that Ava had unsuccessfully tried many pharmaceutical medications. However, with the growing evidence from their clinic, and worldwide, they considered medicinal cannabis to be a safe alternative for patients like Ava. Their knowledge regarding medicinal cannabis was extremely impressive and I tried to soak up all the information and advice.

The professionals in the clinic found it difficult to believe that a medical product like this could cause such a problem in Ireland. They were all a bit puzzled as to why Irish people had to travel as far as Barcelona to access medicine. They treat a large number of people with the oil, after all, and considered it a potentially effective medicine for Dravet syndrome and several other illnesses.

They issued me with a prescription for the THC oil for Ava, which they deemed necessary to continue her treatment alongside the CBD oil. Afterwards, I went straight to a pharmacy and got the bottles of THC oil.

Later, as we all sat outside at a table on some street off Las Ramblas, I thought to myself how very surreal the whole situation was. Here we were, the TD, the MEP and the noisy one from Aghabullogue with their coffee, tea and San Miguel. I'll let you guess who was drinking what. Both Luke and Gino have a great sense of humour, and we had great fun chatting away all evening and watching the world go by.

Tomorrow, we would fly home. I had no idea what my reception would be.

***

I had been nervous, scared and worried to varying degrees throughout the previous weeks, thinking about flying home with the THC oil. At times, I convinced myself that I'd be arrested for carrying the illegal medication back into Ireland. Although I was scared, I wasn't as scared as you might imagine. In fact, as the departure date approached, I felt a strange sense of calm descend on me. After all, the fear of being arrested was nowhere near as serious as the fear of my daughter dying.

That night in Barcelona, I went to bed and slept as well as I could, so as to be ready for whatever the following day would throw at me. Sure, if they arrested me I'd deal with it, although I didn't have any real knowledge of what it actually entailed. Regardless, I was determined to be completely open and honest about Ava's medication. I know many people feel that they can't do this – flagrantly break the law – and I totally understand their predicament. However, I felt that if I managed to bring the medicine home, maybe something positive would be achieved for everyone who needed access. Maybe it would even bring about change.

So, as we arrived in the departures area of Barcelona airport the following morning, Luke, Gino and I did a short Facebook Live posting, stating that we were returning to Ireland with the medication containing the THC oil. As a result, no one was left in any doubt as to our intentions.

Subsequently, I was criticised by some people for not bringing it in surreptitiously, but I felt strongly that the prescription meant something. It validated what I was doing. I wasn't a criminal, I was just doing my best for my daughter. If anything, it was the inaction of the government and roadblocks it set up that were really criminal. The law may have said that I didn't have the legal right to have the THC oil on my person that day in April, but it didn't mean that the law was morally or ethically right. Sometimes, I feel, you really do have a moral responsibility to break unjust laws.

Arriving back into Ireland, we alighted from the plane

with the other passengers. After the normal passport control procedure, we slowly moved towards arrivals. Gino looked back, smiling, and said that he thought we were going to be okay.

Moments later, we saw the sniffer dogs and their handlers approaching. Gino was stunned. As a politician, he travels in and out of Dublin airport quite regularly, but he had never seen or heard of anyone encountering sniffer dogs.

I looked on, absolutely convinced that I was about to be arrested. I wondered what garda station or jail I was going to be sent to. I thought: 'Oh my God, what's going to happen now? What are the visiting hours for the Dochas centre [the prison for women in Dublin] anyway?'

The passengers were all stopped and lined up in single file against a wall. I felt sorry for the other passengers, some of whom appeared slightly distressed by the experience. I knew why the dogs were there. Some people looked apprehensive, while others recognised Luke and Gino and possibly me, and figured out what was going on.

The sniffer dog with its handler approached me. It was like a scene out of *Banged Up Abroad*. A number of faces looked in horror from the handler, to the dog, to me, and then back to the dog. The sniffer dog walked alongside all of us and checked us and our luggage. There seemed to be a brief flash of disappointment in the handler's face as the dog passed me by. The dog didn't 'alert' to the bottles of medicinal cannabis I had in my pocket. Interesting! This would have been a rather amusing development had the whole scenario not been so serious.

Despite the sniffer dog's snub, I remained hostile to the idea of just walking through with the illegal THC oil on me. If I walked past security and said nothing, I reasoned, then Ava's prescription was just being ignored as if it was of no consequence, as if it was nothing. This wasn't on, I realised. This carry-on had to end. Therefore, as soon as I got a chance, I stepped forward and asked one of the customs officials, 'Is this maybe what you're looking for?'

Smiling, the official looked at me and said, 'Yes, hello, Vera.'

'Where do you want me so?' I asked, feeling like this whole situation was just beyond belief.

He seemed momentarily distracted by my Cork accent, but then rather sadly said, 'Would you mind coming with me to the lady customs officials who are waiting over here?'

'No problem,' I replied.

He then asked was I travelling alone. I answered honestly and said, 'I'm not. I'm travelling with Luke Flanagan and Gino Kenny.'

They would never have forgiven me if I had cut them loose, as they were with me come hell or high water. He asked then if the gentlemen would also please accompany me. Again, this was no problem and Luke and Gino were guided away with me.

The other passengers all stared after us as we were led away. A number of them expressed their shock at the unexpected experience. I could see looks which varied from confusion, to anger, to pity. There was no doubt that there was an awareness among many people on the plane that day that we were bringing Ava's medication home. I was grateful for the sympathetic nods and salutes of support.

All three of us were escorted away, to three small rooms, for questioning. I was interrogated by two female customs officials. As I entered, I exchanged 'Good day' with them. I felt it was as easy to be nice and, sure, it never hurts to try. I just thought to myself, 'My God, we are only European citizens when it suits the government.'

I sat down, as instructed, on a rather severe-looking metal chair that had an equally severe- and spartan-looking table in front of it. As I went to pull the chair a little closer in towards the table, I discovered that the chair, along with the table, was bolted to the floor. I nervously laughed and said, 'I won't be pulling any closer to that table today, anyway.'

One of the ladies stifled a smile and as the conversation went on they continually had to pull back from being too friendly. Perhaps most drug smugglers don't mention the weather or how busy they were that day. I forgot on two more occasions that the chair was nailed to the floor and tried to move it, which elicited laughter all round. As the conversation continued, it seemed that I was not going to be arrested, but the medication was going to be seized. It's ironic, I think, to have a medication which would stop Ava's seizure activity being seized.

By this stage the officials gave the appearance of being even more uncomfortable with the interrogation than I was. I think they were mortified that they had to take the THC cannabis oil away from me. As drug smugglers go, I'd say I'm on the mild end of the scale. The customs officials had a job to do, but it was clear from their demeanour that they weren't comfortable with depriving a sick little girl of her medicine.

Next, the searching of my bags and my person began. It was not invasive, but it was certainly humiliating. We were simply not going to be allowed to bring Ava's medicine back into the country. I had the prescription in my hand. I had what Ava needed to get better, but we were not going to be allowed to proceed.

As Luke said at the time, 'There was no strip searches or anything like that. We met a lot of ladies and gentlemen who had a job to do, but you couldn't miss the "we're not comfortable" look on their faces.' But the fact remains that, although I was treated with respect and kindness by the customs officials, I was still subjected to the same process as criminals smuggling drugs.

I was detained for just over an hour and received a 'confirmation note' when the medicine was confiscated. We were all then released without charge. As far as I was concerned, they took my little girl's chance away from her when they refused to give that medicine back.

I was led to believe that the THC oil would be taken to the HPRA for testing, where they'd basically analyse the medicine to see what percentage THC was in it. The process was done so as to establish whether it was illegal or not. If they established that it was illegal then, I guess, the ball was in their court as to what they'd do.

Once we were released by the officials, we went out and spoke to the gathered media, the Facebook Live posting having alerted them to my arrival in the airport. I had got over the detention by this stage, although I was a bit shocked and clearly distressed that Ava's medicine was gone. I was asked why I'd publicised the fact that I was doing this and coming through with the medicine. I replied, 'I wasn't doing anything wrong. I wasn't going to sneak through here like some sort of sleeveen.'

Gino and Luke also spoke to the media and as Luke said, 'Down through history, it takes people like Vera Twomey to change things. Politicians can do this, that and the other, but unless there's somebody directly affected by it who speaks up, it never changes.'

Gino said, 'The bill that I put forward, with cross-party support, last December, would give broad-based access to medicinal cannabis on the recommendation of a doctor, to people who would benefit from using it. People suffering from chronic pain, MS, intractable epilepsy and other conditions can benefit from using it to alleviate some of their symptoms and pain.'

Both of them also expressed their pride in me, and of all the things said, that made me the happiest.

I posted a Facebook request after speaking to the media, asking people to contact Simon Harris's office and ask why a little sick girl with a valid EU prescription couldn't have it honoured in this country? I wanted that medicine back and I felt that I was morally entitled to have it back.

No sooner were we out of the airport and heading back home than I had to prepare for a protest march planned for the very next day in Cork city. No rest, but it was much better to be busy, better to keep trying. The march was planned for the Grand Parade at 2 p.m. With it being only up the road from home, I was hoping that a lot of people could get out and walk. People who weren't able to make it further afield. There's strength in numbers and, you know, we had to keep fighting.

***

We had a fantastic march in Cork city on 22 April. Nearly 1,000 people joined in, to show their support and solidarity for my fight. The streets came alive to the people's chants of 'Make it Medicine, Make it Happen'. Young, middle-aged and older people were all joining together to support a little child.

We were to start on the Grand Parade and make a circuit of the city centre, going down the South Mall, left along Parnell

Place, past the bus station, up Merchants' Quay, and finally back along Patrick's Street to the Grand Parade.

Many people in wheelchairs and with serious illnesses made it along on the day and encouraged us to keep fighting. One wheelchair-bound lady told me that I was a mighty woman to do what I'd done. As I spoke to her I didn't feel very mighty; instead, what I wanted to say was, 'You're the mighty one to keep going in spite of the chronic pain and in spite of it not being mentioned in the compassionate access scheme.'

Lots of people from different walks of life came up to speak to Paul and me. They discussed how medicinal cannabis could potentially help them or a loved one. They told me how much what we were doing meant to them. Their desperation and helplessness was palpable. Some people were frustrated that they couldn't do more than attend the protest because they were so ill themselves. You'd have had to have a heart of stone not to be moved. I was already emotional, but their stories increased it a couple of notches.

The assembled crowd set off from the Grand Parade and quickly took up both sides of the road as they walked down the South Mall. Everyone began to chant, 'Make it Medicine, Make it Happen.' People held banners, flags, posters and purple balloons – purple being the colour associated with epilepsy awareness. I saw the balloons as being important: they were a child-like touch, highlighting that this march was primarily for a little girl who needed this medicine.

The chanting was deafening. I tried to keep it up, but my voice was beginning to go. Thankfully, the other supporters kept it going, in much the same way as they had when we travelled the last few miles in to Leinster House. It was tremendous.

The South Mall is a business street, with lots of solicitors and accountancy offices, so it was relatively uncongested, but as we turned left towards the bus station and Merchant's Quay many more people began to join us. For the most part, those that didn't join us stopped and clapped and cheered as we passed by. It was an extraordinary feeling to have this level of support. Despite somewhat disrupting traffic and making a lot of noise, we didn't hear a single complaint about the conduct of the protest. A lot of cars beeped their horns in support. The gardaí were present and were quite nice, overall. I believe they had a little look at our licence, or whatever was needed to conduct the march, but it was all in order.

Turning left onto Patrick's Street I saw a homeless man sitting over on the footpath near the Father Mathew statue and, my God, what had he, only a poster saying 'Justice for Ava'. He couldn't be passed by without an acknowledgement. I said to Jim Connell or Paul, I'm not sure which, that I'd to run over and thank him. I did so and he said to me, 'She deserves to get her medicine, God loves her.' I told him that he had more on his plate to be dealing with than making posters in support of Ava, but his support was so staunch. What a decent man to be thinking of my daughter when he was so down on his luck at the time and with no home of his own.

Running back to the front of the protest, we continued past Marks and Spencers, Brown Thomas and on up past the Moderne. This is the main shopping street and was thronged with pedestrians, who clapped and cheered as we passed. Several people were doing Facebook Live posts to highlight the event and my friend Siobhan was on hand with her camera, taking pictures and doing short interviews with some of the protesters.

She asked them what message they had for Simon Harris. There was no aggressive talk, just person after person saying, 'Help Ava, do something or find the person in your department to do something for you.'

It was fierce emotional. This was Cork, only down the road from home, and in all my days I had never imagined that I would be standing there in front of hundreds of people for the sake of my little girl's health. What I did know, now, was that the people in Cork would never let it go for an ill child. They came out that day and supported us, with their walking, cheering and clapping, and all without a single complaint. Just like us, they knew that Ava being denied her medicine was wrong, and sure what else can someone from Cork do when confronted by injustice but rebel?

It was hard to keep the tears in check. Unsurprisingly, I gave an emotional speech after the march, the bones of which were: 'You're aware I took a trip during the week?' There was loud cheering and clapping in response. 'Now, the welcome we received in Spain was in stark contrast to the welcome we received when we returned with the medicine. While I was in Barcelona my daughter had four seizures. They've taken Ava's opportunity away from her by seizing her medicine. I can tell you, I want it back.

'It's Simon Harris's job to change the law, to introduce the legislation, for his Fine Gael party members to stop commenting on medicinal cannabis saying, "It'd be an immoral idea to bring it into the country as a legal substance." To stop purporting that we spread fake facts, which is absolutely nonsensical. You know, the nonsense being brought forward from the Dáil is beyond belief.

'I don't want my daughter to die. I don't want my daughter to go back to thirty seizures a day. I want the medication to save her life and the minister has the authority to do that. It has to be allowed. They don't want it to happen. There's no profit for pharmaceutical companies in medicinal cannabis. Stay with us so we can make it happen.'

It was an impassioned speech, but I was bursting with emotion: guilt for failing to bring Ava's medicine home, sadness from the injustice of it being taken away from me. There was utter desperation, too, contemplating a government who had left us in the gutter. It was how I felt on the day; it's how I feel now.

The People Before Profit party were instrumental in organising the march, including the posters, marshals along the route and speakers and other gear for the march. It's these unseen actions which made such a big difference on the day. A tremendous amount of organisation goes into these events. Without this important organisational work, no protest or other such event can succeed.

I wasn't the only one to address the crowd. The previous few days had struck a chord with Gino and he addressed the crowd, saying, 'Anyone in Vera's position would do exactly the same. You know what, bad laws need to be broken to make good laws. People like Nelson Mandela, Martin Luther King and Rosa Parks broke laws to make good laws, and that's what we're trying to do here. Break bad laws to make good laws. People are suffering in this country needlessly. They're being criminalised because they want to access medicinal cannabis. Under the eyes of the law they're criminals.

'That's what my bill is about, it's about decriminalising medicinal cannabis. The government want a highly restrictive

for Ava

"compassionate" access programme that ultimately will mean nothing. What we want for the majority who could benefit is to give them safe access. In this day and age, people should have a choice. If something is working for them, they should have a choice to access that medicine. If we need to break bad laws again, we will break them to make good laws.'

Amen.

Blocking the Gates

'I said: somebody should do something about that.
Then I realised, I'm somebody.'

– Lily Tomlin

The situation at the end of April was that, despite my best efforts, Ava had not been offered or allowed the chance to be treated with medicinal cannabis overseen by a paediatric neurologist in Cork. The medicine Ava needed was being withheld. One member of the minister for health's office thought it was sufficient to pass my messages about another meeting to the minister's press secretary only! I didn't. So, when you can get no sensible contact with the government, what do you do? It's not like I could grow my own cannabis. I mean, I like gardening, but I'm no horticulturalist, and let's be serious, we are dealing with a seven-year-old child whose treatment needed to be supervised by medical professionals. No, once again, I had to take action.

On 3 May, I headed back up to Dublin. My friends Michelle O'Shea, Mags O'Sullivan and Sarah Mahoney came up on the train and met me outside Leinster House. We planned to protest at its gates.

In the morning, prior to the protest, I attended a press conference where Dr Peadar O'Grady, Dr Gareth McGovern and

Dr Cathal O'Sullivan spoke. They discussed the recent motion recommending that medicinal cannabis be legalised, which had been passed by the Irish Medical Organisation (IMO), clearly demonstrating that a lot of the medical professionals in Ireland wanted a more progressive policy.

After the press conference, the girls and I began our protest. We had brought placards, tents and sleeping bags and were prepared for an overnight stay. I'd have preferred to have stood up for my daughter in a more dignified fashion, but we all felt that we needed to do this. We looked at the sleeping bags and back to each other and were saddened by what was ahead of us.

It still felt strange to be protesting at the gates of Leinster House: it isn't something I have ever become totally comfortable with. What I have found, though, is that the solidarity felt between protesters is staggering. No matter if you've a thick Cork accent like mine, or if it is steeped in that of another part of the country, people gravitate together and help out, particularly when an injustice is happening. It brings out the good and the strength in people.

I did a live Facebook post, letting people know what was happening, asking for anyone in the area who could to come over and support us. I also met and spoke to some of the TDs, such as Micheál Martin, Mattie McGrath and Shane Ross, as they entered and left, letting it be known that I needed to speak to the minister for health. Surprisingly, I got a lot of supportive smiles and thumbs up from Fine Gael politicians passing by. A few furtively came over and wished me well, but they didn't linger. They lacked courage. It appeared to be politically toxic for Fine Gael politicians to be associated with me.

It's a sad state of affairs when your only option is to protest and camp outside the gates of your own parliament. We were ready to stay as long as was needed, until we got the respectful response that our kids deserved. We wanted to show the TDs inside the Dáil that there are many people out there in Ireland who need this medication.

I met a lot of old friends and supporters that day. I had encountered a lot of people from attending the various information meetings, rallies and protests, and on the walk, and many called over that day in solidarity. Helen O'Sullivan, Leah Speight and Eamonn McGrath to name a few; Gino and Richard also spent time with us. I also made some new friends that day, including Dawn Connolly and her partner Alan, who came all the way from Edenderry to support us. Their beautiful daughter, Holly, has polymicrogyria and they wanted to support our fight to legalise medicinal cannabis. Holly is another child who could potentially benefit from medicinal cannabis and deserves the opportunity to at least try this medicine.

As Gino said on the day, 'You'd wonder are the people in the Dáil listening? If the medicinal cannabis bill was made law, the people who needed it, or were using it illegally, would be able to access it under medical supervision and in a legal manner. I would break the law tomorrow if I knew myself or my child could actually benefit from medicinal cannabis. Easy. I'd break the law today. The law is an ass when it comes to a situation like this. The medicinal cannabis bill wants to decriminalise the use of medicinal cannabis.'

As the TDs came and went, you'd get a chance to speak to them. Some were more willing than others. The vast majority of Simon Harris's parliamentary colleagues that I spoke to appeared sympathetic to our plight and wanted a solution to be found. Gino met the minister briefly in the Dáil and was told that he wouldn't meet us. No, not even fifteen minutes. Jonathan O'Brien came out for a few words. I told him I really hoped Simon Harris could be persuaded and I'd get the opportunity to speak to him. Jonathan said he could pass a message on to him for us and come back with his response. A glance at Sarah showed that she, like me, felt this was inadequate. I told Jonathan that if Simon hadn't the manners to meet us, even if it was only for fifteen minutes in Buswells Hotel, then passing messages back and forth was pointless.

All of us there that day had kids and we missed and worried about them. But we were ready to wait. It was for their good and for all our families' benefit. We spent the time chatting with passers-by and friends and supporters. People were very good, very supportive. The chats really helped in passing the time and keeping the morale up. Later in the day TV3 came along and I spoke to them.

Michael Collins, the independent TD for west Cork, came out to talk to us several times over the course of that first day. It was around this time that I got to know him well, and since then he has become a great friend. He has highlighted Ava's needs in the Dáil, through parliamentary questions, on several occasions. That day, he voiced his concerns about us sleeping out overnight and said he considered it to be an utter disgrace that it had come to this. During the day, Michael arranged for tea to be brought to us and later in the evening, as the cold and damp started to settle, he started talking about a special hot water bottle. To be honest, it sounded like a damn good idea to me. He arrived back with a large brown paper bag and handed it to Sarah, saying it would keep us warm later. Looking into the bag, we doubled over with laughter. It was a big bottle of Powers whiskey. Wisely, I think, we decided that it wouldn't really help with the tiredness or cold, so we didn't indulge ourselves. All the same, it was a decent thing to do.

Michael has continued to be there for my family up to the present day, both with moral and practical support. All this and we're not even in his constituency and wouldn't have the opportunity to vote for him. He has stepped up again and again to talk to Paul and me, and done all he can to help out. The people in west Cork are fortunate to have a person like Michael representing them, someone who cares enough to get stuck in and make a difference. That night in Dublin his warmth and good humour really buoyed us up.

Another good soul who we met that night was the independent TD for Roscommon–Galway, Michael Fitzmaurice. He brought us over a McDonald's meal, which was a nice touch. You soon get to know the sound ones. My recollection is that it was a 'Happy meal'. I can tell you it was the only happy thing about the situation that night as the cold really started to bite.

The tents were put up and the sleeping mats and bags rolled out. The gardaí outside the gates of the Dáil were very friendly, very decent. Incredibly, it had gotten to the stage of sleeping out on the side of the street for the sake of our children's health. We had hoped that Jonathan O'Brien and Simon Harris could have a conversation that led to us at least sitting down and having a few words over a cup of tea. But it wasn't to be.

Camping outside the entrance to Ireland's parliament with Mags and Sarah will never leave my heart or soul. The looks from some of the people as they passed us on the street – looking us up and down, then turning their heads away in discomfort –

made me realise even more that people who don't have a home need to be gathered into the heart of the community, to be helped as soon as possible. There's an awful unhappiness to being looked down on like that and ignored.

Sarah, Mags and I recall Kate O'Connell, TD, passing us. We had a good view of her as she passed by with a few others. They briefly looked over, saw us and just as quickly looked away. Continuing on, they made their way over to the comfort of Buswells Hotel. We spoke about these glances afterwards and wondered how it could be that we had become people to be avoided. It was unfair: our request for medical justice was not unreasonable or criminal.

You'd be a bit nervous bedding down in the tent on a Dublin street. We were very thankful for the gardaí just beside us at the gates of the Dáil. They said they'd keep an eye on us. It looked like a very tedious, boring post. I doubt they're fighting for that gig.

We quickly found that the mats we'd brought were too thin. Even in summer, the ground was cold and hard. Closing up the zippers we tried to nod off. I had got a loan of a really thick, good-quality sleeping bag, but it was impossible to achieve any level of comfort. The cold from the ground seeped up into my body so that I couldn't warm up at all.

Later on, I heard some men close to the tent talking, and got a little nervous. As I listened, their conversation turned to a discussion of the best means of keeping warm at night. It became apparent then that these were a couple of homeless gentlemen who were preparing to bed down for the night and were discussing strategy. I said to myself that I didn't have a whole lot to complain about, really, after only a few hours of the cold. We had chosen to come up here and protest, after all, while the two gentlemen outside had no choice but to face this ordeal every night.

I don't know how people survive on the streets day after day. It's a frightening thought and it's something that could happen to any one of us. To have no way out must be soul-destroying. Being out in the cold, with the constant noise and lights, the danger and disturbed sleep, is not something anyone should have to endure.

After a period of time, the men's voices drifted away. Soon after, completely exhausted, I finally fell asleep.

***

Thursday morning came around all too slowly. The dawn contained no warmth. We were stiff, sore and badly in need of getting up to move around and generate a bit of heat. I had a chill in the bones that I couldn't shake off. After we awoke we suffered the mortifying experience of people looking at us folding up the tents as they walked by. Like the previous night, some passers-by looked at us with varying degrees of pity or disgust, before they turned their heads the other way.

My 'pop up' tent was misbehaving and refused to cooperate. As I got one bit into the bag, the other side jumped up; when I'd push that down, another piece would pop out of place. Struggling with the tent, I felt even more embarrassed and undignified. Some of the looks we got were upsetting and we were glad when everything was packed away. Standing up and protesting didn't seem to elicit the same reaction as the tents. We found this to be a very strange response, as both sleeping out and standing were a form of protest, but that was our experience of those who passed by that morning. We got sandwiches and takeaway tea from Buswells and a bit of life started to come back into us. As the sun rose we hoped for a better day.

Day two of our protest was now under way.

As you can imagine, there are other protests at Leinster House. People were there that day campaigning on Lyme disease and protesting at the closure of Harold's Cross greyhound stadium. These protests were well attended and we were lost in the crowd. The Dáil wouldn't be sitting on the Friday and wouldn't sit again until next Tuesday. Until I got involved in my campaign for Ava, I didn't realise that the Dáil only sat from Tuesday to Thursday and was closed the rest of the week. It didn't feel like protesting outside an empty building was going to move things forward. I was getting worried that our efforts from yesterday hadn't yielded any meeting and now we were going to be lost in the big crowd for these other two issues. I didn't know it at the time, but Sarah was on the phone, hatching a plan.

As Sarah recalls, 'I started to feel our protest was being over-shadowed by the large groups outside the gates and was losing momentum. You have plenty of time to think at a protest like ours. It mostly involved sitting or standing with our placards and chatting to people stopping by and to supporters. Something needed to be done. People at the gate had mentioned that the garda commissioner, Noreen O'Sullivan, was arriving later in the day, so a lot of media were in the area. This was an opportunity too good to miss.

'I sounded out Gino and Richard Boyd Barrett and they said, "I don't know, I don't know, it mightn't be a good idea. I don't think you should do that, Sarah." They were very cautious, but I had no desire to sleep out in the street over the weekend. I phoned Brian and asked him what he thought about blocking the gates. He said if the opportunity was there to go for it. The politicians don't mind blocking treatment for Ava or Cillian, so why not block the gates for a while?

'I told Vera we needed to block the gates with a sit-down protest. After a small bit of convincing, she was game for it. I pointed out that we had to do something, so that's what ourselves and Mags did. We waited for the opportune moment, made a quick move and sat in the middle of the gates, before the gardaí or Leinster House ushers could stop us. Once we did it, it felt a bit overwhelming. What had we just done?'

After a few moments a large number of gardaí surrounded us, but in fairness they were grand. With the media there we succeeded in highlighting our protest and the need to legalise medicinal cannabis better than a lifetime of sleeping out would have done. My friend Hazel Robinson arrived. She has been a tireless campaigner to get the drug Orkambi made available for cystic fibrosis sufferers and had recently slept outside Leinster House for several days in protest. She's a real warrior and definitely the sort of person you want at your side in a situation like this. She quietly asked did we want her to join us. We certainly did, so she managed to slip in and sit beside us. It's a big gesture to do what she did and show so much solidarity. It says a lot about her great character.

As she said at the sit-down, 'Time is not on our side when we're dealing with children suffering with severe illnesses. We represent thousands who don't have a voice and are left with inadequate care. We want a change.' After Hazel sat down, more gardaí surrounded us, I guess to prevent any further additions to our party.

The People Before Profit TDs Gino, Richard Boyd Barrett and Bríd Smith were all present and supporting us. It wasn't their first sit-down protest or demonstration of defiance. I think they were a bit delighted with our boldness. I can remember looking up at Bríd Smith, who I admire tremendously, and at Gino and Richard, and I felt they were very proud of our bravery and determination to raise awareness and get the attention that our sick children deserved. Sarah joked, 'Gino is starting to realise why Cork is called the rebel county!'

Richard Boyd Barrett said he felt inspired by us. 'They feel they have no choice and have been cruelly betrayed by Simon Harris. His promise to meet wasn't kept. It looks like he's playing a cynical game. It's shameful the way he's treated Vera. We need to support Vera, Mags, Hazel and Sarah and get behind the medicinal cannabis bill.' Richard also brought us over some sandwiches after the initial excitement had settled down.

One of our friends, Brendan Condron, passed us in our mats and also some things from our bags, which was sound as once you're sitting, you've got to sit tight! He also took care of our bags during the sit-down protest. It's worth mentioning that the gardaí allowed him to do this, when they really didn't have to allow it at all. As well as the coverage from the media, blocking the gates prevented the TDs lining up in their cars from leaving the Leinster House car park to head back to their constituencies for the weekend. To be honest, if they spent that short delay thinking about why we were doing it and the delays epilepsy is causing in our children's lives it would be time well spent.

If Simon Harris had honoured his agreement to help progress Ava's access to medicinal cannabis, none of this would have been necessary. Gino summed it up when he said, 'I'm demanding that Simon Harris contact Vera immediately and arrange to meet her and find a way to resolve this matter. He should also return the medicinal cannabis Vera obtained with a prescription, in Spain, without delay.'

There's obviously a protocol for removing sit-down protesters. One of the gardaí came over and explained we'd have to move of our own accord or they'd have to move us. A lovely garda said to us, 'Well, ladies, you've made your point and it's a very good point, but can ye move now?' It was a nice approach. I guess you can catch more flies with honey than with vinegar! We told him that we were sorry, but we couldn't actually move as we were here for our kids. Another garda asked was there anything we needed; tea, coffee? Sarah joked that it would be very useful if we could have his handcuffs! He never did hand them over, though, bless him, he had to stifle a big smile as he stood over us.

I think most of the gardaí sympathised with us and knew there was no badness in what we were doing. Our actions were more due to desperation. They told us the time that they'd move us and explained the process involved, step by step. How two gardaí would come up to us and lift us out of the barrier at the gates.

After blocking the gates for four-and-a-half hours the gardaí finally came along and moved us. Hazel and Mags were walked off, but Sarah and myself held out to the end and had to be lifted. Unfortunately, because we're both so slim and light, that wasn't as much of a problem as we had hoped!

Afterwards, we all felt as though we'd been through a lot over the two days. The Dáil wasn't to sit again until next Tuesday, so we heeded the advice given by Gino and the others to call it a day. The minister for health may have won a small battle by not meeting me, but I was determined to win the war.

for Ava

The past couple of hectic days had made me realise one thing, though: we'd need people's support more than ever, moving forward. If Simon wouldn't take notice of three women camped outside the parliament and four women blocking the gates, we'd need to protest and get out in big numbers to show why we needed this medicine so badly. That was the only way he was likely to listen.

13

Driven from Home

'You must do the things you think you cannot do.'

– Eleanor Roosevelt

Once you raise your head above the parapet in Ireland, you can always expect some begrudger to try and take it off. Some people have an unwarranted, in-built deference to the government and a corresponding aversion to even the mildest form of civil disobedience. And our government love them for it.

I used to be like that myself, to be honest, until fighting for Ava opened my eyes. The walk to Dublin and all the other activity had generated a lot of publicity and overwhelming support. At this stage, there were over 40,000 signatures on the online petition. Along with generating good awareness, however, it also generated unwelcome, nasty attention from Internet 'trolls'. In early May, Paul and I were being 'trolled' quite badly by a number of anonymous people. I responded by asking people who had any doubts about the legitimacy of what we were doing to go to my Facebook page, have a look and inform themselves.

There was no fake news there. Anything I posted was genuine and the reality was not at all like these 'trolls' were asserting. I was worried that some people might believe their nastiness when they said we had some hidden agenda. We barely had time for our own agenda, never mind a hidden one. Fake posts had been put up about us. It was sad to see this type of carry-on, and I really hoped people knew that our motives were genuine. Hiding behind anonymous social media accounts is cowardly and pathetic. I'm prepared to meet and argue the case for legalising medicinal cannabis with anyone, face to face.

Untruths are like an undesirable weed: if you leave them unchecked, they take root and grow. Numerous politicians have insinuated that I've been coached. That I've been guided by other people from political parties. The people who know Paul or know me, though, know they wouldn't really be capable of doing that. I wouldn't be influenced too much by anybody. I'd take advice, sure, but I'd make up my own mind about what to do. I was hurt that some people thought I was being manipulated by others. Therefore, it was important to respond and tell people that my motives were absolutely genuine. I was doing this for Ava, our family, and subsequently for anyone else who could benefit. I knew people knew that, it just had to be said.

***

On a happier note, 13 May was a big, big day in our family. It was Ava's Holy Communion day. It is a significant event in the lives of most Irish children, but in our house it was as exciting as any wedding day. There had been many dark times when she was seriously ill and we'd feared that she'd never get to see this day, but she'd bravely hung on and made it. I was determined to make it a day to remember. There was a little scare the day before, when she had an ear infection, but luckily, with a quick visit to the doctor, she remained stable.

So many people who were following Ava's story on Facebook sent messages of support, prayers, good intentions, cards or gifts on the day. There were dozens and dozens of cards. It was so appreciated, to see the messages and how much people cared. People's kindness and thoughtfulness left me speechless. There were so many cards that I had to do a Facebook Live post to thank everyone, to be sure I forgot no one.

I prayed hard that she'd get through the day unscathed. I think she had a lot of fun; there were plenty of smiles and hugs. It wouldn't have been possible for Ava to have her big day without the support of Father Peadar Murphy and Miss Twomey, who were tremendous in facilitating her taking part in the celebration.

Sophia, Michael and Elvera-Mae were as good as gold all day. They were very well behaved in the church (why can't they be like that at home?) and so happy for Ava being able to put on her white dress and make her Communion, just like all the other children. In spite of the consultants' predictions and all the failures in the medication, she had made it this far. We were so proud of her.

We had a great afternoon in the house, with a lot of people calling over to visit. Overall, Ava was in good enough form. I was delighted that we managed to pull off a Holy Communion day for Ava, without incident. The joy of those few days, their relative normality, was beyond precious for all the family.

***

I attended and spoke at a fantastic meeting in Naas town on 17 May, with a really warm welcome. What I most remember was being introduced to a lovely couple and their teenage daughter.

for Ava

She had had a long and weary battle with seizures. She was a remarkable young woman, in spite of the many thousands more seizures she had suffered when compared to Ava.

They excitedly told me how she had begun taking CBD oil a number of months previously and had experienced a dramatic reduction in the number of attacks. The daughter was even able to tell me a little bit about her success herself and how it felt to be seizure free. I thought about how brave, strong and brilliant this girl was and it gave me hope that someday my own little girl would be able to talk to me like this and tell me how she was feeling. Even something as mundane as 'Hello, Mum.' I longed for that day. That evening reminded me to pull myself together, to be optimistic and know that it would happen. This brave girl achieved it, and so could Ava.

'THE SUPER BOWL'

Around the time of the election of the new leader of Fine Gael, we watched the news, wondering if Leo Varadkar or Simon Coveney would get the top job. I heard the word 'hustings' on the telly and wasn't sure what it entailed, but later found out that it was a large political rally of party members. I realised there was one planned for the Clayton Silver Springs Hotel in Tivoli, so Paul and I decided we'd head over to attend. Simon Harris was supporting Simon Coveney, and although it was an outside chance, I hoped that I might meet him at the hustings.

We ended up getting the night of the event wrong, though, and only realised our error when the live feed came up on Facebook.

I shouted to Paul, 'It's on tonight.'

'What's on tonight?'

'The rally in the Silver Springs.'

'Tonight!'

'Yeah, we'll miss it so.'

'We won't, come on, let's go.'

In less than five minutes we'd explained the change of schedule to my mother, and with three of the four children already in bed we had a chance, so Mother said, 'Off you go and make sure you talk to someone.'

We got stuck behind a slow driver along the road to Dripsey village, so by the time we reached the hotel the rally was well under way. The car park was overflowing. The numerous buses parked up outside resembled Grenagh disco on a busy Saturday night. The only thing was to chance it and go up close to the main door and see were there any vacant spots. Luckily, we found one, parked up and ran over to the doors. When we pushed on them we found that they were closed. I couldn't believe it.

As we stood beside a little table near the closed door, a young fella came over and asked did we need assistance. I told him we were late. When he asked were we members I said, 'Yes, I am.' He told us you needed a wristband to enter, which had me thinking, 'God, the hustings is just like some concert.' The wristbands had been taken away, but the young man went in to check if it was okay to let us in. After getting the green light, the door was opened and in we went.

Paul sat near the back while I made my way up the left side of the room, looking for a seat. The atmosphere was simply incredible. Every row of seats was occupied by crowds of shrieking, cheering supporters. It was almost hormonal. The closest thing I can compare it to would be the Super Bowl in America.

As I gazed at the crowd, I saw grown women jumping up and down shouting, 'Leo, Leo, Leo.' I guess they were the 'Leonettes'. They were committed, they were on fire, but they weren't without competition. As soon as their chant died away, the opposing 'Simonettes' began cheering with gusto, 'Simon, Simon, Simon.' Watching this, I could see where the politicians get some of their oversized egos. There was even some of the Donald Trump-style pointy fingers, saying 'Leo 1' or 'Simon 1', as well as elaborate banners everywhere.

The excitement reached a crescendo as the two leadership candidates came on stage to speak. I was surprised someone didn't faint with the drama of it all. What I witnessed was an adoration I hadn't realised still existed in Irish politics. Some of our neighbours were completely star-struck at being in the same room as the leaders of Fine Gael. I couldn't decide whether I envied them their blind faith, because they didn't realise how little the party really cared, or whether I felt sorry that they couldn't see this. The 'blue haze' still obscured their vision. A couple of years ago I was in the same boat, I suppose, treated as reliable voting fodder. I doubt some people's blue haze will ever lift, at least not until they have some urgent emergency and find their pleas and cries for help going unanswered.

Just then I got a tap on my shoulder. 'Excuse me, madam, have you got a wrist band?'

I replied, 'Hello, no I haven't actually. I was let in, though, and I have my membership card.'

'I'm afraid you need a wrist band, madam.'

I reiterated, 'The gentleman at the door checked and I was allowed in.'

'Well I'm afraid he made a mistake, madam.' The security

guard's hand was on my arm now. He continued, 'I'm going to have to insist that you come with me immediately.'

I stood my ground and asked, 'On what grounds have I to leave? What did I do? I didn't do anything. I'm a Fine Gael member and I have a right to be here.'

He insisted, 'You need to leave.'

'I don't want to leave, I've got a question to ask about my daughter.'

He began again, 'I'm going to have to ins–' but never got to finish his sentence as a hand swept past my face and was placed on the security guard's shoulder. A voice said quietly, 'Leave her alone now, leave that lady alone. Right now, boy.' A Silver Springs staff member, who had been watching the whole scene, decided enough was enough, and was man enough to intervene. The security guard's gaze settled back on me, and with myself and the staff member looking on, he released his grip and shuffled away a number of seats back from where I was standing. He bravely stood there for the remainder of the evening, never taking his eyes off me. I could feel his gaze burrowing into my back.

I turned and looked at my saviour. I was ready to cry, but couldn't because I still had to face the politicians. He had saved me from a potentially humiliating experience. I thanked him for his chivalry and he smiled back, saying, 'You're all right, girl. How's Ava?' My heart nearly exploded with pride, that he knew Ava and that he'd stood up for me because he knew who she was. He realised why I was there that night. I don't think I was ever prouder of the great people in Cork than I was that night.

Both Paul and I were overseen by security for the duration of our time at the meeting. Credit to Conor and Fintan McSweeney of the Saint Olan's branch of Fine Gael, as they both came up and spoke to myself and Paul when many others turned their back. It was good to know that we still had friends prepared to be seen talking to us. Later in the evening, Simon Coveney gave me a few moments and I spoke to him. I appreciated him coming over to talk when other people didn't. It's a shame, though, as other than those short few words, he never did anything practical to help.

***

The vast majority of the public supported our efforts to help Ava, but I know that some people thought I was very unfair on Simon Harris and his team. Mostly people with a leaning towards Fine Gael or poorly informed about events. On one occasion I received a good telling off from a member of the local Fine Gael branch. He didn't hold back and really gave out stink about me not giving poor Simon a chance, going to the papers and highlighting the inadequacies of Ava's care, asking questions of poor Michael Creed. Sure, my behaviour was 'desperate altogether'.

I didn't respond with the same force, as I had respect for his past friendship; instead, I simply listened as he defended his beloved party. I wondered how he could prioritise an unreturned loyalty to a bunch of politicians up in the Dáil over my daughter and a friendship going back decades. He should have known better. When I got home, I just sagged into the chair and recounted the conversation to my mother. Naturally, she was horrified.

Looking back, I'm glad he spoke his mind because it helped focus my own mind regarding priorities and real loyalty. Some people take it as a personal insult if you criticise the powers that be, instead of just passively taking it. To be totally frank about it, Ava's life and the lives of the other people who need medicinal cannabis is the issue. If people are unhappy with me because I fight against an injustice, well good luck to them. Jog on. Paul and I have conducted ourselves with self-control, manners and no aggression. We aren't the ones in the wrong.

I found his comments rather ironic, really, as we had given the Department of Health and Simon Harris years, literally years, of our daughter's life to find a solution. We had placed countless calls, sent numerous emails, contacted politician after politician, and met him several times. In spite of this, no useful progress was ever made.

Negative publicity seemed to be the only thing the politicians would react to. This was clearly seen by the reaction to TV3 news broadcasting Ava having a seizure. This was something we never in a million years wanted to do, but in the end, we had to. The lack of engagement from the HSE and Department of Health compelled us to do it. We were advised that people had to see Ava's terrible reality to truly understand. The media provided the oxygen of publicity, and talking to the various media was a constant ongoing requirement. Reactions would vary: mostly really good and empathetic, but sometimes completely apathetic. *The Late Late Show* displayed a complete disinterest, with thousands of requests from the public to have us on the show disregarded. One friend was advised that my agent should get in contact with them, as if someone like me has an agent. I laughed and told my friend that the only agent I had was for cleaning and I kept it under the sink.

The show had interviewed many prominent people since I'd gone public with Ava's illness. It was even reported that the convicted drug trafficker John Gilligan was allegedly invited on the show. It was bemusing to me why this show, which had showcased so many human interest stories in the past, would not have me on as a guest. Ava's serious illness and my struggle to achieve medical justice has impacted many people. I couldn't and still can't understand why RTÉ didn't seem to want to hear my child's story, particularly when the issue of medicinal cannabis affects so many people. I'd always thought growing up that that was what *The Late Late Show* prided itself on: discussing the topics of the day. Instead it seems to me to have become one interviewer interviewing another staff member of RTÉ about their 'journey'.

***

On 27 May, we held a very well-attended rally in Tralee. On the same day a vigil was held in the square in Portarlington to support Ava. When people take time out of their busy days to attend a rally or protest, it's a great gesture of support. I always try to make it worth their while attending, by keeping them informed about how Ava's doing and if there's been any progress in obtaining the medicine.

I told them, 'Last week, Ava had a particularly bad seizure. I went to her, caught her and held her in my arms. With the power of the seizure, I couldn't hold her, she started to turn around in my arms. That's why Paul and I are fighting to achieve medicinal cannabis for our daughter, because pharmaceutical medications have not worked. CBD on its own is working to reduce the severity of her seizures, but we need the addition of THC to assist in controlling and reducing her seizures.

'It's not just Ava. A couple of weeks ago, my friend turned forty and the following week he was diagnosed with MS. He's another person who'll need the likes of medicinal cannabis to ease his spasms and suffering. He's been in pain for a long time, but only got the diagnosis now. This is the answer to ease the pain and other symptoms of so many different conditions. I look with utter envy at the people with access to this across the world. People who can get this medicine from pharmacies. We want access in our own country. That's not too much to ask, is it?'

People agreed with loud shouts of, 'No.'

There was plenty more talk about Paul and me on Facebook by this stage. There was a bunch saying that I had 'Munchausen syndrome by proxy', that I was imagining my daughter's illness. Well, I can tell you, I don't have an imagination that could conjure up witnessing twenty-three, twenty-four seizures a day, and neither does Paul. There were others asking who was minding the children when I was on a bit of a walk up to Dublin? Did I care about my children at all? I'd say to them, I wouldn't have walked to Dublin unless my children were my whole life. We're going to Tralee, Cork, Dublin because we have to do it. The responsibility of minding the children falls on my mother, friends and family during these times, and we're lucky to have them. Without that help, we wouldn't have been able to go anywhere.

Still, despite all the help and the campaigning, all the options for getting Ava what she needed were proving impossible to achieve. All the options, that is, bar one. And by May it was to that final option that we grudgingly turned our attention.

***

By the middle of May, it was becoming increasingly clear that we had no choice but to leave, if Ava was to receive treatment. The progress of the 'Cannabis for Medicinal Use Regulation Bill 2016' was being blocked and delayed at every opportunity by the government. Meanwhile, we were looking at Ava's precarious health and, simply put, we had to move. We had to pack up and go.

The government and HSE were demanding that we provide clinical evidence that THC oil would work for Ava and, based on a review of that evidence, we could then apply for a licence to legally bring the medicine into the country. The sting was that, to obtain the clinical evidence abroad, Ava would have to become a medical exile for several months. It trips off their tongues so easily, in a few short seconds: 'Just obtain the clinical evidence.' But to actually achieve it, with the way the system is stacked against you, is a Herculean task, involving huge financial and emotional hardship.

It is a disgrace and totally unnecessary to force people to travel abroad to obtain clinical evidence, when there is so much evidence already out there that medicinal cannabis can work. Advanced, first-world countries and regions like Israel, the Netherlands, Colorado State and Canada all prescribe it, and why? Because it works for many people to alleviate pain and reduce seizure activity.

At the time, I asked people to stick with us, saying, 'I'd hope, if Ava has to leave, like it seems we will, that you won't lose heart about this situation. I think now it's even more important that we, as a community of people in this country, stand up for the rights of others to not have to leave and go abroad to get medication. Although we're going now, your niece, aunt or uncle could be the next person to go through this. It is time to end this upheaval and distress to gain access to medicine, be it for epilepsy, MS, chronic pain, or other conditions where THC oil and CBD oil can help.'

If we were going, it was going to be all of us: Paul, myself and the four children. I certainly would not want to leave with Ava alone, and have my three smaller children remain behind in Ireland without their mother. That would be hugely upsetting. No, we'd go as a family; we'd go together.

By late May, Paul and I were busily trying to establish the most suitable location. It wasn't easy. We had to do pretty much all the work of finding out where to go ourselves. The public sector medical professionals provided absolutely zero help. Isn't it a terrible thing to be told, 'There's nothing more that we can do for Ava' and then have them provide no assistance in helping us to help her?

Word of mouth is often the most reliable advice. In sourcing the treatment, we preferred the idea of a personal recommendation, from a trusted friend or acquaintance. I asked on Facebook if people with experience of obtaining treatment with medicinal cannabis, particularly in Europe, would contact me and give me their thoughts. It was very difficult to be on the Internet, trying to find somewhere suitable.

In extremis, Spain was about as far as we'd chance bringing Ava. It was our initial destination of choice. After all, the Kalapa clinic had experience prescribing medicinal cannabis to children with Ava's condition, and they'd been very professional to work with when I flew over. And it was not realistic, really, to imagine we could go to Colorado or Canada. They were too far away and the plane trip over would be too full of uncertainties and risk.

Eventually, however, we selected an unexpected location. As some question marks were raised about the government accepting the type of medicinal cannabis prescribed in Spain, and in order to avoid any uncertainty and ensure that Ava accessed a treatment that would be accepted as providing clinical evidence, we ended up turning to the Netherlands.

Medicinal cannabis had been allowed, on prescription, in the Netherlands since 2003 and cannabis research was booming. The Dutch are rightly proud of their advances and achievements using medicinal cannabis in the treatment of intractable epilepsy.

I spent a lot of time researching the facilities and the care options available, talking to those over in the Netherlands who had any knowledge and experience with the programme. To be honest, it was the best option available. We thought it was just about close enough to drive and not pose an unacceptable risk to Ava's health, although any long drive is tiring and tiredness can bring on Ava's seizures, so it was a genuine risk. But due to the government's lack of action it had to be taken.

'What is wrong with this country's government?' I asked the question on Facebook in early June, as Paul and I finalised our plans to leave Ireland for medical exile. The vast majority of Irish citizens and most medical professionals, many of whom had told me they were keen to prescribe medicinal cannabis, supported us. No – the intransigence and blockage lay with the government. I asked people to send Ava's petition to as many people as possible, to Facebook pages, support groups, politicians and senators, anyone who might help.

It was clear that there was no welcome in Ireland for a seriously ill little girl. Only away with you and find a solution, or don't, elsewhere. What has happened to this country?

Many of the local politicians also supported Ava. Around this time, I was heartened to see that Councillor Ted Tynan proposed a motion that 'Cork City Council calls upon the Minister for Health, Simon Harris, to support the legalisation of the use of cannabis for medical purposes. The benefits of medicinal cannabis have been demonstrated by independent medical experts, such as Professor Michael Barnes [author of the 'Barnes Report' on medicinal cannabis] and Professor Finn [professor of pharmacology and cannabinoid research]. Medicinal cannabis is available in other EU states. I salute the courage and determination of campaigners such as Vera Twomey, who has campaigned tirelessly on behalf of her daughter Ava.'

We had set up a GoFundMe page to help with covering the costs of travelling to the Netherlands for Ava's treatment. Setting up a page for donations was the last thing we had ever wanted to do, as it acknowledged the failure to receive the treatment in Ireland. We had wanted to believe that the government wouldn't be wicked enough to drive Ava from home, that, morally, they'd do the right thing. My God, were we wildly off the mark. We were so very sad that we had to leave the country and become medical refugees. What else could you call it?

The response to the GoFundMe page was absolutely amazing. We discovered that the ordinary, decent, real people of Ireland were still just that – really decent. The support and donations just blew us away. They were the real saviours of our little girl. Our friends, Mags and Owen, kept up their support by organising a motorbike charity run. Friends around the country had coffee mornings. Every single one of these acts of kindness made Ava's treatment abroad a real possibility.

The fundraising only began because there didn't seem to be

any chance of receiving assistance under the treatment abroad scheme or the 'treatment access fund'. In reality, there wasn't any assistance provided by the government bodies. I think, as with the compassionate access scheme, the government needed to be able to claim that a scheme was available, but when you tried to avail of it, you soon discovered that the terms and conditions made it all but unavailable.

We didn't know how long we'd have to remain abroad, but it certainly would be more than a few months. How do you budget for a stay of indeterminate length? It took a lot of organising to suddenly stop one's life in Ireland, transplant the family abroad and then pick up the strands of a new life in the Netherlands. We hoped to head off as soon as the arrangements were completed. I prayed for the strength to keep going and make the right decisions on the difficult journey ahead.

Ava had a terrible day on 13 June. That day she suffered several bad seizures, and I ended up taking her to the doctor that evening. There was nothing, such as a cold or infection, that they could pinpoint as actually being wrong with her. That was extremely worrying, as it meant it was solely down to the Dravet. Later that night, as she rested in bed, exhausted, drained and white as a sheet, I realised that we had to go straight away.

14

Medical Exile

'Lord, won't you give me the strength to be strong and be true.'

– Damien Dempsey

I put a call out to the Irish community in The Hague for help in locating a rental property. I worked from sun-up to the close of business to secure accommodation; it was not an easy task at the best of times, but in a big city, during peak holiday season, it was a hard slog. Not knowing how long we'd need to rent for, and not being in the country to view properties, made it a very challenging ordeal.

All that we could take for the next several months was crammed into every available space in the car. We picked the toys carefully, ones the kids loved but which wouldn't occupy much room. Their lives were going to be turned upside down, away from Nana's hugs, their familiar beds and everything that was home. Leaving had to happen, but there was no doubt that the kids were going to suffer. It made me so angry that I was compelled to disrupt my children's lives because we had to save their sister's life.

It was undoubtedly going to be an extremely long and taxing journey in the car, with disrupted sleep, in unfamiliar surroundings and lacking any routine, but on balance it was the best option. If anything happened to Ava on a plane it could be life-threatening and we couldn't risk it.

We were desperately sorry to go, especially to leave my mother. She is a fiercely independent, loving, wonderful woman and her heart was breaking at our departure. She worried endlessly about Ava. Now she'd be concerned about all of us and only able to contact us by phone. With tears barely held at bay, she put her arms around me, saying, 'I'll be praying for ye and I'll be praying to your father to look after ye.' We should have been the ones making her life easier; instead it was mostly the other way around.

It was one of the most emotionally upsetting nights I'd experienced, preparing for the journey. The back of my throat was tight and I felt an emptiness in the pit of my stomach. I distracted myself with the task of moving bag after bag into the car. Luggage would be arranged, then rearranged, trying to fit in more stuff. Leaving, we gathered the kids in our arms and they sleepily hugged Nana, having already said a proper goodbye before they went to bed. I wrapped my arms around my mother, telling her, 'I'll work so hard to get us home.'

She said, 'I know you will girl, mind yourselves, I love ye.'

And with that, we left our home, Cork and Ireland. Driving out the lane that night, I thought, 'What has become of this country or was it always as bad and I never realised?' Our hearts were sick with worry, but we jollied each other along in the front of the car, Paul and I, pretending it was okay for the sake of each other.

Part of the reason we remained resolute and strong was the steadfast support of the ordinary Irish people. They certainly hadn't forgotten about Ava, because the donations to the GoFundMe page had been amazing. We wouldn't have been able to move abroad without that support.

***

The drive up the motorway was completed without incident. Arriving into Dublin port, the huge ferry loomed up in front of us, with a long queue of vehicles snaking back, waiting to board. Sitting in the car, I thought of all the other Irish people forced to travel abroad for opportunities over the years.

The sailing was an exciting event for the children; the smaller ones ran around, while Ava arranged herself on a seat and played away with her LEGO. The boat took a couple of hours to reach Holyhead and all the kids took turns at having small naps, while Paul or I entertained the rest.

After disembarking in Wales, we had a long drive to Harwich ahead of us. We planned to make a few stops along the way, to break the travel up and provide the kids with as fun a trip as possible. Wales was in the midst of a heatwave, lovely for relaxing on the beach, but not great when cooped up in the car for several hours. We were worried that too high a temperature could trigger a seizure. I thought, 'This is just great, we arrive in Wales on the one day of the year when it's over thirty degrees.' It just left myself and Paul with the usual nervous anxiety, waiting for something to happen, as the car steadily got hotter and hotter. Thankfully Ava stayed seizure free the entire time.

The kids enjoyed themselves, but questioned why Nana wasn't there. I explained again that we had to go to the Netherlands to get Ava's medicine, because Simon wouldn't let her have it at home. Nana had to stay home to mind the house and pets.

It was a conversation that never got any easier, but bless them, they accepted it. This discussion seemed to make a big difference as, now that we were on the road, they appeared to accept the situation, even if they didn't really understand all the details.

Ava had been enjoying herself, looking out the window of the car, watching everything around her. I so wished she could tell us what she was thinking. Hopefully, that would start to happen soon. She was smiling and having a great time with her brother and sisters. They played well together, making Ava feel at ease in the unfamiliar surroundings. They all had an awareness, even little Elvera-Mae, of the need to be more gentle with Ava and that was very apparent on the trip. Late that evening, we reached our destination, a Holiday Inn twenty miles or so outside Harwich.

We had chosen the hotel on the recommendation of a friend. We'd booked a family room but, my goodness, it wasn't suitable and more like a hostel than a hotel. The room size was totally inadequate and there was no restaurant. In fact, a hostel might have been a better option, because the room had no working air-conditioning and the windows barely opened. Already warm, with our arrival, it rapidly became suffocatingly hot.

The kids were so tired by the time we found somewhere to eat that they were getting upset. It had been a long few days and Elvera-Mae took ages to drift off to sleep in the travel cot. No doubt she was overtired. As usual, Ava took much longer to settle, but tiredness eventually overcame her and she, too, drifted off.

Initially, the plan had been to rest for a day, before getting the ferry, but we decided remaining wouldn't be restful, so we resolved to travel on in the morning. I got on the phone and rearranged the ferry booking. With that, and after a poor night's sleep, we checked out. I felt sorry for the receptionist; it was early when we left, but she had already received half a dozen complaints about the lack of air-conditioning.

I gasped out loud when I saw the ferry in Harwich. The boat crossing the Irish Sea was big, but this one was absolutely enormous. I just thought, wow, the volume of traffic between the United Kingdom and the continent must be colossal. We had reserved a cabin and I was expecting the worst, that it would be tiny and have us sitting one on top of the other. When I opened the cabin door, though, I received such a pleasant surprise. There was plenty of room, a television and en suite. I wonder what the luxury cruises are like, because this was way beyond my expectations and it was just a regular ferry. Aside from the cabin, there were cafés and restaurants galore and a really nice play area for the children.

We spent our time on the ferry resting, exploring the amusements, on the viewing deck and eating in the café. Beyond that, there wasn't much to do, but the crossing seemed to melt away and before we knew it the coastline of the Netherlands appeared on the horizon. There it was, our new home for God knows how long.

***

Sailing towards land, I looked at the long stretch of coast and thought again of emigrants arriving in new lands. Emigrants, or more accurately medical exiles, was what we were: arriving with no job, home or long-term accommodation. The rental had fallen through when we found out that the minimum let was for six weeks at a cost of five thousand euros. That expense was out of the question and left us wondering what on earth we were going to do now. The one bright spot was that we had arrived in one piece.

It seemed the only option was to find a cheap hotel for the night. I thought, 'Oh my God, more disruption for the children.' It looked like we'd have to find an Airbnb, but looking online they appeared to be extremely expensive. Also, we had little understanding of the areas where the different accommodations were available and of their suitability for the children.

The previous week, Luke Flanagan and I had spoken, and he had given me the contact details of a friend of his who was living in The Hague. This thoughtful gesture turned out to be one of the most important ever made to us. Because it was through Luke that Paul and I were introduced to Edelle.

Paul and I felt quite alone and weighed down by the journey, so we were grateful to have anyone to contact. We got out Edelle's number to ask her for advice on where to stay for a few days. We'd spoken briefly the previous week. The next phone call was a revelation.

'Hi, Edelle, how's things?'

'Great, girl, how are you?'

'We've landed in Holland.'

'What! That's fantastic, we have to meet up, as soon as possible.'

'Definitely. Only one thing, the accommodation has fallen through, it was five grand for –'

'How much?!'

'Yeah, very expensive, we couldn't stay there, so I wanted to ask you, do you know of any budget hotels till we sort out a rental?'

Edelle was adamant, 'You can't stay in a hotel, you can't do that.'

I was flummoxed. I didn't yet know Edelle that well and asked, 'Why not?'

'No way. You can stay with me.'

I was gobsmacked. 'We can't do that, Edelle. It's not just me. Paul and the kids are here. Sure, that's six of us and we can't …'

Edelle interjected, 'Vera, you're not staying in a hotel, you're going to stay with me. Vera, you can and you will.'

That was the marvellous conversation I had only twenty minutes after arriving in the Netherlands. Little did I know that I had made a firm friend, who is one of the most fantastic ladies I have ever had the privilege of meeting.

Just two hours later we were sitting in a restaurant with Edelle and her friends. Paul and I were dazed and tired; with all the travel it was a bit of a whirlwind. We tried to explain our story, but as we spoke their looks of incredulity and horror only increased. Initially, they didn't get it. They couldn't believe that we'd had to go into exile to obtain treatment. Ultimately, when they got their heads around it, they were absolutely furious at the reality of our situation. They were all expats who had left Ireland over the last ten to twenty years to work and build a life in The Hague. Their addresses may have been Dutch, but they were Irish through and through, and to see us exiled to obtain treatment for Ava brought many of them to tears.

Edelle professed herself to be deeply ashamed by our treatment. One by one, each of the guests said that such a thing would never happen in the Netherlands; it simply would not be allowed to happen to a child. A solution would have been found long ago. We had no good answer, other than official intransigence, as to why a solution couldn't be found back in Ireland.

We explained that it was only the generosity of ordinary people that had enabled us to travel, and their continued generosity that would allow us to stay. Thankfully, the fundraising events were ongoing and donations continued to come in. In June, there was a motorbike drive in Cork and Kerry, and in July, a big event in the Tivoli theatre. The night we left for Holland, there was a night of music in Curtin's pub in Grenagh, and months later, when we were in Holland, they also held a fashion show. Musicians of the calibre of Mick Flannery, Kíla, Paddy Casey and Susan O'Neill had gotten behind the 'Party for Ava'. Shay Cotter and a range of comedians also performed at the Tivoli event. There were more coffee mornings in Aghabullogue, and hunter's trials organised by Tom Healy. Griffins Garden Centre in Dripsey had a choir singing. People's efforts were unbelievable, and it was only matched by their utter horror and disgust at our exile.

Later in the day, Edelle welcomed us home, where we were finally able to properly relax over a cup of tea and a chat. The kids really enjoyed the homely environment; it was the ideal place to stay for those early days. Not wanting to lose any time, Paul and I arranged the doctor's appointment for early the next day. We also didn't want to abuse Edelle's generosity and immediately began to research various rental properties. Many were unsuitable, though, either being too small, too large or too expensive. The numerous first- and second-floor apartments were out of the question. Ava could easily fall down stairs or off a balcony. Despite the abundance of rentals, once we whittled them down to those suitable and affordable, the list was substantially smaller.

We persevered and after about two weeks of emails and phone calls, we rented a lovely apartment as our long-term accommodation. In that time, Edelle had made us feel very welcome and took the pressure off having to rush trying to secure a rental. She wrapped her arms around my family in our time of need, both in inviting us to come and stay with her, and by doing everything she could to help. She wasn't kidding about her generosity, and throughout our stay became one of our 'go-to people' for advice or just a cup of tea and a chat.

We eventually met Sandra, our landlady. Thankfully, she disregarded the advice of her estate agent, who thought that it might be foolish to rent the apartment to a family. She was visibly upset by our story. She was a GP, which made our conversation even more interesting as she explained how she was well acquainted with THC oil and CBD oil and their medical benefits. In her career, she'd met children with serious epilepsy who had seen other medications fail. She pointed out, 'If it can reduce the seizures and pain, why do other medications have to be tried first?' She felt that it 'was a shame it was a final choice'. Not knowing how long we had to stay was a shock to her, too, and she allowed us to draw up a six-month lease, with the option of renewing it if we hadn't yet received the licence. It was a lifesaver to have the accommodation sorted for the duration of our stay.

It felt like all the prayers and good wishes that were sent Ava's way began to reap rewards once we arrived in The Hague. The attitude was much more positive. Things were beginning to work out and we looked forward to the appointment that had been arranged with the doctor.

***

for Ava

Meeting the GP was scary as so much depended on its outcome. And what was the doctor going to be like? I lay awake into the early hours prior to the meeting, running through these thoughts on a loop.

It was emotional beyond belief when the actual meeting took place. All I can say is, 'What a man.' The welcome the family received was warm, and rather Irish, with the offer of a cup of tea as we waited. This was a pleasant surprise. I thought about all my meetings and scheduled appointments in Ireland. They certainly didn't include refreshments.

The GP's approach was professional, considered and compassionate. He had carefully read Ava's notes. That in itself took a long time, as you can imagine, as they were extensive. We had a long discussion about possible options, his advice and recommendations. His judgement was that she had exhausted all the conventional avenues and it was shameful that we'd had to leave Ireland with the children, especially Ava. We explained to him that we needed a paediatric neurologist to come on board, as soon as possible, and he assisted us in expediting an appointment.

He felt that the CBD oil alone might be sufficient; however, with the experience of Ava's recent seizure activity on her present level of CBD oil, we felt that it was essential she be prescribed THC oil alongside the CBD oil. He was impressed by our knowledge and understanding of medicinal cannabis in relation to its potential impact on Ava's illness. For us, we were delighted to finally meet a doctor who was so knowledgeable about medicinal cannabis and who prescribed it regularly.

At one point he asked why consideration hadn't been given to prescribing CBD oil and THC oil back in Ireland, considering all other avenues had been exhausted. Where do you start in answering that! We tried to explain the illogical resistance of some of the Irish medical profession and the Irish government. As we spoke, he'd shake his head. He'd been to Ireland on a number of occasions and couldn't fathom that such inaction could be displayed by a country with such warm and friendly people.

His compassion was too much for me and the tears started to flow. Here was a man who was listening to us. He was a good man, looked warmly at Ava and was appalled that she had to leave Ireland to receive treatment. He expressed concern for all of us, advising that we take care of ourselves and rest as much as possible after such an ordeal. We must have looked as worn out as we felt.

Ultimately, the doctor was satisfied, based upon Ava's history and previous experience, that treatment with a combination of THC oil and CBD oil was an appropriate option. Therefore, we were given a prescription for Ava to receive THC oil, as well as the CBD oil.

Just like that it was done. No drama, no hostility, no poorly masked disapproval. What the Irish government had refused to allow had just happened so easily in the Netherlands. You'd almost expect the sky to fall in, but no, life continued on outside the window. The only difference was that Ava's had gotten a lot brighter.

I was crying again, but this time it was tears of pure relief.

***

It was so nice to deal with such positive, progressive people. They used to laugh when I said that; they just saw it as common sense. It was more that Ireland's officialdom was regressive and stuck in an out-dated, grudging mindset. Even the ordinary Dutch people we spoke to thought that medicinal cannabis was a fantastic treatment. It redoubled my determination not to give up on legalising medicinal cannabis in Ireland. We could have that positive mindset, particularly as most ordinary Irish people already do.

After receiving the prescription, we made our way to the Transvaal pharmacy. The pharmacy had been another revelation, as they'd already been extremely helpful with their advice over the phone about the various cannabis medicines that were available. Now that I was here, I was excited to meet them all. It was so strange to find people willing to help, rather than come up against opposition and roadblocks.

The prescription medication was issued the next morning and at long last Ava began her treatment with a mixture of cannabis THC oil and CBD oil. She had been doing okay over the last few days, but I was really looking forward to her getting going on it. People throw around the term 'been on a journey' for quite minor events. But for us to get to this point had been a 'journey' in the truest sense of the word. We still had a long way to go, of course, but that was still a good day. A number of supplements, including Krill oil, vitamin D3, zinc, coriander and chlorella were also given to aid Ava's long-term well-being. This holistic, health-based approach was great. Diet was never a treatment priority in Ireland. You were left to figure that out for yourself.

I did have concerns that the addition of the THC oil might not help, of course, but I knew that we had to try. From that first day of treatment, though, there were no more tonic-clonic seizures. I'm not a doctor, but no one is more attuned to Ava's health. I could see for myself that when we first began the CBD oil the number of seizures had decreased enormously. Now we were beginning to see similar marked improvements. Time would tell as to their extent, but it was heartening to see an immediate response.

Sadly, we didn't get any support whatsoever from Ava's public sector medical team in Ireland during this period. They had said that there was nothing more they could do for Ava in Ireland and now they did nothing to facilitate her receiving treatment anywhere else. You'd expect Ava's medical team to be her greatest champions, her firmest allies, but the reality felt very different.

Meanwhile, with the politicians, we were told that it came as a shock to many of them that we had actually gone abroad to obtain treatment, while the people who'd supported Ava all along continued to support her. I actually got several phone calls from Fine Gael politicians during the medical exile. Each professed their private moral support, but they didn't feel they could go further, for fear of damaging their standing in the party. If only that passive support could have translated into action.

***

We loved getting to know our neighbours, Roo and his family. Having the neighbours so close was different to the farmyard at home. Not only was Roo beside us, but there were floors occupied above us, and houses at the bottom of the garden. Two gardens away, there was a more modern building with five floors of apartments. You'd be out in the garden and unexpectedly hear a 'Good morning.' Part of me liked the new experience, but a bigger part of me wanted the familiar view back home of Aghabullogue peeping through the trees.

I knew we weren't part of the long-term community, but the neighbours were welcoming and friendly. Roo became our 'go-to man' and any problems were rapidly sorted with his sound advice.

I had brought over my favourite mug, but I used to get so emotional looking at it. I didn't want it here, I wanted it at home, where I'd chat to my mother at the kitchen table. Our neighbours back home were shocked once they learned of our departure and they rallied around my mother, calling for tea when they could, to have the chat and keep her company.

Some days you felt you were living in a parallel reality to Ireland. One of those days was 12 July, when we learned the disappointing news that the Health Committee in the Dáil had recommended that the 'Cannabis for Medicinal Use Regulation Bill 2016' be rejected. I felt the committee members were very negative, not looking at the bill's potential benefits, the increasing use of medicinal cannabis abroad, or showing any inclination to amend the bill to make it more generally acceptable. While that charade was taking place back in Ireland, here we were in the Netherlands, with Ava receiving top-class care and starting to experience the real benefits of medicinal cannabis.

We were seeing so many improvements in her. By 19 July I was able to report that Ava had 'essentially no seizures since she started the medicinal cannabis with THC. She's counting to twenty. Before that she couldn't count to five. She's feeding herself, visibly brighter, her appetite is excellent, her sleep has improved and her balance is better. She's putting on weight.' Ava also started to use some new words that she hadn't used before. This was very significant for someone like Ava, who was largely non-verbal and who didn't have a vocabulary with which to express herself.

Worryingly, Ava caught a bit of a bug for two days around the middle of July. Despite this, there were no seizures. Considering how sick she was, I think if she had been at home without the THC oil, she'd have had at least six or seven tonic-clonics. Over the following few days she bounced back really quickly, which was another new development. She was bright-eyed, looked great and was rock solid walking around the house. It only confirmed that going to The Hague had been the right decision.

By 9 August my little girl was twenty-one days seizure free. She had changed before our eyes and was going from strength to strength. Every day Ava was feeding herself independently in the morning, afternoon and evening. She was running around in the garden and was out in the sunshine and able to enjoy it. Before the treatment began she wouldn't have been able to enjoy the hot weather, but here in The Hague, with the temperature at twenty-five degrees, our little girl was actually getting a tan.

As well as playing in the garden, there was more dancing, playing with LEGO and with jigsaws. She was doing them in a different way; there was so much more awareness. One day I followed her and witnessed her climbing the stairs in the house. I hadn't realised she would attempt it and was delighted, if a little scared. She was able to go out in the car and enjoy things and contribute in a way she couldn't do before.

I was beginning to see my child in a new way. For example, it turned out that her facial features had been affected by the seizures, but now that this was fading I could see a resemblance to relations that I hadn't noticed before. All this was extremely emotional; we were just so delighted, but so sad that even her beautiful face had been frozen and affected all this time. We were getting to know this little girl in a way we had all wished we could for such a long time. She could let us in now. I could honestly say that I had not seen any negative side effects. One day she heard a song on the radio and began to happily sing along. That was something we could never have even dreamed of happening previously. Her progress was so visible.

Despite having an ear infection in the middle of August, there were no seizures. This was her second bout of minor illness since the treatment began and she was able to fight it off. It was another hurdle successfully passed. Ava was soon back out playing and enjoying being with her family. The stair climbing was also becoming a regular habit.

***

In all the time we spent in The Hague, the first meeting with Ava's paediatric neurologist was possibly the most emotional and certainly one of the most important.

It was with a great deal of anticipation and trepidation that we made our way over to the hospital, hoping it wasn't going to be as fraught as some of our experiences in Ireland. We had previous experience of the hospital in The Hague, as we'd visited it to check up on my knee, which had never totally recovered from the walk and had been a bit painful while I was there.

Upon entering the hospital, we checked in at the reception. Ava's details were taken, her passport was requested, as were the details of the doctor treating her. A card was then prepared with her photo and patient information, and that remained in our possession from then on, to be produced at each subsequent appointment. The card could be scanned at one of seven machines placed inside the doors of the hospital. Once scanned, it pulled up all of Ava's details, such as the time of the appointment and who the appointment was with. The machine also printed out a slip with a barcode and directions to the location of the consultation. Upon arriving in this location you encountered another machine which scanned the barcode and printed off another slip directing you to the room and waiting area of the appointment. After arriving there you took a seat. The reception staff were alerted to your arrival on their system and the waiting time prior to the appointment never exceeded fifteen minutes. If it stretched to twenty minutes, the staff would come out to speak to you and apologise for the long delay. It was a novel experience to attend a hospital when fifteen minutes was considered the maximum waiting time and twenty minutes cause for an apology.

Our neurologist introduced herself to Paul and me and then put her arms around each of us in turn, saying, 'I support one hundred per cent what you are doing for your daughter, and before we even begin I want to tell you I will do everything within my power to help you, by whatever means possible. I want you to tell me everything, from the very beginning, leave nothing out. We have as much time as you need.'

Being spoken to with such compassion made it a struggle to keep the tears from our eyes. I start to well up even writing about this, as it was so different from many introductions we'd experienced over the years.

Paul and I began to recount Ava's history of Dravet syndrome, her medications and all the other relevant details. The neurologist had received all of Ava's medical notes already, but wanted to hear the whole story in our own words. It took a considerable amount of time, almost two hours, but there was never any sign of the neurologist, or the paediatrician and the epilepsy nurse who were also present, wanting to hurry us.

As Ava's story was told, the neurologist's and the epilepsy nurse's jaws dropped lower and lower. Her coma, the heart attack and the long list of all the medications had all three clinicians visibly shocked. The neurologist said, 'I do not understand why they [the Irish neurologists] would not consider medical CBD and THC oil as the next option. You have exhausted every other avenue. Why not then medical CBD and THC? It is the next logical step.'

I told the neurologist about the time that it had been suggested that a VNS (vagus nerve stimulator) machine be inserted into Ava's body to try to counter the seizures. Every year, many children in Ireland have VNS machines placed in their bodies. We didn't, however, as we'd been told when Ava was about two that it wasn't an option for kids with Dravet. But, in 2014 or 2015, it had suddenly been suggested as an option. At the time, we told the neurologist that if it wasn't considered safe before, it couldn't be safe now either and that we felt a VNS was, therefore, a bad idea. The suggestion was dropped and never mentioned again.

When we had finally finished recounting all that we had been through, the neurologist said, 'We will do everything to help Ava, she is a beautiful little girl. We hope she will do well, she is doing well already and we will work with you on the necessary programme.'

The neurologist told us that the process would take three months and that the supervision would begin that day. She would work with the GP who had prescribed Ava's medication, with a view to the neurologist becoming the prescribing doctor for her medication moving forward. There would also be a coordinated approach between Ava's private paediatric neurologist in Cork and the paediatric neurologist in The Hague. (Ava's Irish private neurologist was able to help in overseeing Ava's care as long as she wasn't prescribing the cannabis; it was a fine distinction but a major one, in that it allowed her to overcome the indemnification insurance issue.) Ava's progress would be monitored carefully, with regular EEGs (electroencephalograms) and appointments to review her progress.

The neurologist cautioned that we must be realistic, but Paul and I had no problem being realistic. What was meant by this was that our expectations could not, nor should not, exceed the possibilities of success. Paul and I are realistic people – we weren't expecting a cure – all we hoped to achieve for our daughter was a healthier life, with less pain and fewer seizures.

It brings to my mind the Irish doctors and politicians who have commented about people describing medicinal cannabis as a panacea. I don't know if they're referring to myself and Paul, but we never expected a cure for Ava, just the best chance for her to have as few seizures as possible; to have a life, some fun and be happy with her family.

The neurologist stated that speech and language therapy and occupational therapy would also be arranged as a matter of urgency. They would look into the organisation of a school place and they wanted to know immediately if we needed anything to help with Ava's care during her stay in the Netherlands.

We were both exhausted and emotionally spent after the meeting. After working so hard and for so long to achieve this result, we felt that it had been a great day. More than that, it had been an achievement. It had also been a team effort – my mother, Paul and myself, together with the support of a tremendous number of people. Our unity allowed us to move forward, fighting for Ava to the best of our abilities. We couldn't have reached this stage without the support of our friends and the indignation of the country. People had watched, supported, hoped and prayed for Ava to legally get the medication she deserved, overseen by a medical consultant. That day, she finally got it. The next battle was to get the licence and end her medical exile.

***

Despite the elation we felt after such a positive meeting with the neurologist, there was a dark cloud looming on the horizon. Sophia and Michael were scheduled to start school in September. Paul and I had already decided that I would go back with the children for the start of school if our stay extended past 1 September. There was no other viable option. Enrolling the children in a Dutch school would have entailed a whole new set of challenges and, without the licence, Ava couldn't leave. We had hoped to get Ava into school, but as we would not be there for the full, year-long term, that had proven to be impossible.

There had been some mention by the HSE of a three-month period of time to gather the clinical evidence, so we had hoped to establish the three months evidence from our arrival in June to our September school deadline. However, it had taken a long time to meet with our paediatric neurologist, so our three-month period didn't start until early in August. This was distressing, because we could clearly see the evidence of Ava's day-to-day improvement since she had begun taking Bedrocan CBD oil and THC oil.

All this meant that every day was now a day closer to separation. It was another unnecessary challenge. As if we hadn't faced enough to last a lifetime. Ava would have to try to maintain her progress without the people around her whom she had never been away from for any significant period of time in her life. It was impossible to gauge what effect it would have on Ava's mental health, and we were concerned for her and for all the children in that regard.

Where does this go? That was the question I asked myself as the separation approached. A few days previously, Ava had been reading a book and out of the blue said, 'Where does this go?' It was a question I often asked myself. I didn't have a firm answer, but I knew we were heading in the right direction.

It was a privilege to see Ava improve every day. It was something we had dreamed about for so long. I was so upset that I wouldn't be able to help with her progress because I had to go away and leave her there.

Packing bags had never been as heartbreaking. I placed the little tops, children's shoes and teddies in each of the children's bags. I constantly looked at Ava's face and tried to soak up every gesture.

Michael, Sophia and Elvera-Mae were tremendously excited, unaware that their joy in returning to see Nana would be quickly replaced by missing their dad and sister. The Netherlands had been an adventure for the first few weeks, but they were missing the familiar surroundings of home.

Paul had a sad look in his eyes, but he tried to remain cheerful and positive. It wasn't just the separation; Michael's fifth birthday was coming up and the party would be a hollow affair without his dad. Paul was also going to miss his first day at school. Those occasions are never repeated and Paul wouldn't get them back. These were the occasions of which the government and HSE deprived our family.

15

Separation

'Being deeply loved by someone gives you strength,
while loving someone deeply gives you courage.'

– Lao Tzu

It was a very upsetting separation in the airport. Sophia was inconsolable, her little face was red with tears streaming down her cheeks as she hugged Ava and her daddy tight. Paul wasn't able to hold his composure either as he held Ava in his arms. To see him crying was very upsetting. Michael was totally confused and stared at what was happening around him. He didn't have Sophia's understanding and repeatedly asked for Ava and Daddy to come home. Elvera-Mae only wanted to run in every possible direction. She was happily unaware of the impending separation, but I knew she'd soon be asking where 'Dadee' and 'Aba' were.

It was unnatural for a family to be split up like this, and totally avoidable. Ordinary people could see that and reacted to it. TV3 had travelled over to the Netherlands to cover the story. Both Zara and her cameraman, Conan, were incredible. It was a pleasure to have them there. There were over one million views of TV3's coverage of the sorry event. It was difficult to have such sad family events filmed for public broadcast, but it needed to be done to show how callously we were being treated.

Our friend Teresa, who had been a great support to us during our stay, spoke about Ava's success. Teresa was a tower of strength and support the whole time we stayed in The Hague, not only with the hospital, but also with the day-to-day adjustments that came with living in a different country. Once again, the good nature of Irish expats came to the fore.

Zara and Conan also paid a visit to the Transvaal pharmacy and saw the laboratory where the medication is produced. TV3 contacted the government and found that the HSE had only sent a couple of very basic emails to their Dutch counterparts regarding the construction of a compassionate access programme for medicinal cannabis in Ireland. The HSE had one of the most experienced countries regarding medicinal cannabis practically on their doorstep and they hadn't taken advantage of their expertise and knowledge. If the HSE had a real interest in contacting the Dutch and asking for help, they'd have been delighted to show how treatment is managed with such professionalism and care.

Once we arrived home, the kids were constantly asking when Daddy was coming back. The idea that he'd be gone for so long hadn't sunk in. Young children find the idea of months and longer periods of time hard to grasp. Sophia kind of understood, but Michael and Elvera-Mae were just too young to appreciate the situation. My mother and I dealt with it as best we could and hoped that the routine of school would help settle them. The day before school started, Sophia and Michael both decided to put Ava's cup on the table along with all the others because as Sophia said, 'We can't forget about Ava.'

Ava was well aware that we'd gone. How could she not be, given that we had always been such an inseparable part of her life. She didn't sleep well for several days after we left. This was potentially very serious, as good sleep is essential for any child with epilepsy. Now Paul was doing all the minding on his own and, believe me, those of us who care for very sick children know that twenty-four-hour monitoring involves no half days. It required constant attention and must have been exhausting, especially when Ava's sleep was disturbed.

Michael's first day at school was grim. It was also his birthday, which made the absence of Ava and his dad all the more deeply felt. Mother and I didn't let him see our sadness, however, as we put the finishing touches to his new uniform and school bag. It was a big day for him, the start of many new adventures.

We slowly strolled down to the school and as he excitedly entered the building, I left fairly quickly. The other parents delighted in their child's first day and hung around chatting at the gates as I would have done in normal circumstances. With Paul and Ava far off in the Netherlands, however, it didn't feel normal to me, and so I had to go. Some of the parents had a few tears, but if I'd stayed I would have been howling in the car park.

I returned home and sat in a kitchen chair, thinking how even the little, simple pleasures were tarnished. Paul and I couldn't even enjoy Michael's first school day as a family. I felt so miserable. I sat for a while, but not for too long. The longer you allow the sadness to fill your head, the more you have to empty out again. I busied myself instead, baking his birthday cake, putting up balloons and making his after-school party as enjoyable as possible. He had a memorable day, but missed his daddy.

That was a tough day.

***

On 12 September I was delighted and humbled to receive the news that I had won the 'Outstanding Recognition Award' at the 'Hidden Hearing Heroes' awards. These are organised every year to recognise ordinary and extraordinary acts of kindness and determination. I invited Gino, Lindsey Graham and Sarah Mahoney to accompany me to the reception.

As I was presented with the award, Stephen Leddy, Hidden Hearing's managing director, had some very kind words, saying, 'Vera has battled exceptional challenges and fought for the best chance for her severely ill child. It is in adversity that our traits of courage and determination come to the fore. Vera Twomey's love for her child and anguish at her suffering produced a real hero, who is fighting, not just for her own child, but to address a medical question and a legal situation that has far-reaching implications for many people.'

Now, if only I could get the powers that be to see things as clearly as Stephen.

***

Ava continued to show great progress throughout September. Each day appeared to bring on small incremental improvements. Paul was giving me daily updates and I'd smile, trying to visualise what he was describing. She still wasn't getting tonic-clonic seizures, which was just amazing. The worst that happened was that she gave small shudders if she had a high temperature.

She would now look at Paul so clearly and start singing, something she had never done before. Before The Hague, she had never been able to recall a song that she had heard an hour earlier and still have it in her head. Her balance continued to improve and Paul discovered that, like any little girl, she loved to dance and spin around while playing. Dancing and these simple enjoyments hadn't been possible in earlier times because her balance had been far too bad.

Paul recounted one little incident around about this time when the music on the radio changed suddenly as Ava was dancing. Ava identified this change and reacted to it negatively – she didn't like the second song as much as the first, so she stopped dancing. When the first song came on again later, she started to dance again. These little things, which parents take for granted with a healthy kid, were all revelations and sources of wonder for us.

Before we went to The Hague, Ava would never respond to her name. I would always have to call her several times to get her attention. By the end of September, however, she would turn and respond when you called her name. She appeared to have much more understanding of what we were trying to communicate. Ava's eating also continued improving, day by day. She took her time, but if meals took a little longer, that was okay, because she was heading in the right direction.

Ava's personality was revealing itself more and more. She was an easy-going little girl. She would take her time, but that was just her. Her demeanour and stance had markedly improved and you could see that she was less constricted and not in pain. She was constantly running around in the garden. In previous years, if she was out in the garden, she might want to run and try to run, but invariably she'd topple over and her joy would end in tears. It wasn't like that any more.

Despite all the progress, I was unable to get any concrete indication about how long Ava would have to remain in the

Netherlands before the Department of Health would accept the clinical evidence from their Dutch colleagues and agree to issue a licence for Ava to receive medicinal cannabis in Ireland. The talk of a three-month time period for gathering clinical evidence being acceptable for the HSE wasn't set in stone, after all, and so I dreaded that Ava's exile could drag on interminably. The constraints were essentially governmental by this point, as our private Irish neurologist had built up a very positive relationship with the Dutch consultant.

Ava worked hard for her progress. Everything that she achieved – every word spoken, jigsaw completed, little storybook read – she had to work at it a hundred times harder than a child without learning difficulties. She needed help and support. She needed the love of the people around her and the love and affection of her brother and sisters. If she were back at home, they would be all playing together and constantly interacting and stimulating Ava's development. The additional pressure being put on her, being away from her loved ones, was nothing short of disgusting.

A protest rally titled 'Bring Ava Home' was organised for 17 September at the Garden of Remembrance on Parnell Square. It was a very fitting and appropriate location, I felt, as it meant that people could remember Ava at a memorial dedicated to remembrance. Supporters travelled from all over the country to attend and stand in solidarity with my family. It made you feel like you weren't alone and let the government know that we needed medicinal cannabis legalised. They had to be constantly reminded of that fact, and that we weren't going anywhere. This medicine had changed my daughter's life; it had given her a chance at life.

I spoke about hope at the rally, because I needed to feel some hope. 'We all have hopes in our own lives, for our future and for our children's future. Sometimes things happen that make life so, so difficult, when you're in a situation like my daughter was in. One medicine after another didn't work. Time goes on and you lose hope because you say, "What am I going to do?" But, for Ava, after doing my research, it was clear that medicinal cannabis was her hope, our hope. It was the light at the end of the tunnel. We can't give up on getting this medicine because for some of us it's our only chance left and we have to have it. For others, it's a medicine that could enter their lives sooner, before things become more serious and before more unnecessary damage is done. They deserve that right. Everybody deserves the right to something that'll give them hope.'

I read out a quote attributed to the Greek poet Aeschylus: 'There is no pain so great as the memory of joy in present grief.' That described the situation that my family had been put in. We constantly remembered the good times at home, when everybody was together, even as we had to tolerate the injustice of our current separation. No matter what Ava was achieving – the walking, speaking, dancing, singing, answering her name when she's called – it shouldn't have been happening in the Netherlands. It should have been happening at home. All Paul and I want is for our kids to reach their potential. Our little girl isn't going to go to Trinity College or UCD, but that doesn't mean she doesn't have the right to reach her full potential.

One evening in September, I was standing at the front door feeling very lonely. I looked up at the sky, thinking about how that same sky was looking down over my little girl and Paul. It was now the only connection we had in common – that we could both look up at that same sky. I had as much chance that night of holding my little girl's hands as I had of pulling one of those stars down from the sky. I wasn't there to bring Ava a glass of milk, or fix her blanket. I wasn't there to talk to Paul about how she was doing and about how he was doing. Sure, the phone and Internet were great, but they couldn't replicate the physical and emotional connection of being together.

Still, it wouldn't be much longer before I was over there again. We had decided that, once the children had settled down in school, I'd head back over to The Hague and swap places with Paul, so he could come home and get back to work. After all, his income was essential to keeping the whole show on the road. We were heading into the fourth month of Ava's medical exile now, and had still failed to establish exactly what the Irish government wanted in relation to her supervision by a neurologist. Paul returning home to work was the most practical and realistic way of helping Ava stay as long as might be required.

***

The flight into Amsterdam was uneventful, but I now had to factor in extra time for my bags to be searched. Of course it was all random, but since Barcelona my bags always seemed to be the ones selected. It's like my name's on a list!

I was so excited to see Paul and Ava in the arrivals area. As I ran over to them, Ava reacted to my hello and turned her head. She looked, and a great big smile erupted from ear to ear and her eyes sparkled with delight. She held out her hand and said, 'Mammy.' It was the very best of welcomes. She held on tight as she hugged me. It was clear she'd missed me and no doubt she still missed her siblings and Nana. She looked even better than I'd imagined; I was so proud to be her mam.

Once Paul left, it was just Ava and me in the apartment. It had become a much quieter, more lonely place compared to when six of us had filled it with energy. I tried to make the days as stimulating as possible for Ava. We'd go for short walks to the local shops or visit the little café halfway up the street. I'd while away the time over a coffee and a juice for Ava. I could buy most of what was needed in the small, local shops, which was very convenient. The bigger, weekly shop became a lot easier once I'd gained confidence driving on the other side of the road. It opened up so many more opportunities for us.

One of our best days in the Netherlands was when we drove to Haarlem, which was about one hour's drive away. Haarlem is a beautiful city, with cobbled streets and an enormous cathedral. We just strolled around looking at the sights and I tried to keep Ava amused. It mightn't seem like much, but we were together, having a carefree day and enjoying the sun. The sheer uneventfulness of the day was to be savoured. As I wheeled along the buggy, Ava was clearly enjoying herself and had a broad smile on her face. It was wonderful to see her so happy.

We had a big appointment with some of Ava's medical team in early October. She was getting to meet the speech and language, occupational therapy and physiotherapy teams. I was excited to be getting this essential help, and it was a real tonic to see how easily the sessions had been organised. There were no long waiting lists and referrals. The various strands of the medical care seemed to be well coordinated and very much patient centred. All the staff were located near to each other. Within a day or two, there were already plans in place to organise the therapy for Ava, which was so important for her development.

A beautiful little incident happened in early October, which has always stayed with me, as it really touched my heart. Ava and I were walking as far as one of the local grocery shops, Ava skipping along holding my hand. Down the street she pulled at my hand and as I looked at her she said, 'Did you have a nice day?' Of course I said, 'Yes, I've had a brilliant day, Ava, did you?' Ava continued to look up and with a big smile said, 'I had a nice day, yes.' With those few words it became a really great day. We might have been alone and far away from home, but those words showed how far Ava had come. She was happy and making progress; I had to remain strong.

A lot of people held a 'cup of tea for Ava' day in mid-October. This was another effort to highlight Ava's exile and it got tremendous support. I saw on Facebook that my other three beauties had a cup of tea for their sister. It was hard to look at their lovely smiling faces and be so far away. Thanks to everyone who posted pictures for Ava all over Ireland, England, the Netherlands, France, the USA, the Canaries, Riga and even the Dominican Republic that day.

I tried to keep positive during this period, but the demands of being Ava's lone carer in a foreign country were very draining. A typical day went something like this: I'd get up before seven o'clock in the morning, wake Ava and give her the medication. Every day it had to be administered punctually. After that, I made the breakfast. There was no radio or television worth listening to and no papers. The quietness was crushing as I'm used to a noisy house with a lot of hustle and bustle.

I would watch the neighbours heading off to work and a little later I'd WhatsApp my children at home, have a short chat and tell them to have a great day. I would always try to be smiling and positive. I felt it was vital to keeping them going in a happy frame of mind. It could be quite honestly unbearable, seeing their little faces and hearing all their stories.

Ava's jigsaws, LEGO kitchen and picnic basket were then set up in the sitting room, to see which one she wanted to play with. These were the only ones, of her favourite big toys, we could fit in the car when we came over in June. I had to consider what to do next. Could I grab a quick shower? Ava needed supervision 24/7, after all; there was no one to watch her if I did chance the shower. It was these little things that became such a hassle to achieve when you were minding her on your own.

Going shopping for food was also a real challenge, at times. Ava had a cold one of the weeks, with a high temperature. It would have been unwise to take her out, so I couldn't get out to buy some essentials that she needed. Being alone with Ava every single day, and without friends calling, was awfully hard. There were no chats, no bits of news. It made the calls from friends back in Rylane, Aghabullogue and elsewhere so special. People had no idea what it meant to get that phone call. If I closed my eyes I could almost imagine I was back home.

The day would be organised entirely around Ava and her care. We did jigsaws, read book after book, watched *Peppa Pig*, and if it was mild we'd go out for a cycle or walk. I'd attached a special seat onto the bike so we could both go for a spin together. She loved the bike and would smile with delight as the wind blew through her hair.

After supper, around half seven, it would be Ava's bedtime. If I was lucky it would take one to two hours for Ava to settle to sleep. She often had quite interrupted sleep and there might be further visits to settle her down again. She'd usually wake again around five o'clock for a chat, then rest again, until the medication had to be given at seven. With that, the daily routine would repeat for a new day. It was 'groundhog day'.

When Ava had settled in the evening I'd go down to an empty, deathly quiet kitchen. The evenings with Dutch television were just a non-event. I'd sit for a bit anyway and then it was off to bed to look at Facebook until I was tired enough to fall asleep. Before I went to sleep, every single night, I thought about how the only thing stopping Ava and me from being at home in Ireland was the signature on a piece of paper from a young man in Dublin called Simon.

Sophia had turned six in June. Perhaps because of having to deal with Ava's illness all her life, she had become a very sensible, mature little girl. The 'big sister' that Ava loved being around. She has a bubbly, chatty character and a fair fire in her at times. However, that October she wasn't happy. My mother could tell something was bothering her and with a bit of gentle coaxing got the reason out of her. She said Halloween wasn't going to be any good at all without Ava. 'Why can't Ava come home for the Halloween party?' My mother tried to explain, but as she said, 'I'm trying to explain to the child something that makes no sense to anyone.' Sophia reiterated her view that 'Simon Harris is a bad man.' She stated that she'd make up the licence and Nana and Daddy could take her up on the train to Dublin to give it to him.

Now, this was a six-year-old child trying in her own way to fix the problem. I wondered did the powers that be know or care that they were putting such a heavy burden on a small child? Did they realise that she worried so? Sophia didn't enjoy that party the way she should have because her sister was missing. At the time, it broke my heart in two not being there for her, to comfort her and tell her everything would be okay. As her mother, that's what I should have been able to do. All my other three children wanted in the week before the party was for Ava to be home and be able to join them. I'm so proud of Sophia for trying to come up with a plan. She is so thoughtful and has a beautiful soul.

**

The months crawled by and eventually October had come and gone. The family hadn't been together in over two months and the pressure was taking its toll. Ava hadn't seen her grandmother in almost five months.

The 'compassionate' access scheme was supposed to be launched that October, but, surprise, surprise, there was no sign of it. And because THC oil was not even being considered for inclusion, potential progress would be denied to other people under this wholly inadequate scheme. I felt more strongly than ever that it had to be part of the programme and allowed, via legislation, in Ireland, just like in the Netherlands, in Germany, in Canada, in Israel. We couldn't once again be left ten, fifteen years behind the progressive countries in Europe. That was not what our sick children and adults deserved.

I had needlessly been concerned when we left for the Netherlands that people might gradually forget about Ava, but thankfully the support for her had continued unabated. On 21 October the Northern Ireland 'Rats' motorcycle group had a fundraiser for Ava and a motorbike was donated for the night, which was just unbelievable. Several of the fashion and clothing shops in Mallow town – Luna Bella boutique, O'Flynns footwear and Barry's menswear – held a fashion show for Ava in Grenagh in Rathduff hall. In Westport, Naomi Clarke organised a 'yellow ribbon' event where they festooned the trees along some streets with yellow ribbons to symbolise Ava's exile. It was such a brilliant idea, peaceful, but powerful. Yellow ribbons to bring Ava home. There really were so many people, many I didn't even know, who were supporting us and wishing us well.

I had a lot of time to think over those long, lonely months. I tried to rationalise how we had ended up in this predicament. Had we made the right decisions along the way? Much of the time there had been no right decision, really, and we had just tried to select the least bad option. Paul and I did what we did because we wouldn't have been able to live with ourselves if Ava died and we hadn't tried to the best of our ability to help her. The public health system had essentially written her off, but we were never, ever, going to write her off.

I suppose it boils down to love. There is no man that you have ever seen, or ever will see, that you would love in the way that you love your children. You love them, and they need you, so you do what you've got to do. Your children can't get help for themselves, especially someone as sick as Ava. It's your job to stand up and do something for them. When there is such a need, when you have someone that you love so much, it means that you can't give up, no matter what the cost is to yourself.

I think the connection between you and your son or daughter is a very powerful thing. We all have a sense of duty, but there is something within women that is an instinct. It's there and it's very real. They are your children and your responsibility to protect. Living with Ava's seizures, there was a constant throbbing terror in my chest. I was on edge and I got used to living on the edge. It became part of me, because I was never relaxed, ever. The worry was crippling; it assimilated into my day-to-day life, a normal part of an abnormal existence. I only really noticed the weight I had been carrying all along when, after several weeks of successful treatment in the Netherlands, I realised I wasn't constantly preoccupied with Ava's seizures for most of my waking hours. I could physically feel the tension in my shoulders easing up.

Ava had a great spell in early November. We also received some very welcome company, when Gino came over to visit us. I think Gino making that effort, despite his hectic schedule, showed a lot about the type of person he is. We brought him along to the Transvaal pharmacy. He remarked in a Facebook Live posting, 'The procedure is so straightforward. It's literally just a couple of minutes. The prescription is given to the family and people get on with their lives. Families having to emigrate to be medical refugees makes me so angry. When you see it up front, it makes me ten times angrier.'

The period of monitoring Ava's response to the treatment continued. Like some Chinese water torture, the medical exile seemed never-ending. The Dutch neurologist was delighted with Ava's progress at the next consultation. At the time I was delighted to be able to report on Facebook that when counting the period between seizures, 'It's not days any more, we've gone into several months.'

All around, things had improved. The only problem was that we were in the wrong location. There was a real possibility that I might not get home for Christmas. The stress and pressure in my head was unyielding every waking hour. If forced, the family could probably have gathered in the Netherlands for Christmas, but the frustration was building because, as a family, we couldn't make any firm plans for the immediate future.

***

On 9 November I made a flying visit back to Dublin. A trusted, dear friend, who knew Ava well and with whom Ava was very comfortable, minded her for the day. Briefly leaving was a big deal, but after much thought I felt that I could travel to Dublin for the day. The reason for returning was that Gino's bill on the regulation of cannabis for medicinal purposes was being debated prior to the vote at the second stage in the Dáil. All the indications were that it was going to be voted down and rejected. The government certainly would try to achieve that. Thankfully, given that it was a minority government, there was still a chance.

I began conversing with Micheál Martin again around about this time. I was able to tell him about Ava's progress and the opinions of the Dutch consultants. I also had a very welcome phone call from the leader of Sinn Féin, Mary Lou McDonald, where we had a long conversation regarding medicinal cannabis. I felt like she really listened to the facts surrounding Ava's treatment.

Advocates for medicinal cannabis had organised a protest outside the gates of Leinster House and I spoke to the crowd of well over two hundred people. I was as honest as I could be and told them how difficult it was in exile. 'There is nobody I would wish this situation on, nobody. What we are going through over there, what we are dealing with is absolutely criminal.' As the crowd applauded, I added, 'It's so wrong; people deserve an opportunity to try this medicine.'

Minding Ava on my own over the last few months had been exhausting, especially if she had trouble sleeping. I was worn out even before I travelled over from The Hague. I was 'burning the candle at both ends', as they say, and something had to give. Unfortunately, it gave outside the gates, shortly after my speech.

One moment I was chatting away to some friends and the next thing I know I'm in an ambulance. I had collapsed; the strain and pressure had gotten to me. I ended up being rushed to Saint Vincent's hospital, where I convinced the staff that I was feeling better and got back to the Dáil in time for the reading of the bill.

The cross-party health committee had already recommended that the bill not proceed, a move that Gino described as 'sabotage'. In the weeks and days leading up to the vote, he'd continued to plug away at persuading the bigger parties to vote against the recommendations of the cross-party health committee and to allow the bill through. As it transpired, the government didn't challenge the People Before Profit party's counter motion, in which they proposed that the bill should proceed to the next stage of the legislative process. I guess they had read the tea leaves and knew they'd be outvoted. Fianna Fáil and Sinn Féin gave a 'qualified support', but were seeking amendments to the bill. Pro-cannabis campaigners in the public gallery cheered loudly at the decision.

The bill could now proceed to the third stage. It was an extraordinary turnaround given that the health committee had unanimously recommended that the bill should not progress. I think all the public pressure, canvassing of the political parties, and Ava's story had swung the decision. Gino was pretty upbeat: 'This morning I thought it was the beginning of the end for the bill, but tonight it's only the end of the beginning.'

I think I may have had a very mild concussion after my collapse, but after numerous cups of tea, I was revived and feeling right as rain – particularly given the turnaround in support for the bill. I returned to Ava later that night. It was literally, as well as figuratively, a flying visit.

Arriving back in The Hague I took up where I had left off. A few days after coming back we walked to the shop for milk. As we were leaving, Ava turned to the shopkeeper and said, 'Bye-bye' and blew him a kiss. His face erupted into a big smile; he was thrilled. I was so proud of her ability to make this lovely gesture.

In mid-November I was sent a copy of a letter the pupils from Aghabullogue national school had sent to Simon Harris. It said, 'Can you figure out what is missing in this picture?' The children had drawn a picture of my family, minus myself and Ava. 'Compassion? Fairness? Love? All three; also missing are the mother and sister of our friends, who have to live in another country, splitting up a family, because you can't do the right thing. Do the right thing. Bring Ava home.'

You have no idea how appreciative we were that the children did that. It was very important to know that people at home still cared. I'll never forget that night, sitting on the stairs, reading out that message. I couldn't keep the tears at bay; I felt very lonely and isolated, but that support showed we weren't alone, people were with us in their hearts.

The third weekend of November was not one I ever hoped I'd be facing in a foreign country, because that was the time of my dad's anniversary. He was a wonderful man who, along with my mother, worked so hard all his life. Mam and I spoke and agreed that the behaviour of Fine Gael would have broken his heart. It had broken my mother's and she said that, in a way, he's lucky he didn't experience it, because his loyalty lay with Fine Gael.

Dad was strong, hardworking, fiery and funny. When he laughed, he laughed heartily, and when he got cross, which wasn't very often, the memory would remain with you for some time. It was upsetting to be away from home on the day of his anniversary. For him, and maybe because of him, I was going to persevere. He'd have said, 'Dig your heels in and get the job done. Never, never, give in.'

And we weren't the only ones digging our heels in and not giving in. One of our neighbours in The Hague had been driven into medical exile from England for the sake of their little boy. Alfie and his mother, Hannah Deacon, had become another 'cannabis refugee' family, forced away from home to gain access to potentially lifesaving medicine. He was doing great when I got to meet both of them. As Hannah said, 'The hardest part is that Alfie and Annie [her daughter] do not understand why they can't see their grannies, who are a big part of their lives. They're very confused.'

Medical exile was so tough; we all just wanted to go home – even Ava. Soon after arriving in The Hague, I had asked Henry Murphy, our local pharmacist in Macroom, if he could send over one of his calendars. We always had one of his calendars up at home in Aghabullogue. One evening in late November Ava walked over to the calendar, pointed up to it and said, 'Home.'

***

for Ava

Ava's eighth birthday was on 26 November. I tried not to focus on the absence of the rest of the family, but rather appreciate the love and good wishes. Ava enjoyed the cards and the candles on the cake. She was able to celebrate her important milestones now. She received an enormous mailbag of cards and presents. Such was the amount, I felt under some pressure to acknowledge everyone's kindness. I really hope I managed to reach out to everyone, as we really appreciated that people had remembered her in their thoughts and actions. Coming up to her birthday, I had received the sad news that some people believed I was actively looking for cards and gifts. The only thing I was looking for was a licence. I had mentioned my dad's anniversary and Ava's birthday to highlight how deeply wrong it was to be away from home on two such important dates. I guess anyone who could come to the conclusion that I'd use my little girl's birthday to look for gifts will never see the real me.

We attended another series of appointments with Ava's neurologist just before her birthday. I was apprehensive. Would her improvement be apparent in the examination? Another EEG was going to be conducted – there'd already been one done earlier in the summer – to determine if there was a reduction or improvement in the seizure activity in her brain. The neurologist would also provide an overall assessment of progress to date.

We arrived at the hospital and within twenty minutes were seated in the EEG room. A large number of sensors were placed on Ava's head. These measure the electrical activity in the brain and help in determining the normality of that electrical activity. It's a painless process, taking about forty minutes, though it can be a challenge to get a young child to remain still and allow the clinician to attach the sensors. The EEG was a key part of the clinical evidence.

Three days later, we were back at the hospital to meet with the neurologist. I was quickly put at ease by being told that the improvement from the initial EEG, conducted earlier in the summer, to the one performed three days ago was remarkable. The seizure activity in Ava's brain had significantly reduced. The neurologist said, 'I can tell that the child is now totally with us in the room today and much more able to engage than she was previously. Before I even ask you any further questions, I can see for myself that Ava has made a staggering improvement.'

You can't begin to imagine my joy at hearing such a positive assessment. I had waited so long to receive news this good, and it was a tremendous relief. Ava's improvement was being acknowledged by an eminent paediatric neurologist. All that remained was to assemble the doctor's assessments and clinical evidence and apply for a licence. Before, daring to hope had been dangerous and had resulted in so much disappointment, but my little girl was doing so well that this time daring to hope could actually be okay.

The neurologist advised me that in the next week a report on Ava's condition would be completed and sent on to the Irish private neurologist, and that from there the licence would be applied for. Ava's Dutch neurologist felt it would be logical for the application to be granted, considering her significant improvements.

The clinical evidence was submitted and the licence applied for very shortly after the Dutch consultant sent her report to Ireland. As you can imagine, I was very keen for a decision to be made.

for Ava

What happened next was ... nothing. For several weeks the HSE were 'reviewing the evidence', which was an extraordinarily long time to review such a concise document, especially considering the situation we were in and given the fact that Ava had experienced such a profound improvement.

I am deeply indebted to the politicians who helped me at the time. I was in regular contact with Luke, Richard, Gino, Mick Barry, Aindrias Moynihan, Martin Browne, Michael Collins and Micheál Martin. Listening to their assessment of the situation, and receiving word that they were pushing for a successful resolution, helped me to keep going. Alongside these conversations were the more ordinary ones with my friends and family, keeping me connected with life back home and reassuring me that, after coming so far, I could get through these final few steps.

At the end of November, Micheál called to reassure me that progress was being made – more slowly than hoped, admittedly – but it was being made. He came into his own at this time and it was wonderful that even in the midst of a scandal surrounding the Fine Gael politician Frances Fitzgerald, he still found time to advocate for Ava. He couldn't give any date for a resolution to our exile, but the promise that progress was being made lifted my spirits.

It was becoming clearer and clearer that we were on the cusp of success. I could sense it was coming; Ava was going to get the licence. Despite all the roadblocks and unhelpfulness, the Department of Health and HSE could no longer deny medicinal cannabis was working. But when would they stop their delaying, finish their review and make a decision? I was so excited about the thought of getting home and ending our medical exile.

16

'We Have it Now'

'It always seems impossible until it's done.'

– Nelson Mandela

It was early on Tuesday 28 November that the phone rang and I saw the by-now familiar number. I rushed out of the bedroom where Ava was sleeping, so as not to wake her, and answered the phone. The call wasn't made by Simon Harris, or even by an official in the department or HSE; instead, it was made by Micheál Martin.

'Hello, Vera, this is Micheál.'

'Hi, Micheál, how's things?'

'Good, good.'

'Have you any news, Micheál?'

'I have a little bit of good news: the licence has been granted.'

'Oh my God! Are you sure?'

Micheál gave a small laugh. 'Yes, Vera, I'm sure.'

'Of course you're sure, I don't know why I asked that. Oh my God!'

It's fair to say that, over the last few months, Micheál had gone out of his way to help. The amount of time he spent on the phone with me was only surpassed by Gino. His involvement certainly helped to expedite the licence, and without his help I may well have been forced to spend Christmas in The Hague.

The conversation continued on for several minutes and I thanked him and told him I was very grateful for his thoughtfulness in letting me know as soon as possible. My head was in a spin, but grateful doesn't even begin to describe how I felt that morning. I don't think there's an adjective big enough to describe my emotions at the time.

At long last, Ava's licence was granted. I held off announcing it until I received the official confirmation. Then, I quickly did a live Facebook posting so I could get the news out. People had been very good and I wanted them to know as soon as possible. It's been mentioned to me by a couple of people that I don't smile enough during my Facebook postings. Often there was very little to smile about – if anything, most days I was doing well not to cry – however, this day I was beaming. In fact, I couldn't get the grin off my face. I think about ten years dropped off my face that day with the enormous weight that was lifted off my shoulders.

'It's really, really good news. Ava's been granted the licence and we're coming home. I just want to thank everyone and, you know, the support and everything. We'll be home for Christmas. She's doing really, really well. I just can't wait to get back to Aghabullogue and she'll do even better there.'

The congratulations were quick to arrive. Some of my closest political supporters, who were now very good friends, issued press statements. I've always enjoyed reading Luke 'Ming' Flanagan's views. In this case, he cut away at all the official waffle and exposed the core of the issue, saying, 'Hats off to Vera Twomey. She has achieved what myself and others have failed to achieve. One gets a feeling that today is a milestone in the cannabis debate. She shamed Minister Harris into granting a licence. He couldn't leave Ava in The Hague for Christmas. This is a great day for those who need medicinal cannabis.'

Gino was obviously very pleased and thought that, 'No family or individual should ever have to go through what the Barry family have gone through in the past five months. They sought out clinical evidence in a different country, in order to come back to Ireland to prove this treatment works. This treatment should be prescribed and available in Ireland by a trained medical doctor. If there's a lesson to be learned from all this it's that the current licensing system by the minister for health is not fit for purpose. The "compassionate" access scheme is too restrictive and cumbersome and it will be unable to provide access. The only way to guarantee broad-based access is via primary legislation in the form of the "Cannabis for Medical Use Regulation Bill 2016".'

Once the news got out I was inundated with congratulations, emails, phone calls and by various media contacting me to talk. I had a really great chat with Neil on Red FM. He ended up giving the family tickets to the Fota Island 'Santa experience', which was a lovely gesture. It promised to be a great Christmas, more than I'd dared hope for only a short time ago. I had a lot to say and a couple of times felt like I was fighting back tears, but for once they were tears of joy. 'I can hardly believe it, we've got there in the end. I'm so, so happy that finally we're able to come home. She can get the medicine that works for her at home. It's just fantastic.'

I was thinking of all the good people who helped achieve this great day and others who didn't do what they could have done, what they should have done. 'We got tremendous support from Gino Kenny, Mick Barry and Michael Collins. Aindrias

for Ava

Moynihan was listening to me endlessly and was a great help. I should add that I thought, naively, Fine Gael were the good guys. But, unfortunately, I was wrong.'

***

People were naturally interested in how Ava was doing. Some people thought of the medicinal cannabis as a 'magic wand' which could sort everything out. For Ava, I had no doubt it had been a lifesaver, but I needed to temper their thinking with the reality, which I described one evening on Facebook Live: 'Ava will always be a more vulnerable girl than other girls. If she gets a cold, or an ear infection, or the flu, her temperature increases and she going to be more prone to seizures. That's always going to be the case. I've never said that this is a cure, but what the medicinal cannabis has done is brought the seizures under control and it's giving her the space to be able to grow.'

Seeing your daughter go from fifteen to twenty tonic-clonic seizures every day to a position where you're only watching the clock to give another spoon of Calpol at the right time is life-changing. That's about as tough as things are now, and for us that's not that hard.

Medically, the THC oil and CBD oil had undoubtedly changed Ava's life, in the sense that over in The Hague her cognitive ability, balance, dancing and speech had all improved. On top of that, her appetite, sleep and awareness were all so much better. I had started to discover that Ava could be a bit of a rascal. (I think she gets that from my mother!) I found that if the mood wasn't on her, it was next to impossible to get her to sit for a live Facebook posting; she'd be up and off to play with her toys. I wasn't complaining, though; this whole new side to Ava is what I had been fighting to see, to allow her to show us.

Meanwhile, as Ava continued to improve, the kids were delighted with the news that we were coming home. They were constantly saying to Paul and my mother, 'When is Ava coming? When is Ava coming?' It was so important, both for Ava and her siblings, for us all to be back together. They're all very small, and Ava and I hadn't seen them since the mid-term holidays. Although Ava didn't have a full awareness about going home, I knew that she would understand when we got there and she saw Michael, Sophia and Elvera-Mae again.

By 1 December all the loose ends and paperwork were in order and finalised, and I was ready to come home. We finally had the licence in our hands, after it was issued by the Department of Health. I made my final visit for quite a while to the Transvaal pharmacy. I picked up Ava's prescription and got to thank Arwin and the other fabulous people working there for all their help and kindness. The people in the Transvaal pharmacy didn't know me or my family when I first approached them for guidance and help, but they didn't hesitate and they were invaluable to us during our stay in The Hague. Collecting Ava's medicine that day was our happiest day in the Netherlands.

Paul had come over to help with the move, and because Ava was doing so well we had decided to fly back the next morning from Schiphol airport to Cork. We'd have the medicine with us as we travelled and, as we didn't want a repeat of the carry-on in Dublin airport in April, it was important to have all the paperwork with us. I really didn't want to be detained this time. Looking back, April felt like such a long time ago – another world.

Flying wasn't even something we had dreamt about doing when we travelled over in June. Ava's health had been much too fragile. It just goes to show how far Ava had come, how much better she was. I really didn't want to forget to tell anyone the good news, and so I posted the details of our arrival on Facebook. That way anyone who was following would be able to see our plans.

Only one more day and we'd be back in Ireland and back in Aghabullogue with my mother and the kids. How many days had I sat and imagined it? I thought of some of the things I'd been through. It felt like years since I had walked from Cork up to Dublin. It was two years since we started the petition on Change.org and that felt like a lifetime ago. Every single day had been phone call after phone call, email after email, Facebook update after Facebook update. On and on and on. It was going to be a big change to just have what we needed for Ava.

The following morning had the feeling of Christmas morning as a child. The big day had arrived and I could hardly believe it. We were leaving behind a great, welcoming city and great people like Edelle, Roo and his family, Sandra, Teresa and all the other people who did so much to help, week in, week out. How would I have survived without meeting up for tea and chats with Edelle? I simply couldn't have coped without all the help. The explanations and help with the letters and post written in Dutch. I knew I'd miss the laughs, chats and common sense. The visits filled up the emotional 'tank' again and again, and almost made living there seem normal. We love you all. All we can offer is our thanks and our friendship, which you'll always have. Yes, I had met some great people, but it was time to go home.

There was such a sense of relief, of being freed. Ava could

now come home, safe and secure, and with her future treatment being overseen by a neurologist. I was really excited for her to get back to school and to see how much more the teachers would be able to draw out of her. My joy was, however, tempered by the experience of medical exile and a realisation that not everyone would be able to leave the country, to be away from their families.

There was a hollow sound in the kitchen of our apartment that morning: the shelves were empty, the cupboards were bare and everything was packed up or eaten. As I held on to my cup of tea, it hit me that I hadn't fully taken it in, that we were finished in the Netherlands, that we were leaving and that there would be no further drama to stop us. It felt like it was happening to someone else and I was just observing events unfold. I looked out the window at the little garden, and the lavender plants we had planted with the children in a modest attempt to brighten up the place and put our touch on it. I hoped the next family would mind them and a little something of us would remain behind in The Hague. Maybe this was the start of the nervous breakdown some of my cheery friends suggested I'd be having at some stage. I put down the cup and went off to find some job to completely occupy my mind.

I heard Paul calling my name from the hall, which pulled me out of my reverie. 'Vera, there are a couple more bags to shove into the car, was there anything else to go in?' No, after one final check for missed items we were done. The front door closed behind us and we headed for the airport and home.

I had tears in my eyes during the drive. Was I mad? No, I was simply grateful for the help and friendship we'd received. The kindness of the Dutch people and Irish expats I encountered was a wonderful revelation and would be missed.

We couldn't help but notice the thick fog as we crawled up the motorway to Schiphol airport. 'A bit foggy, Paul, I hope the flight isn't delayed.'

'Nah, don't worry, girl, sure you know how it goes. It usually burns off sometime in the morning, we'll get there.'

We had discussed the possibility of being stopped and questioned about the medicinal cannabis in our possession. Paul was confident it would be grand now that we had all the paperwork; however, any hold-ups could make us miss the flight. I didn't want Ava exposed to any stressful situations or interview rooms. She was in great form that day, but we never wanted to push our luck too far.

As it turned out, there was no problem bringing the medicinal cannabis onto the plane, but the fog did end up delaying our departure. What's an extra hour or two after several months of exile? I had become used to the anonymity of The Hague over the previous several months, but as I waited to get on the plane I realised that no matter how much some politicians ignored Ava, the ordinary decent people hadn't ignored her. There were smiles and nods of support and shy little waves from the other passengers. They'd glance from Ava to Paul, to myself, and then back to Ava. Their eyes would light up with happiness to see Ava looking around, taking it all in and smiling away.

One woman walked up and started talking away: 'I just had to come up to say, well done. You did a great thing for your daughter, she's lucky to have you.' Then she unexpectedly gave me a big hug before walking off again. If I was told I was a 'mighty woman' once that morning, I was told it a hundred times. Others, not one bit shy, said, 'I've followed you on Facebook since the start. God almighty, they really put you through hell. They'd no right forcing a sick girl and her family abroad to receive medical treatment. Those politicians only call around when there's an election, that's all they care about.'

One lady was interested in the medicine and shocked at the small little bottle I produced from my pocket. 'Is that it? But it's tiny. I thought it'd be a huge bottle; to be honest, I don't know what I thought. So much trouble and upset over so little a thing; it's a crazy situation.' More people crowded around to see the THC oil. Showing people the medicinal cannabis and the small number of drops that need to be administered always surprises people. It bursts the bubble of medicinal cannabis's undeserved negative reputation. 'My God,' they'd say, 'only a few drops to stop her seizures. They're a bad bunch to stand in the way of that.'

When we finally got onto the plane we were treated really well. Several cups of tea were sent over from other passengers and Ava got to take it all in on her first trip in a plane since travelling to Spain as a very young child. She even got a quick look at the cockpit on the way out.

Staff from the airport greeted us off the plane and we sailed through the customs without any unnecessary delays. From there we were brought to the VIP lounge to meet the media and politicians who'd supported Ava's fight over the years.

Ava had received tremendous help from several politicians and it was only right that they were invited to her homecoming. Gino was there, as was Luke Flanagan, and we were delighted to see Michael Collins smiling broadly as we turned the corner, standing alongside Aindrias Moynihan and Micheál Martin. Martin Browne, who had proven such a stalwart during the walk, was also there, with a fine head of pink hair which he was planning to shave off for an upcoming charity event. Even though

Fine Gael support had been absent, as a gesture, I had invited the local Fine Gael politician, Simon Coveney; however, he declined as he had a prior engagement. As I put the phone down I said to myself, 'Well, boyo, you can't say you weren't invited.'

Zara King was there to record our arrival and was as delighted as we were to meet up again. She'd been to several of the most notable events: attending the walk, travelling over to the Netherlands to see us in medical exile and the Transvaal pharmacy, and now finally our arrival back on Irish soil. Ava also got to meet Santa, while I spoke to several newspapers. It was all a bit of a blur.

After maybe twenty minutes with the media and politicians, we walked down the corridor and emerged into the arrivals hall. As the sliding doors opened, we were greeted with loud cheers, clapping and the smiles of our friends. They had been waiting for several hours due to the delays. I later learned that to amuse themselves they had started cheering and clapping all of the passengers as they passed through the doors. There was Lindsey, Michelle, Nathalie, Sarah, Maura, Deirdre, Mags and Owen to name a few. Great people, whose help and support had kept us going during some difficult times. I had the licence in my hand and dizzily all I could think of was to wave it in the air. I looked across at Paul with Ava in his arms and the happiness in their eyes said it all. I think Ava knew she was home and would soon be seeing her nana again. As they say, it's all in the eyes.

The crazy journey continued beyond the massive hugs, laughter and tears. I got to chat to people I hadn't seen for several months. It was a great welcome and it didn't stop at the airport. Several of our friends from the motorbike club had organised an escort all the way back to Aghabullogue. The cavalcade of bikes and cars was a surreal spectacle to witness as it wound its way back home. Looking out the window, the Irish countryside looked oddly unfamiliar, which is always the way when I return after being away for any length of time.

Approaching home I started to see yellow ribbons tied around the trees. Later, I found out that some friends had come over earlier from Tralee to put up the ribbons, and the Aghabullogue parents association had also put up posters and balloons. They stood in the freezing cold to welcome us home. That was my only regret for the day, that we couldn't stop to hug and greet everyone like they deserved. Ava had become really tired after such a long, eventful journey and really needed some rest and quiet time. I hope everyone there realised how much we appreciate their kind and thoughtful gestures.

Turning the corner into the farm lane I could see that nothing had changed in the old place. The rain was falling in a typical Irish welcome and the dogs and chickens were still wandering around like we'd never been away. After a few cautious sniffs the dogs were satisfied that it was really us and order had been restored. Walking up to the house I saw the door open and the children and my mother coming out. This was the moment I'd been waiting for and dreaming about. There were tears and smiles and, despite the rain, some mighty long hugs as the family was reunited.

17

Make it Happen

'We should legalise medical cannabis.
We should do it nationally and we should do it now.'
– Dr Sanjay Gupta, chief medical correspondent, CNN

I spoke too soon about Ava being free, as it turned out. While Ava could legally come home with her medication, we didn't yet have all she needed. Shortly after we returned home, a friend asked me, 'What exactly does having the licence mean?' I had been so focused on obtaining the clinical evidence and applying for the licence that I hadn't dwelled enough on what it actually provided. You might think the answer would be obvious, but the system is very opaque and firm answers can be hard to obtain. I suppose we could have tried to nail down every detail, but the pressure and strain of the medical exile had been taking a serious toll on me towards the end. My burning focus was on getting home to Ireland and reuniting the family for Christmas.

The question sent a chill down my spine. Sure, it allowed us to legally import the medicinal cannabis back into the country, but that was it. There was no mention of any assistance in funding the medication. As a lifelong illness, epilepsy medication is covered under the 'long-term illness scheme' and Ava's prescribed medicines have always been covered by this scheme. Our naive assumption was that the new medication would also be covered, but we should have known it wouldn't be that easy for us, not with medicinal cannabis. Now we made the shocking discovery that the medicinal cannabis was not going to be covered.

This cynical move I absolutely could not accept. I began to make enquires with officials in the Department of Health and the HSE about how the cost of the medication would be covered. I was hoping it could be sorted out quietly and amicably, but by late December I had received no positive response and decided to tell people of Ava's predicament.

'It turns out that, moving forward, we will have to meet the costs of all Ava's medication and travel over to Holland every three months to collect the medication and attend our appointment with Ava's neurologist. There's no support from the government. The elation of having Ava's medication, legally and above board, is indescribable; however, it has been tainted by the worry of how the financial burden can be met long-term. Long-term, it must be met under the long-term illness scheme, or by some other avenue, so she has the security of knowing the costs are covered, like they would be were it any other anti-seizure medication. We will be trying our best to sort this out.'

Just before Christmas, Ava had an appointment with her Irish private neurologist, which went really well. The neurologist had seen my daughter when she was really ill, so was delighted to see her doing so well and was extremely impressed by her progress.

And she was doing well. Ava had quickly fallen back into life at home. She was becoming a 'little Miss Independent', was much more determined and physically stronger. She had the strength now to keep demanding what she wanted, which was really good to see. She was very aware of the phone camera, and if she wasn't in the mood it was a challenge to get her to do a Facebook Live post.

Over the Christmas holidays, I tried to temporarily forget about the looming problem of paying for the medication. I just wanted to relax and enjoy it. Christmas Day was just as I'd dreamed. The entire family at home. It was loud, wild and so much fun, being filled with happy children. The four children were no longer separated but playing together as they should be, all delighted that Santa came. I thanked people for their unbelievable generosity in giving Ava presents, because she's a huge fan of *Peppa Pig*. We didn't do anything different, but it was probably the most special Christmas I had ever experienced. It was quieter than a lot of years; we didn't go out much or go too far, but just being home was such a relief.

After the holidays and into 2018 I resumed my efforts to get the costs of the medication covered. A friend told me, 'You know, Vera, you might have to start campaigning and fighting again, from the very start, in order to get any movement from the government.' The worst thing about this comment was that I knew he was right. I greatly respected my friend's judgement. He'd a lot of professional experience of dealing with the HSE and had never been wrong about anticipating their next move. It was a daunting thought, but a licence that is unaffordable is just not an acceptable type of licence. If I had to start campaigning again, so be it.

I spoke about my family's experiences at another well-attended meeting that was held on 18 January by the People Before Profit party in Cork. Gino updated the attendees about the progress, or lack thereof, of his bill in the Dáil. The legislation was being held up in limbo by the latest government trick called a 'money message', where a bill which may cost the state money is held up and its progress stopped. It was ridiculous. I mean, what about the money that could be saved? How much did the drugs that Ava tried, which failed, cost? Ava hadn't been admitted to hospital by ambulance or as an emergency since October 2016. That time period corresponds with the time she began receiving medicinal cannabis. Previously, she'd have spent anywhere up to five to six months of the year in a hospital bed. Medicinal cannabis can ease suffering, replace more expensive drugs and free up hospital beds. The 'money matter' tactic needs reversing; instead, let them figure out how much medicinal cannabis could have saved the state in the past and would save the state in the future.

Meanwhile, Ava continued to come on in leaps and bounds. She was managing to drink her cups of milk independently, which was a huge achievement for her. Her visit to the dentist went really well. It was a big deal to be able to go to the dentist. Previously, she wouldn't have been able to do something as simple as that because of the seizures. She also held her ground during one rocky period when she had a cough and a high temperature, which would previously have landed her in hospital on an IV drip. We were also able to drastically reduce her one other prescribed medication, Zonegran, down to a very low dose.

One of my friends phoned me in late January. She had spoken to her child's neurologist and been told that there was no sign of the 'compassionate' access scheme happening in the foreseeable future and 'there was nothing to offer them'. There was no positive news or timeline for it to begin operating, or any information about available medicines. The fact that there was no sign of the scheme becoming a reality was really upsetting.

I got a terrible fright in late February. Part of Dravet syndrome is an inability to control body temperature. Both Sophia and Ava had ear infections and were poorly. In a matter of seconds, Ava's temperature shot up from normal to through the roof. I rushed to the doctor's for an antibiotic to fight the infection and help bring down her temperature. It worked, thank God, but I had flashbacks to previous unhappy days when a similar event would have inevitably triggered a tonic-clonic seizure.

One day in March I asked Ava, 'Are you okay, girl?' She turned and looked right back at me, replying, 'Yeah, okay,' then proceeded to walk across the room, pick up her book and start to point out the animals to me. That was a happy, happy Tuesday.

Through all this, the continued inaction of the government to pay for Ava's medicine was becoming very, very upsetting. I could see how much benefit the medicinal cannabis provided, but its long-term access was being put at risk by the cost. We were using the remaining money from the GoFundMe donations to pay for the medication, because we'd been so careful in spending it while in exile in the Netherlands; however, the fund was rapidly depleting because the monthly cost of the medication was around 1,500 euro. No family can sustain that type of expense on top of all the other normal day-to-day outgoings.

The time for being quiet had passed by mid-March. I told people on Facebook, 'The HSE and Department refuse to meet their policy responsibility of covering the reimbursement of Ava's CBD and THC medication. I have quietly tried to work with them, but they have not stepped up to meet their responsibility. We need to campaign again for justice for Ava and we will. She deserves better than this.'

To help move things on, a press conference, hosted by Gino

and Luke, was held on 23 March. I once again faced the assembled media and outlined Ava's situation, and how her access to medicinal cannabis was being put at risk due to the government's inaction. A request I had made to meet with Minister Harris was being considered. The impasse was purely bureaucratic, nothing more. There had never been a problem covering the cost of the eleven drugs which had failed to work, after all, so surely the one medicine which did work for my daughter should be funded. Luke felt that Ava 'had climbed a mountain; we are now asking the minister to help her over a little hill'.

I liked his analogy, and was sanguine that, however difficult it would be, the medicinal cannabis would eventually be funded. Their position was simply indefensible.

The HSE were saying that 'market authorisation' was the reason the Bedrocan product couldn't be funded under the long-term illness scheme, and suggested Ava try a medicinal cannabis product produced by Tilray and available in the Czech Republic. This was simply incredible; after spending most of 2017 stating that prescribing medication was an issue for the consultant and patient, here they were trying to make Ava use a medicine which was not recommended by her consultants.

Ava's neurologist told us it would be extremely unwise to change her medication from one that clearly worked to one that may not. Neither of Ava's consultants supported any change in the medication and these concerns were put in writing, as achieving seizure control for a person with intractable, drug-resistant epilepsy is a remarkable achievement and not something to be played around with for the sake of paperwork.

The press conference went well and was a positive, initial start to what may have been a long campaign. I was also blown away by the deluge of supportive messages from the public, who were disgusted by the carry-on. People had thought that Ava's plight was sorted and were very angry to discover that more roadblocks were being erected. Despite this support, though, there was no movement from the government in the following week. They still continued to recommend that Ava change her medication, knowing full well that there was no medical support for making the change.

To build momentum and raise more awareness another press conference was held, on 5 April, this time in Cork city. Mick Barry, Gino and Jonathan O'Brien hosted it. Little did I realise it would be the last one in the campaign, because the very next day I received the thankful news that the government would fund the costs associated with Ava's medicinal cannabis after all. Sense had finally prevailed, thank God.

I couldn't wait to tell people on Facebook. 'I just wanted to do an unusual live with some good news. I've been having a lot of phone calls today and we've had some fantastic news, that Ava's medication is going to be covered. The Department of Health and HSE were on to us, they phoned us this afternoon to tell us that Ava's THC and CBD oil is going to be covered. I thought nothing could top getting the licence in December, but the worry of this has been immense. We have absolutely what we need for Ava, we're so thrilled. It's not down to us, it's down to everybody, everybody that supported Ava from the very beginning to these last few days. Without you, we wouldn't have got this, I know we wouldn't. It's from the heart we're so grateful.'

***

The Rehab 'People of the Year Awards' were held on 15 April, having been postponed due to the heavy snow in March. It was a great honour to receive an award, even more so because it was members of the public who had voted. I had a great day and was delighted to share the occasion with Mags, Edelle, Gino, Sarah and my cousin Pat, who accompanied me up to the Mansion House in Dublin.

Never let slip an opportunity to advocate for your cause. People shouldn't be placated by the tiny number (seven) of licences granted to use medicinal cannabis, not when thousands deserve the opportunity to see if they could benefit. Ava's success should be viewed as a stepping stone to more people obtaining access and legislation being enacted.

As I was speaking to a friend, I noticed the Taoiseach, Leo Varadkar, enter the room. I walked over, politely introduced myself and asked, 'What progress can be made on the medicinal cannabis legislation?' He glanced at me and replied, 'The bill is going nowhere. I'm on a tight schedule with RTÉ, I've got to go.' I returned to my table on the verge of tears, shaken by this apparent dismissal of a bill that held out such hope for so many sick people. With a few minutes to spare I decided to rewrite my acceptance speech, imploring Leo directly, on behalf of those who needed a voice.

It was a little nerve-racking to be speaking to such an illustrious audience, and I knew the people watching at home numbered in the hundreds of thousands. Anyway, my speech went like this:

'I want to dedicate this to my husband, Paul, and to my mother, Katty. They can't be here tonight, they have to mind the lads at home. I want to dedicate it to my daughter Ava, as well and to thank Rehab for the honour of presenting me with this award. This award is supposed to be for extraordinary people, but we're just ordinary people put in an extraordinary situation, where we had to fight to get what Ava needed. We've been let down by the government, but we were never let down by the Irish people, who supported us the whole way through this for the last two years.

'I'd like to say, because Mr Varadkar is here tonight, that the outstanding issues must be resolved. The outstanding issue is legislation for medicinal cannabis in Ireland. We need legislation to access treatment properly. We do not want pain; we want our rights. We do not want the pressure; we need our medication. We want the government and opposition to work together to give the people of Ireland the gift, because it is a gift that Ava has received, and that is her freedom. Freedom to live her life free from seizures and free from pain. To live and grow and to be happy, with a brighter future, because everybody deserves that right, now and into the future. Not just the seven people who've been granted licences in Ireland to date, but the thousands of other people who are watching here tonight, hoping and praying that legislation would be brought through to ease their suffering and pain.

'So, I would ask you, Mr Varadkar, to lift the money message on Gino Kenny's bill, to move it forward and to support legislation for the people of Ireland into the future. We want it now and you're the man to do it. We want you to do it immediately. Thank you.'

The speech touched a chord with the people in the room, and I got a standing ovation from the assembled audience and lots of positive comments on Facebook. Now, RTÉ had never been overly interested in covering Ava's story, so it was no surprise to find that my speech was edited, to remove my direct address to Leo Varadkar, in the highlighted video of the awards which they uploaded onto YouTube. At least they're consistent; we mustn't show even the mildest form of criticism of the government on the national broadcaster, now, must we?

These awards felt like the end of a chapter in our family's life. It had been an eventful and unforgettable period, but as we turned the page I felt full of hope that Ava had been provided with the best possible opportunity to be well, happy and to reach her potential.

My greatest regret is that we weren't able to access medicinal cannabis sooner. We had faith in our doctors and neurologists for such a long time, thinking they'd eventually come along with the right combination of drugs. What actually happened was that Ava staggered from one pharmaceutical medication to the next. At one point she was on five different drugs and was taking sixteen tablets daily. The doctors took the side effects of the various drugs in their stride. These negative effects didn't seem to discourage them from trying the drugs or increasing the dosage. It was such a contrast to their unwillingness to try medicinal cannabis, despite it having such minor reported side effects. For anyone who says that medicinal cannabis is detrimental to the brain development of the child, I would point out that one of the pharmaceutical drugs that we used left Ava unable to walk or speak, and none of them stopped the seizures. I'll never really understand the reluctance to embrace medicinal cannabis, particularly when we had expended all the other options.

Our success in accessing medicinal cannabis is somewhat bittersweet, however, because I've met so many people who desperately need the same chance. At the time of writing, in early 2019, the government continues to use their 'money message' tactic to cynically block any progress of the 'Cannabis for Medicinal Use Regulation Bill 2016', forcing people to break an immoral law, go into medical exile or continue to suffer. For these people, the fight to legislate for medicinal cannabis will go on and I'll of course continue to make my contribution. I strongly believe, from my experience, that medicinal cannabis should be a first choice medicine in cases such as Ava's, not a last choice. Nobody can contradict me when I say it can work; I've seen it first-hand. We've just got to keep going and 'Make it Medicine, Make it Happen.'

And it will happen, we can make it happen.

Acknowledgements

Without the support and help of so many people Ava wouldn't be here with us today, it's that simple. The rallies, protests, walks, fundraising and various other activities were successful because people supported them and made them a success. I've met so many great people over the last few years, that I'm afraid I haven't remembered everyone. Thank you Maura Macaulay Walsh, Anne Williams, Luke 'Ming' Flanagan, Mark Gaynor and his brave son Ronan, Lindsey Graham, Tom Curran, Michelle O'Shea, Tom Barry, Mags O'Sullivan, Owen O'Sullivan, Sarah Mahoney, Brian Mahoney, Terry McMahon, Henry Murphy, Melanie, Mary O'Sullivan, Danny, Leah Speight, Deirdre Kennedy, Gillian O'Riordan, Paddy O'Brien, Fachtna Roe, Nuala Fenton, Brendan Condron, Sandra Classen, Eamonn McGrath, Hazel Robinson, Edelle Croghan, Teresa, Roo, Richard Boyd Barrett, Bríd Smith, Damien Dempsey, Mark and Jim McDonnell, Jesse and Joel Stanley, John Delea, Jimmy O'Driscoll, Prof. Mike Barnes, Dr Cathal Ó Súilleabháin, Dr Gareth McGovern, Mick Barry, Jim Connell, Michael Collins, Martin Browne, Micheál Martin, Aindrias Moynihan and Jonathan O'Brien. If I forgot to mention anyone and your kindness in the book, I apologise, and I want you all to know that I'm very grateful for your help and the solidarity shown.

A special mention must be made for Gino Kenny. A kind man with a big heart. He literally walks the walk. If there were more politicians like Gino, Ireland would be a better place.

I can't say a big enough thanks to the amazing ambulance

crews I've met over the years. They saved Ava on so many occasions and do an incredible job in the worst of circumstances. Jenny, Brian and Michael, thank you.

We were very grateful for the support of TV3, in particular Paul Byrne and Zara King. Without their help Ava may not have got any coverage on television. Neil Prenderville and Colm O'Sullivan of Red FM and TheJournal.ie have been tremendous from the start. The *Irish Examiner*, *Evening Echo*, *Irish Independent* and *Cork Independent* have also provided invaluable coverage over the years.

Writing this book has in many ways mirrored the journey myself and my family had to take over the last few years. At the beginning, with a blank page in front of me, it appeared to represent a daunting, insurmountable task. Without the help of my friends, in pulling the material together from various sources and forming it into a comprehensible narrative, it would never have happened. But, page by page, the manuscript filled up with the events of the last few years. I experienced a myriad of emotions during the process. It was upsetting to remember the low points, like when Ava was really sick and was barely hanging on, but it brought a smile to my face to remember the highs, which were mostly centred on the great people I met, their compassion and their unwavering support. Thank you Sarah and Maura O'Sullivan for proofreading my work.

Several publishers told me my manuscript was too controversial and harrowing to ever be published, so credit must be given to Ralph Riegel for seeing its potential and Mercier Press for having the courage to publish it. Pat O'Donoghue, Noel O'Regan, Wendy Logue, Deirdre Roberts and Sarah O'Flaherty have been a genuine pleasure to deal with, as was my proofreader,

Bobby Francis. Their unfailing good humour, understanding natures and astute editing were instrumental in providing a polished sheen to my writing. I hope the photos kindly provided by Siobhan Walshe, Joy Orpen, Fachtna Roe, Gavin Monaghan, the *Irish Examiner* and *Hot Press*, amongst others, convey some of the drama of the events as they unfolded.

On the day that Ava was diagnosed with Dravet syndrome I was left lost for words and without any real guidance. Learning about other people's experiences would have really helped me in finding my footing and making sense of my new reality. If this book can provide help to even one person when making that difficult journey, then it will have been worthwhile writing it. Keep fighting!

Love, Vera xxx